Desig

Landscapes & Gardens
in the South

David W. Marshall

Who This Book Is For
And How to Use It

Having been a University of Florida IFAS Horticulture Extension Agent in Tallahassee, Florida for almost thirty-six years, the author has answered thousands of questions from gardeners. He knows what beginning gardeners want and need to know, but he also knows the needs of more advanced gardeners. This book is simple enough that beginning gardeners can use it as your guide. Yet it's also filled with the type of detailed information that advanced gardeners will reach for as a reference time and time again, too.

Design & Care of Landscapes & Gardens in the South is a holistic approach to gardening. Its goal is not to give the most detailed information on any one topic, but rather to serve as a guide and a reference for gardeners in your day to day gardening activities. It is intended to be your most important reference, a reference where you can quickly find an answer without having to spend hours searching online or through numerous university Extension publications or gardening books. Using this book as your reference, you will be prepared when you go to your garden center to buy plants or gardening products.

This book was written especially for those of you who live in Zones 8-9, as defined by the new 2012 USDA Plant Hardiness Zone Map shown on the book's back cover. Zone 8 is the tan-green area which covers coastal North Carolina; most of South Carolina, Georgia, Alabama, and Mississippi; northern Louisiana, southern Arkansas, central Texas, southwest New Mexico, southeast Arizona, and parts of California.

Zone 9, represented by the golden-tan area on the map on the back cover, covers northeast and central Florida, southern Louisiana and Texas, southwest Arizona, and most of the coast of California.

The author is based in Tallahassee, Florida, which is in the southern part of Zone 8 (Zone 8b), almost to the northern part of Zone 9. So those of you in Zone 8a need to realize that winter will come just a little earlier, last a little longer, and be a little colder than in Tallahassee. Consequently, some plants that may come back after a Tallahassee winter may not come back so readily in Zone 8a. Those of you in Zone 9 will enjoy a little milder weather, so you can more easily grow most of the plants in this book and even more. Just consider north Florida the mid-point, and remember that the further you go north and south, and the closer you approach Zones 7 (light green area on map) and 10 (the orange area, south Florida), the more differences there will be.

The author has included the botanical name of most of the plants. Photos of many of the plants will be in Volume II, the accompanying volume which has color photos of many of the plants. But, if a particular plant sounds interesting to you, and it's not included in Volume II, simply use your favorite search engine on your computer or smart phone and type in the plant's name. Use the search engine's "Images" mode to find photos.

If you don't have access to a computer, then take this book to your favorite local nursery. The personnel there should be able to help you find the plants you're interested in, if they stock them. Not all of the plants in the book are you likely to find at any one nursery at any one time. Even if your nursery doesn't have a particular plant though, you can always ask if they can get it for you. If they can't, then look for online sources of the plant. The same principle applies to other products you may see mentioned in this book. Some of the recommended fertilizers, for example, may not be stocked in your local nursery. But they may be able to find the fertilizer or something very similar for you, or, using the internet, you may be able to find another source.

Color Photos Are in Volume II

The companion to this book, Volume II, is where the color photos are, illustrating many of the plants that are discussed here in Volume I. Volume II will give you ideas for your own garden as you see how the plants can be used in the landscape.

Color photos were not included in Volume I in order to make the book more affordable. It was more economical to offer the photos in a separate volume rather than include them in this longer volume. Look for Volume II wherever you buy Volume I. Volume II will give you tons of ideas for your garden.

About the Author

David W. Marshall was born in Augusta, Georgia and grew up in Appling, Georgia in Columbia County. He always had a strong interest in nature, so after trying several majors in college, he eventually went to University of Georgia to study Landscape Architecture. There he made one final switch in majors, to horticulture. He graduated from University of Georgia with a Bachelor degree in horticulture, then later received a Master of Plant Protection and Pest Management degree, also from University of Georgia.

After receiving his Master degree, David came to Tallahassee, Florida as a Horticulture Extension Agent for University of Florida. He served in that position from 1976 until he retired in June 2012. As Extension Agent, he wrote thousands of newspaper garden columns, taught thousands of Master Gardeners, and taught hundreds of classes for nursery and landscape professionals. He authored two books, *Design & Care of the Southern Landscape* and *Tallahassee Gardening*. He also did a number of radio and television shows on gardening. But one of David's favorite projects was working with Master Gardeners in maintaining a demonstration/trial garden consisting of thousands of types of plants. He continues involvement in the garden after retirement as a volunteer because he believes the garden is a tremendous learning and teaching tool for north Floridians.

David writes the monthly garden tips for the Florida edition of *Southern Living* magazine as well as the bi-monthly garden almanac for *Florida Gardening* magazine. Available for landscape design work and consultations, he may be reached at davidwm777@gmail.com

Since 2000, David has developed an interest in Latin America, particularly in Colombia, the country where he met his wife and has traveled extensively. As part of a team from University of Florida, he also taught several horticulture classes in Costa Rica in cooperation with EARTH University. David has been intrigued with the variety of plant growth in Central and South America and particularly in the variation with altitude changes. There are plants such as *Phormium*, for example, that grow well in the eternal springtime weather of Medellin, Colombia (altitude about 5,000 ft.), yet won't hold up in the hot, humid summers we have in the southeastern U.S. Intrigued by the plants of Colombia, David has found that there are a number of tropicals that do thrive during our summers in the South. Some even will come back after our mild winters. They make excellent choices for our summer and fall gardens. Many are discussed in this book.

Acknowledgments

This book is an update of my previous books, *Design & Care of the Southern Landscape* (1991) and *Tallahassee Gardening: Design & Care of the Southern Landscape* (1994). This revised edition, *Design & Care of Landscapes & Gardens in the South*, is for all of you who have urged me over the years to update and release my book again. Thank you for the encouragement and the motivation to do so. As you can see, I have added a lot of new information in this edition. Life is a continual learning process, and I am excited to share with each of you who read this book.

I just recently retired (June 2012) after almost 36 years as an Extension Agent for University of Florida's Institute of Food & Agricultural Sciences in Leon County, Tallahassee. I would like to express my appreciation to UF-IFAS Extension and Leon County, my co-workers, and to all the people I served, for a fulfilling and educational career. I especially want to thank the thousand-plus Master Gardeners I trained over the years, for I learned from you, too. Likewise, I want to thank the nurseries and landscape companies with whom I worked over the years. I learned much from you, too, and you made it fun. Tallahassee, and the South in general, is fortunate to have some very good horticulturists. It has been a pleasure working with you all. I thank you for your cooperation, your help, and your friendship.

I dedicate this edition of my book, as I did my last, to my late parents. It was my parents and my grandparents, as I grew up in Columbia County, Georgia, who instilled in me a love for the outdoors and the value of stewardship of the land.

When I started the update of this book, there were no electronic files of the 1994 version from which to start. So I am very grateful to my wife, Maria Isabel Marshall, for typing in the whole 1994 edition and starting the ball rolling on this update. I ask her forgiveness for the many, many late nights and weekends of work I have put in on the revisions over the last year.

The cover design was done by the very talented Michael Meissner, husband of my niece, with 30 years of design experience and doing business as iMountain.net. I thank Michael for his quick turnaround on the project when I discovered at the last minute, though I had the cover photo, I needed help with the design layout.

I'm grateful to University Press of Florida for extending me an offer to publish this book. Though in the end I finally decided to publish through CreateSpace, nevertheless I do very much appreciate Meredith Babb, the UPF Director, and their editorial board taking the time to evaluate the book.

Last, but certainly not least, I want to thank my Lord, Jesus Christ, for all. The older I get, the clearer becomes the significance of His grace.

Contents

1
Design of the Garden & Landscape
Ideas for Getting the Most out of Your Landscape

YOUR LANDSCAPE SHOULD FIT YOUR NEEDS

Some people relax by working in their yard. Others hate yard work. Still others spend months traveling around the world and have no time for yard work, at least part of the year. The same landscape will not fit the needs for all these people.

Home landscapes need to reflect the needs and desires of the homeowner. But, many homeowners end up with a landscape that is a reflection of everyone else's landscapes rather than a reflection of their own needs and desires.

It makes little sense today to not make better use of your landscape. A home and property are expensive. So you need to make the most of them. A good landscape plan helps you to do just that.

A good landscape plan can pay off in financial terms when you sell your home too. No one will dispute that an attractively landscape home will attract more interest, and usually sell more quickly, than an identical house with a less attractive landscape. Many studies show that, in most cases, you more than recoup the money invested in landscaping.

FINDING HELP IN DESIGNING YOUR LANDSCAPE

So, you agree that it makes good sense to put a little extra thought, money, and effort into your landscape? But, if you're like most homeowners, you really don't feel competent at developing a landscape plan. There are professionals that can help you.

Contact several professional landscape designers or landscape architects. Find one that you like and with whom you'll feel comfortable working. Have them design a plan that you can either plant yourself or have a landscape contractor plant. And have them give you advice on how to phase in the implementation of the plan. Few of us have the time or the money to do it all at once. Besides, it's more fun to do it over time than to try and do everything at once.

Don't trust all decisions to the landscape design professional. You don't call a building architect and simply say, "Design a house for me." Nor do you contact a real estate agent and say, "Pick out a house for me." You tell them what you expect. You read, learn about the choices, meet with the architect or agent on numerous occasions, and have continuous involvement in the selection process. The same must be true of a landscape design. No one cares about what you want as much as you do.

The sooner you involve a landscape design professional in the building process, the better. A good landscape design professional knows much more than a building architect, engineer, or a building contractor about landscape considerations. A good landscape design professional can help prevent costly mistakes in tree protection, soil grading, house orientation, or other areas that crop up in the initial stages of home building or even smaller building projects. You might even consider involving a landscape design professional during the process of shopping for a home site. A good professional should be able to help you avoid buying a poorly drained site or other such problem site.

SELECTING A LANDSCAPE DESIGN PROFESSIONAL

How do you select a good landscape design professional? My advice would be to interview several. See what they know about local soil conditions, how to protect trees during construction, drainage, local plants, and landscaping for energy conservation. As you narrow your selection of a professional, ask to see other landscapes they designed and had planted one to three years ago, and talk to the homeowners. Evaluate how well you communicate with the landscape design professional. If they don't understand you, or you don't understand them, there will be problems with the end result.

All this will take some effort. But you won't have to pay for this time. Later, once you're paying the professional for their time, you may whish you had spent more time at this stage.

You may wonder about the difference between "landscape designers" and "landscape architects". Laws vary from state to state. But, basically landscape architects have completed a five or six-year degree in landscape architecture from a university. The course work is heavy in design, but usually very low in horticulture. On the other hand, there are generally no training requirements for someone calling themselves a landscape designer.

This is not to say, however, that there are not experienced and talented landscape designers who will not do a better job for you than many landscape architects. The key to selection lies in the interview and investigative steps just outlined. Don't let your decision be swayed by low prices of an unqualified landscape designer. Likewise, don't be swayed by the high title of a landscape architect who doesn't really know much about plant requirements and may draw a beautiful plan on paper that just doesn't work in real life. Interview, and talk to past clientele. Titles guarantee nothing.

IF YOU DECIDE TO DESIGN YOUR LANDSCAPE YOURSELF

Some of you may have a natural ability for design, and so, for you, designing your own landscape is fun. If you want to do the design work without the help of a landscape professional, do your homework. Use the plant lists in this book. Visit your local University Extension website to obtain reading material about plants suited for your area (see the websites listed at the end of this book). Talk to reputable local nursery people. Ride through neighborhoods to spot landscapes that appeal to you. Take pictures. Talk to the people who care for the landscapes. Spend plenty of time planning your landscape before you start planting it.

Put your landscape plan on paper, drawn to scale. Otherwise, you will likely find that you will move plants a number of times trying to get the landscape to look just right.

You may even consider hiring a landscape designer to do a concept plan on paper, outlining different areas of the landscape, bed lines, general sizes and shapes of plants that will give certain effects, etc. Then you can gradually fill the landscape in with plants that you select.

Many nurseries will send a designer out to your house for a landscape consultation at an hourly rate. If you decide to plan the landscape yourself, I strongly urge you to at least take advantage of this modestly priced service before you start planting. A designer's second opinions may be save you from costly mistakes.

SOME PRACTICAL TRENDS YOU MAY WISH TO FOLLOW IN PLANNING YOUR LANDSCAPE

Smaller lawns. People are tiring of mowing large lawn areas that serve no functional purpose. Many still want and need some type of lawn – for children to play, just for looks, whatever, - but they're making that lawn area smaller and more functional.

Retention of more natural areas in the landscape. What's the point of scraping an area clean of existing trees and brush with a bulldozer only to have to replant it, especially when that scraping process harms trees that you may wish to save?

Existing trees have roots out three times the width of their branch spread. So, if it doesn't need to be cleared with a bulldozer in order to place the house, plant a lawn, or plant something else, then ask yourself why you're clearing it.

Lots of small trees left on sites. The intense landscaping with lawn, foundation planting of shrubs, etc. may be done close around the house. But further out from the house, and buffering the house from the street, remain natural tree areas with a forest floor and lots of young trees in addition to the big trees. If you remove all these young trees, you lose the buffer they provide, the home for wildlife they provide, and you lose the future generation of your forest. Remember, trees don't live forever. You need replacements for those that will die along the way. It makes for a very beautiful, serene, at harmony-with-nature landscape. Contrast this to the sterile landscapes that often result when everything is cleared and an acre of lawn grass is planted. Whereas the new trend of landscaping works with nature, the old method of landscaping struggles against nature.

Increased use of groundcovers.   While the amount of space devoted to lawns in landscapes has been reduced, the amount of spaces devoted to groundcovers has been increased. People are discovering the advantages of groundcovers. They're easier to maintain than a lawn. And, they add a richness to the landscape with their varying textures. Also, as in the case of shaded areas, they'll often grow where lawn grass won't grow well. So, even though groundcovers are often more difficult to plant and establish initially, they're generally less demanding over the long run than is a lawn. Hence, the trend toward smaller lawn areas and larger groundcover areas has grown stronger.

Groundcover bed under trees

Use of more color in the landscape. Color attracts the eye in the landscape. Just about every home gardener plants at least a few flowers. But, not only are people planting more flowers, they're becoming more sophisticated in their use of flowers and plants with colorful foliage. They're using a wider range of annuals and perennials to extend flowering over most of the year. And, many people are carefully designing their flower beds with color schemes, flower heights, and foliage textures taken into consideration.

Color is provided not only from flowers, but from foliage colors and berries as well. People plant trees such as 'Bradford' pears because of their fall leaf color. Other plants, such as "Savannah" hollies, are planted for their generous production of colorful berries. And 'Burgundy Wine' euphorbia obviously is planted for its rich, burgundy foliage in the spring, summer, and fall landscape.

Use of more drought-tolerant plants. Long periods of dry weather over recent years have made drought-tolerant plants more popular. Don't be mistaken. Drought-tolerant plants still need water during their establishment period. And they may need water during extended droughts, even after well-established. But they can go longer between waterings. To make maximum use of drought tolerant plants, group them in the landscape. One of the main principles of xeriscaping is having different zones of plants with different water needs. Generally it makes the most sense to have the plants that have higher water needs nearer the house. Then further out in the garden, have some areas that can go long periods without supplemental watering.

Agave americana (century plant)

Use of micro-irrigation. Micro-irrigation puts water where it's needed, greatly reducing wasted water. Components are available at many garden centers and big-box stores, and the systems can be installed by anyone, hooking directly to a water spigot, just as you would connect a garden hose. In fact, that's pretty much what makes up micro-irrigation... flexible hose, with emitters being added wherever you need them. Such a system is relatively inexpensive and is great for watering new shrubs, flower beds, vegetable gardens, etc.

Micro-irrigation spray head

Use of more native plants. Using native plants allows us to bring a touch of our natural landscape into our own home landscapes. Donna Legare, co-owner of Native Nurseries in Tallahassee, says that she loves holly fern, an exotic fern, when she sees it in someone else's yard. But, inspired by what she sees in nature in Florida, she chooses Christmas fern and shield fern for her own yard. She bases much of her personal landscaping on the inspiration of nature, as do most native plant gardeners. Another good reason to plant native plants is that our native wildlife, from insects to birds and animals, depends on them.

Native plants must be placed in the proper habitat to grow well, though. They're no different than exotic plants in that regard. Whether native or exotic, pick the right plant for a given site.

Use of more trees. Ever since energy prices

began rising, people have been more concerned with planting shade trees. In fact, trees should be one of the first things you plant in a new landscape. It takes some years before most trees make an impact. So start them early.

Use of improved cultivars of plants.   With advances in plant breeding and plant propagation, a dogwood is no longer just a dogwood.   People are learning the advantages of planting improved cultivars of dogwoods, such as 'Weaver' or 'Barton', over just planting a seedling dogwood.   The same is true in the case of many other plants.   Improved cultivars can offer many advantages over seedling plants.   An improved cultivar has been selected for some special characteristic and has been propagated to retain that characteristic uniformly from plant to plant.   With seedlings, however, there is no uniformity.   A seedling may or may not have the desired characteristics. There can be much variability among seedlings.

Use of more mulched areas.   Every square inch of the landscape does not have to be planted with groundcovers, lawn, shrubs, or flowers.   Some landscapes have large areas of mulched ground with no plants except the large trees above.   This protects the tree roots, keeps your soil from washing away, and recycles nutrients to the trees. It also saves you a lot of work, because you don't have to rake leaves. You can just use the lawn mower to blow the leaves back under the trees when you mow the adjacent lawn out in the sunny areas. And, lastly, it just looks good. Good, clean mulched areas are attractive.

Large naturally mulched area under live oaks

Avoidance of pest-prone plants. Heavy reliance on pesticides in the landscape is out of favor today. Therefore, home gardeners tend not to select plants that they think will have many problems with insects, diseases, or other pests. For example, many home gardeners have opted not to plant hybrid tea roses, peach trees, or even gardenias because of certain pests which are common on these plants. Nurseries no longer sell redtop photinia, once popular in our area, because of a fungus leafspot disease that became a serious redtop pest. No one wants to spend their life spraying pesticides.

Water gardens.   Many home landscapes now include some form of water garden. The sound of running water adds a soothing touch to the backyard landscape. And, as long as there is a shallow area in which they can stand, birds will often be attracted to water.   Small, relatively inexpensive recirculating pumps, pre-formed pool liners and an assortment of aquatic plants are readily available at many garden centers.

Gardening for wildlife. Birds, butterflies, and many other forms of wildlife bring added dimensions to the garden... song, color, movement, and interest as well as other advantages such as natural pest control. So planting for birds and butterflies is a natural part of gardening for many. But we've also learned the value of brush piles and leaving old, dead tree snags where they're not a hazard because they provide homes for birds and other wildlife too.

Landscape lighting.   As we've become more sophisticated in our use of interesting plant forms, we've also become more creative in our use of landscape lighting.   The landscape can take on a completely different character when illuminated by night lighting. Lighting the landscape at night extends the length of time in which we can enjoy the landscape. It also can serve as a crime deterrent.

Compost areas.   Most of us like to do the environmentally correct thing, so we're beginning to make compost piles at home. It's not necessary that you have a fancy compost bin. What is necessary, though, is that you have an out-of-the-way place to pile the excess leaves, prunings, kitchen scraps (except meat), and other stuff that can be composted. This place needs to be close to a source of water (so it can be kept moist but not wet), and, if possible, should be in full sun. It also needs to be where you won't forget to turn it every month or so with a fork. When the composted material begins to look like soil, you can use it to mix into flowers beds, vegetable gardens, or other areas to be planted. Don't confuse compost with mulch, though. Well decomposed compost is used as a soil amendment, mixed into the soil to improve nutrient-holding capacity, aeration, and drainage. Mulch consists of larger particles of organic material, such as leaves, bark, or wood chips, used on the surface of the soil to hold in moisture, keep out weeds, reduce compaction, etc.

2

Soil Preparation & Planting

Successful Landscapes Build from the Ground Up

(Don't Skip This Section; You'll Be Sorry if You Do)

PREVENTING SOIL RELATED PROBLEMS

I t's an extremely common problem. You plant new trees or shrubs, but the plants just never seem to thrive. A few months later some of them may even have some dieback. And further down the road, some of them may die totally.

Plant roots need oxygen. Oxygen space is limited in hard, compacted soils and also in poorly drained soils. The best way to ensure that the soil has sufficient oxygen is to dig a wide planting hole, at least 2-3 times the width of the root ball of the plant. The digging aerates the soil and helps the plant to get off to a good start.

The other thing that you can do to help ensure that the plant roots have plenty of oxygen is to not plant the plant too deeply. Don't dig the hole any deeper than it needs to be. The old advice used to be to plant the plant at the same depth in which it was growing in the container. The latest research tells us to actually set the plant a tiny bit higher than it was growing in the pot. This is to allow for soil that will tend to get pushed up around the plant or mulch that will be placed over the plant, and also for any settling that will occur.

Planting hole 2-3 times width of root ball.

HOW TO LANDSCAPE SITES WITH POORLY DRAINED SOILS.

Some sites have poor drainage. This also results in low oxygen levels for the roots. Water will actually drain into the planting holes and stand there. Of course, this also tends to rot the roots because of the anaerobic conditions.

Plants such as dogwoods, azaleas, junipers, boxwoods, and many other commonly used landscape plants just won't tolerate such poorly drained conditions.

Before doing any planting in an area of suspected poor drainage, dig an 18-inch deep hole after you've had a good rain, preferably an inch or more of rain.

Fill the hole with water. If it takes more than several hours for the water to rain, then you should select plants that will tolerate poorly drained conditions. For lists of plants for wet sites, see the lists in the chapters on trees and shrubs.

Poorly drained soil

Raised beds can also help. But the beds have to be raised considerably, more than six inches, to have a significant impact.

When adding small amounts of soil (less than a foot), try to rototill the added soil into the existing soil. If the existing soil is hard and compacted, you run the risk of having water perched above the old soil unless you break up the old soil first.

SHOULD YOU USE SOIL AMENDMENTS? (PEAT, COMPOST, ETC.)

For years, it was recommended that you mix one part peat or compost with the backfill soil when planting a shrub or tree. Research has changed that recommendation.

Using a soil amendment to change the soil composition of an individual planting hole creates a bath tub effect. During rainy weather, water from the adjacent soil will drain into the coarser-textured amended soil area and stand there around the plants roots. The oxygen in this waterlogged area will be limited. As a result, the plant roots will begin to die and the top of the plant will exhibit the symptoms as leaf margin burn or limb dieback, maybe even as complete plant death.

During dry weather, the amended soil in the planting hole tends to dry out quickly because it has larger pore spaces. So, the plant can suffer from drought stress even when the surrounding natural soil has plenty of moisture.

The current recommendation is not to use soil amendments in individual planting holes. If you wish to change the soil composition in a planting area that is poorly drained, has had its topsoil layer stripped away, is compacted, or has extremely sandy soil, add the amendments to the whole planting bed and rototill them in. If you're planting an individual tree or shrub and wish to change the soil composition, create an amended planting bed large enough to accommodate future root expansion and plant the shrub or tree in the middle of the bed. Never just amend a small individual planting hole.

Much of the time there is no need to use soil amendments anyway. That's what University of Florida research has shown. Pick a plant that can tolerate the type of soil on the site.   Then take the time to thoroughly cultivate the soil for an area three to five times greater the size of the root ball.   The plant should grow well if it is given adequate care following planting. And you can save the money you would have spent on soil amendments.

It's when you try to plant a plant in soil unsuitable for that type of plant, or when you dig a planting hole little larger than the pot in which the plant was growing, that you'll have problems.

THE WRONG LOCATION CAN KILL A GOOD PLANT

Sometimes, even with reasonably good soil preparation, a plant just doesn't grow well. Provided it was a healthy plant in the beginning, it is probably just not suited to the site on which you planted it.

One lesson I've learned over the years is that if a certain type of plant doesn't grow well on a certain site, then it's foolish to keep trying to grow that plant there.   Simply find another plant more suited to the site.

Plants differ in their tolerance to light levels, soil conditions, and other such factors. For example, some plants such as wax myrtles will tolerate the extremes of either dry sites or poorly drained sites.   Other plants, such as azaleas will tolerate neither extreme.

Too often we put plants where they're really not happy. Dogwoods and azaleas don't like hot, dry sites.

Other plants, such as crape myrtles or oleanders would tolerate hot, dry conditions much better.

Take time and forethought to match the plant to the site. Use the lists in the following chapters to pick the proper plant for the intended spot. I've tried to provide information to help make the job of finding plants for a given type of site a little easier.

DON'T NEGLECT PLANTS ONCE THEY'RE PLANTED: MULCH, WATER, AND FERTILIZE PROPERLY

Once you put plants in the ground, don't leave them on their own. You'll need to mulch plants for a generous distance around them with pine straw, leaves, or other organic mulch. The mulch will conserve moisture, reduce weed competition, moderate soil temperatures, and provide some nutrients as it decomposes, not to mention protect the plant from mechanical damage from weedeaters and mowers. At least annually check the mulch. You should maintain the mulch at about 2-3 inches deep. Don't let it get too shallow. But, don't get it too thick either. Leave a space of several inches around the trunk free of mulch to prevent trunk rot. Mulch piled up around the trunk is a common maintenance error that should be avoided.

New plants require frequent watering. Check the moisture of the root ball of the plant. It will dry out much more quickly than will the surrounding native soil because the nursery potting medium is of a coarser soil mix, usually of something like peat, sand, and bark.

Pore spaces are bigger, providing good drainage and oxygen levels. But the larger pore spaces also result in the root ball drying out quicker than the surrounding native soil.

During the summer you may find it necessary to water new plants every other day, or maybe even every day in very hot, dry weather. During the spring and fall you may be able to go a little longer. And during the winter, intervals can probably be stretched even further. But don't think that just because it's winter that plants don't need water.

There is no substitute for sticking your finger in the root ball and checking the moisture level from time to time. Be very attentive to water needs of new plants for a year or more after planting. Remember, the roots need to grow out into surrounding soil. And it takes time to develop a good root system in the surrounding soil. Larger tree specimens will take several years before they become well established.

When you water, make sure you apply enough water to thoroughly wet the root ball. You won't provide enough by standing there spraying with the garden hose. If you're trying to do so, you're under-watering. You have to let the water run in one place long enough to thoroughly wet the soil four to six inches deep.

A good way to water new plantings is with a micro-irrigation system. A micro-irrigation system is essentially just a flexible ½ to ¾ inch hose that can be attached to your water spigot. Then, into this hose, you insert a spaghetti tube with an irrigation head on it wherever you want water. It's a flexible, relatively inexpensive and easy-to-install system that you can purchase from your local garden center or big-box store.   It enables you to water new plantings effectively and efficiently. And, if you want to make the job even easier, you can put a battery-operated timer on it and program it as desired.

Vortex micro-irrigation head is for
watering individual plants

Once plantings are well established, a year or two down the road, they will require less supplemental watering. But be aware that even then, especially during prolonged droughts, supplemental watering can help plants tremendously. And in some cases, it's the difference between life and death.

Water is needed year-round, not just during the spring and summer. Plants will use less water during the cooler seasons, and less water will be lost from the soil to evaporation then. But, there will still be times that the soil will become dry and you'll need to water during fall, and even during winter.

Supply added nutrients to the plants in the form of fertilizer. This is especially important in the early establishment years.   Follow   the   fertilization recommendations given in this book in the chapters on various types of plants.

Soil testing is available through your local extension office, a branch of your state's land-grant college. Soil testing can tell you what the major plant nutrient levels are in the soil and if you need to add fertilizer.

180 degree spray head is good for
watering groups of plants.

3

Plant Problems
Preventing Them Before They Start

The reason that this chapter on plant problems is so near the front of this book is not to discourage you as a gardener. Rather it is to help you make your life as a gardener easier, by helping you to understand what causes most plant problems, before you start selecting plants and planting. As they say, an ounce of prevention is worth a pound of cure!

When a plant is growing poorly, we tend to assume the problem is caused by some pest, such as an insect or disease. Usually, though, that's not the case. More often, plant decline is caused by the two factors discussed in the last chapter: either poor soil conditions, or trying to grow the plant in an unsuitable site for that particular plant.

So, YOU can prevent most plant problems by: 1-Selecting the right plant for the site, and 2-Following proper soil preparation and planting techniques.

Another common cause of plant decline is poor care. Just as plant selection is YOUR responsibility, so is the plant care. Is the plant base free of weeds and does it have mulch around it? Do you periodically fertilize the plant, and do you water it when rainfall isn't adequate? Do you prune it with care, or do you haphazardly shear it without much thought as to where you're making the individual cuts?   Remember, plants are living creatures. Neglect or abuse, in the form of competition from weeds, inadequate moisture or nutrition, and careless pruning or other types of wounds, take their toll on the health of plants. You can even kill a plant with too much care... too much water or too much fertilizer.

So often, such stresses weaken a plant and pave the way for the development of disease or insect problems.   Just as when you or I get run down, sickness often follows.   The same principle applies to plants.

Rather than just relying on pesticides to manage pest problems, we need to use what is called Integrated Pest Management (IPM). IPM involves such common-sense approaches as making the environment less favorable for the pest organism. For example, you may decrease watering frequency and therefore lower the humidity which favors fungal disease development. IPM also uses principles such as sanitation or removal of infected plant parts and frequent monitoring to catch pest problems before they get out of control. To have a plant pest problem, you have to have three things: a host plant, a pest organism, and a favorable environment for development of the pest. IPM involves manipulating all these factors to more effectively manage pest problems you may encounter in the garden. Though pesticides are mentioned in this chapter, always try other methods of control first.

So, when trying to diagnose a plant problem, first look for the obvious and the most common problems. Examine the growing conditions of the plant and the care the plant has received.   Then, look for the presence of insect pests, which you can often see. Finally, consider the possibility of a plant disease.

INSECT PESTS

Often with insect pests, you'll be able to see the culprit on the plant. Be careful, though, not to assume that just any insect you see on the plant is a pest. Some insects are not only harmless; they're actually beneficial in that they feed on pest insects.   You certainly don't want to kill these good guys needlessly!

Basically, pest insects are of two types. There are the chewing insects, and there are the sucking insects.

CHEWING INSECTS
(CATERPILLARS, LEAFMINERS, AND BEETLES)

Damage of chewing insects is usually in the form of chewed holes or notches in leaves. In the case of leafminers, the damage is in the form of chewed trails or blotches in the interior of the leaves, between the two surfaces of the leaf.

Not all insects chew. Only certain kinds, such as caterpillars and beetles, have mouthparts that facilitate chewing. Other insects, such as moths and butterflies, have harmless siphoning mouthparts which they use in gathering nectar from flowers. And, still other, such as aphids, have piercing-sucking mouthparts which they use to suck sap from plant parts.

It takes quite a bit of damage from chewing insects to cause significant harm to a plant. A few chewed leaves here and there aren't worth worrying about.

However, if the damage is severe, insecticide control may be warranted.

Chewing damage in lawn from sod webworms.

Insecticide sprays are generally safer and more effective than dusts. Be sure to spray the undersides of the leaves as that's where the insects usually are found. Insecticides such as *Sevin®; malathion; Ortho Max Lawn & Garden Insect Killer®; Spectracide Triazicide Insect Killer Once & Done!®; Ortho Tree and Shrub Insect Killer; Bayer Advanced Fruit, Citrus & Vegetable Insect Control;* and *Bayer Advanced Tree and Shrub Insect Control* are effective against many chewing insects. Be sure to read the insecticide label to ascertain that it's okay to use the spray on the type of plant you have. Also, follow all precautions and directions on the label for your safety and for effectiveness of the product.

Most chewing insect plant pests are **caterpillars**. *Bacillus thuringiensis* is the active ingredient in several insecticides that are very effective against most caterpillars. Dipel®, Thuricide®, and Biological Worm Spray are several possible tradenames of products containing BT. Use BT for caterpillar control whenever possible because it is not harmful to beneficial insects, to man, or to animals.

One unusual type of chewing insect is the *leafminer.* Called a leafminer because they mine or tunnel between the upper and lower leaf surfaces, they are the larvae of certain kinds of flies. The adult fly lays her eggs in the leaf and the hatched larvae spends its life tunneling between the surfaces. Other types of leafminers just leave blotches.

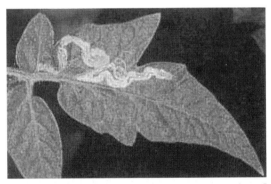

Leafminer damage in tomato leaf.

Leafminers are best controlled with a systemic insecticide such as Bayer Advanced Fruit, Citrus & Vegetable Insect Control; Bayer Advanced Tree and Shrub Insect Control; or Ortho Tree and Shrub Insect Killer.

Systemic Insecticides enter the plant's system rather than just staying on the leaf surfaces.

One type of chewing damage sometimes attributed

to insects is not caused by an insect at all. *Slug* damage appears as chewed leaves, especially on tender flower plants or vegetable plants. But, you'll see no insect and won't see the slugs either, because they feed at night. *Slugs baits* are available from garden centers. The paste kind, such as Deadline Slug and Snail Killer, work very well, but be careful to read the directions and use only around plants specified on the label. For example, Deadline cannot be used around vegetables or fruits. Slugs can also be killed by using sunken bowls of beer in the garden. The slugs are attracted to the beer, and when they fall in, they cannot crawl back out. Diatomaceous earth is another possible control for slugs.

Beetles are another common type of chewing insect pest. Many beetles feed at night. If you note chewing damage on a shrub or tree, yet you can find no chewing insect pest, it is a good possibility the damage was done by beetles.

BEETLES THAT BORE INTO TREES

Beetles that bore into trees, usually only attack stressed or weak trees. The stress may be from such factors as drought, construction damage, or lightning. By the time beetles attack the tree, it is often so weakened that it would die even without the damage from the beetles.

The group of the beetles known as the *pine bark beetles* operates in a similar manner. However, the pine trees these bark beetles attack sometimes would not die unless the beetles attack. Most pine bark beetles attack quickly and in large numbers. Often the trunk has many of the little balls of sap from the beetles' entry holes.

Once you notice the signs of the pine bark beetles' attack, it will be difficult to save the tree by spraying. The beetles have already begun tunneling out beneath the bark, making egg-laying galleries. Soon there will be so many of these tunnels that the tree's circulatory system (located just beneath the bark) is disrupted and the needles of the tree will begin browning. At that point, it is definitely too late to save the tree.

However, Onyx (active ingredient, bifenthrin) is an insecticide that can be used to protect high-value pines adjacent to infested pines. Onyx must be applied by a professional, licensed pest control operator who can do lawn and ornamental pest control.

SUCKING INSECTS (APHIDS, SCALES, LACEBUGS, MEALYBUGS, WHITEFLIES AND MITES)

The most common insect damage you'll encounter on plants is from sucking insects. Aphids, scale insects, lacebugs, and mealybugs, as well as mites (not really an insect), all have sucking mouthparts that they use to suck plant juices. The sucking of the plant sap results in various types of damage. Usually there is discoloration of the leaves. Often new growth is distorted and deformed.

Aphids (plant lice) are often seen clustered on new, tender leaves and stems. Aphids are most often light green, though some types are other colors such as gray. Often you'll see old, white shed skins around the pin-head size aphids. Another sign of the presence of aphids, whiteflies, or soft scales is the presence of sooty mold, a black film on the plant foliage or surrounding objects. The sooty mold is a fungus that grows in the sweet juice excreted by these sucking insects as they feed. To rid a plant of sooty mold, you must simply bring the sucking insect problem under control.

Scales are usually found on the undersides of leaves or even on stems. Scales are insects with coverings, ranging from the appearance of tiny turtles (as with magnolia scale) to a sticky coating of snow (as with white peach scale). Scale insects really don't even look like insects because the insect itself is beneath the covering. Only when scales are young, before they form their coating, do they move around. Once their coating is formed, they are stationary.

Tea scale on underside of camellia leaf.
Photo from University of Georgia

Mealybugs are closely related to scales. Instead of coverings, though, mealybugs excrete a white sticky coating in which they are free to move around. Mealybugs are white and have two tail-like appendages extending from their rear end. There are also small appendages around all sides of the mealybug's body.

Citrus mealybug
Photo from University of Florida

Lacebugs, practically always found on the undersides of leaves, are common pests of azaleas, sycamores, lantanas, and some other plants. Their damage is first noted as a speckling of the top of the leaf. Close inspection of the undersides of the leaves may reveal the tiny, lacy-winged insects or specks of their black, shiny excrement.

Azalea lacebugs on underside of leaf. Note the characteristic shiny black specks of excrement. Photo from University of Georgia

Whiteflies appear just as their name implies. Certain plants such as gardenias and ligustrums are favored hosts. The adults don't feed, but the young, developing in small, round, flat cases on the undersides of the leaves, do feed. And, like aphids and soft scales, they excrete a sticky juice in which the black, sooty mold fungus likes to grow.

Mites are not insects. But their feeding damage is similar to that of sucking insects. Plant-parasitic mites are generally too small to be easily seen on a plant. The first sign of mite damage is usually a yellowish speckling on the upper surface of leaves. Also, on broadleaf plants, the new growth may be curled and distorted because of feeding during the development of the leaves. Webbing is sometimes evident with spider mites, especially if the mite population has reached high numbers.

One way to check for presence of mites is to rap the damaged plant parts onto a piece of white paper. If mites are present, you'll usually see them as tiny pin-point-sized dots crawling around on the paper.

Whitefly pupal cases and an adult whitefly.
Photo from University of Florida

INSECTICIDES FOR SUCKING INSECT CONTROL

Whenever you find damaging levels of sucking insect pests and have to use a pesticide, try to select the pesticide that poses the least risk to you and the environment.

Insecticidal or horticultural oils are great for controlling many sucking insects such as scales, aphids, whiteflies, mites, mealybugs, and lacebugs. Insecticidal oils generally are safer to the applicator and the environment than many traditional chemical insecticides. Some of the older types of oils specify on their label that the oil not be used when excessively high temperatures are expected.

New lighter insecticidal oil sprays are now on the market. These sprays should pose less risk of burning plants at high temperatures than previous formulations. High temperatures are usually interpreted as those over 85 degrees.

Year ago it was common practice to pour the dirty dishwater over the foliage of plants, such as gardenia, that had whiteflies or aphids. Soap is an effective and environmentally safe insecticide and can help control many insects, especially the sucking insects such as aphids or whiteflies.

Label from one brand of horticultural oil.

Commercial soap insecticides, formulated

specifically for safe use on plants, are available from most garden centers as various brands of insecticidal soap.

Be sure to follow all the directions and precautions on the soap formulation labels, though, just as if you were using any other pesticide.

When the soaps and oils don't work, you may have to resort to regular pesticides. Just use them carefully, according to label directions.   And, except for rare cases such as when growing peaches or nectarines, don't use them preventatively.   Normally, it's much wiser to wait until an insect problem develops before you spray. Many of the same insecticides that you can use for chewing insects can be used for sucking insect control: *Ortho Max Lawn & Garden Insect Killer®; Spectracide Triazicide Insect Killer Once & Done!®; Ortho Tree and Shrub Insect Killer; Bayer Advanced Fruit, Citrus & Vegetable Insect Control; and Bayer Advanced Tree and Shrub Insect Control.* There may be other brands of these insecticides with the same active ingredients. Just make sure the label specifies directions for the site or type of plant where you intend to use the insecticide.

Never use an insecticide, or any pesticide, in a manner inconsistent with the label on the pesticide container. To do so can be a violation of Federal law and could be hazardous to your health.

PLANT DISEASES
Before jumping to the conclusion that an ailing plant

has a disease, remember to first look for more common and obvious causes of decline such as poor drainage or compacted soil.   Once you've eliminated such causes of decline and determined that there are no insect pests present, only then should you consider the possibility of a plant disease.

Most plant diseases are caused by one of three types of microscopic organisms: either plant-parasitic fungi, bacteria, or viruses. Fungus diseases are most common, followed by bacterial, and finally viral.

There are some chemical fungicides on the market that will help control certain fungus diseases, but there are very few bactericides and no viricides. And, a particular fungicide only controls certain fungus diseases. That's why it is important to correctly identify the specific disease.

Making chemical fungal disease control even more difficult is the fact that not many fungicides are curative; they don't cure the plant once it is infected. Most fungicides work by providing a barrier on the plant surface that prohibits the germination of fungus spores and subsequent penetration into the plant. In other words, fungicides are primarily preventative agents, not curative agents. If most of the leaves of a plant already are infected with a fungus disease, then it is too late to spray. Spraying will only help prevent the infection of new growth and growth that is not already infected. Spraying is not usually a cure-all.

MAJOR GROUPS OF DISEASES

Stem Diebacks: The most common type of plant disease encountered is the stem dieback. With a dieback, tips of branches, entire branches, or even entire plants die. Dieback diseases, though, are not usually even actually true diseases. That is, the primary cause of the problem is not usually a fungus, bacterium, or virus. Most often, the problem can be traced back to poor soil conditions, poor care, or the plant being planted where it really doesn't belong. Pesticide sprays often do no good for such diebacks.

Sometimes diseases do cause diebacks. In such cases, pesticides still do little in controlling the problem because the disease organism is either in the vascular system of the plant or in the root system. The best thing to do is to cut back the plant, cutting into healthy tissue and removing the diseased portion.

When cutting back a diseased plant, you must be careful not to spread the disease organism from the diseased wood to healthy wood with your pruning tools. You will do just that unless you sterilize the pruning tools with alcohol or a 10% bleach in water solution between cuts.

Try to make your cuts six to eight inches below any signs of dieback. Examine the interior of the stem where you make the cut. If it is discolored, indicating disease activity, cut back several inches further. But, be sure to sterilize the pruning tools before making that last cut. Continue this procedure on each affected limb until you reach healthy wood.

Root rots: There are several types of fungi that will

cause root rots. Some of these are fungi that are favored by poor drainage. But mushroom root rot is a common disease that can infect woody plants on any type of site. If you have a well-established woody plant that suddenly dies, and you can find no visible above-ground symptoms, you may be dealing with mushroom root rot. A trained person can sometimes find white fungal material just below the bark of the lower trunk or larger roots that flare from the trunk. So called because at a certain stage of its life cycle this fungus does generate small tan-colored mushrooms, mushroom root rot cannot be treated with a fungicide. It is best to replant with a different type of plant, preferably not a woody plant.

White fungal material just beneath the bark in plant with mushroom root rot. Cornell University photo.

Leafspots: There are many types of leaf spot diseases caused by a wide range of fungi and bacteria. Some, such as black spot on rose are so common that you may learn to identify them by sight. But most will require diagnosis by a trained person such as an experienced Extension horticulturist, nursery operator, or landscape pest control person. Or, they may even require laboratory diagnosis. See your local Extension agent to arrange laboratory diagnosis through your state university plant disease lab. You must correctly identify the leaf spot disease and causal fungus to know which fungicide to use.

Fungicide sprays will help with many leaf spot diseases if applied soon enough. But, don't wait until every leaf on the plant is severely affected and leaf drop has occurred before starting sprays.

On the other hand, don't become overly alarmed just because you see a few leaf spots on a plant. No plant is blemish-free, especially late in the summer. Most leafspots on plants never develop to a serious enough degree to warrant applying fungicides.

Consider the time of year, too. There's little to be gained in spraying a deciduous plant, such as a dogwood, in September, when it will be losing its leaves in a month or so anyway.

There aren't many cases where spraying for leaf spot diseases is really needed on ornamental landscape plants. There are some exceptions, such as with roses being grown for show. And some fruit trees need preventative sprays to prevent leaf diseases.

Powdery mildew: Powdery mildew can be a significant leaf problem on some plants such as roses, crape myrtles, and euonymus. As its name implies, this fungal disease looks like a white powdery mildew growing on the leaves. The leaves soon yellow and fall. Fungicides such as Bayer Advanced Disease Control for Roses, Flowers, and Shrubs (containing tebuconazole) are available to control powdery mildew. Be sure the fungicide you select has the type of plant you wish to spray listed on the label.

Viruses can cause leaf problems, too. Again, the rose is a common host. Virus-infected rose plants usually have leaves with distinct bright yellow mottled patterns. There is no chemical control for viral diseases. Do not prune a virus infected plant and then prune a healthy plant without sterilizing the pruning tools first. You'll spread the virus. Aphids can spread some viruses, too. It's advisable to remove virus-infected plants from plantings of roses.

Camellias sometimes get similar virus leaf mottling. Do not propagate from such infected plants and, again, be careful about spreading the virus by pruning. Otherwise, the virus on camellia doesn't seem to cause significant damage. In fact, sometimes viruses have resulted in desired variegation in the flowers.

Azalea or camellia leaf galls are diseases that look worse than they are. Common especially during cool, rainy springs, these diseases cause thickened, distorted, and discolored leaves on azaleas or camellias. The affected leaves are quite shocking to most home gardeners, convinced their plant has some rare and terrible malady.

Azalea leaf gall. University of Illinois photo.

Once you find the disease in the spring, the infection has already taken place and there's nothing you can do to remedy the situation. Nothing, that is, other than pick off all the affected leaves, put them in a garbage bag, and get them out of the area so that they cannot provide inoculum for next year's infection.

Azalea or camellia leaf galls don't kill the plants or cause any serious damage other than the only slightly unsightly presence of the deformed leaves.

Lichens: A lichen is gray or greenish fuzzy, crusty growth often found on the bark surface of many plants, especially declining plants. A lichen is a combination of a fungus and an algae. The fungus anchors the algae to the plant, and the algae, being a green plant, manufactures food for the two. Lichens are not parasitic to the plant on which they are found. They are only using it as a home. They would be just as happy on an old fence post or a wooden roof shingle, two other places they're commonly seen.

Lichen. University of Illinois Extension photo.

Unfortunately, because lichens are so often found on declining plants (probably because it's easier to become established on a plant that's growing and expanding so slowly), they're often blamed for the decline. Most often the decline is caused by poor growing conditions or poor care. Have the plants been fertilized and watered as needed? Are they mulched? Are they growing in an extremely sandy soil or in an extremely compacted soil or a poorly drained soil? The decline can usually be traced to such conditions.

No fungicide control is generally recommended for control of lichens.

MISCELLANEOUS PESTS

Moles: Moles are small, tunneling animals that make tunnels just beneath the soil surface in search of soil insects and earthworms. In the process, moles sometimes uproot small plants or cause uneven surfaces in lawns. Mole traps are available from many garden centers. Though difficult to catch, moles are not impossible to catch using such traps.

Don't waste your money on the poison baits sold for mole control. Moles only eat live insects or earthworms and such bait isn't attractive to the moles.

One or two moles, because of moles' wide-ranging activity, often give the impression that many moles are present in a yard and that a serious problem exists. Often, though, the few moles will soon leave an area for new feeding grounds and the problem will end quickly. So, considering the difficulty with which moles are trapped, patience is often the best remedy when moles are active in your yard.

Armadillos: Damage from armadillos digging in your yard may occur, especially if you live adjacent to a wooded area. The armadillos are primarily nocturnal, so you may not see them. But, you may be troubled by the holes they leave behind in your yard as they dig for insects and worms.

As with moles, though, there is not an easy solution to stopping armadillos from digging in your yard. If you live out in the country where it's legal, you might resort to shooting them. You might also try trapping the armadillos in a live trap. But, then what do you do with an armadillo once you catch it? It is my understanding that the correct procedure is to humanely dispose of the armadillo. The armadillo being a non-native nuisance animal, your state Division of Wildlife prefers that you not release them where they will become a nuisance to someone else. So, only if the armadillos are causing a tremendous problem for you would you probably want to resort to trapping and disposing of them. The whole procedure could become rather involved and troublesome.

Deer: As our suburbs take over deer habitat, deer are becoming more and more of a garden pest. There are many home remedies we hear: soap bars hung in plants; human hair hung in nylon stockings among plants; adding a beaten egg to a gallon of water and spraying it over the plants. One gardener even says used kitty litter spread around the affected plants works wonders – and really doesn't smell that bad once spread. There are commercial repellents such as Hinder that do seem to work but that require regular application. Nothing seems to work in all cases. Deer seem to have varying sensitivities to the various remedies. The only sure remedy seems to be a fence, 8-10 feet high, around the garden.

Deer also seem to have varying tastes as to what plants they will and will not eat. Deer in one area may not eat impatiens. But your deer may love them. Deers' taste will also vary with the season. They may turn up their noses at pittosporum this year, but next year when the woods are dry, your succulent pittosporum tips may be irresistible. So, a good list of deer resistant plants is all but impossible to develop.

There always seem to be exceptions to the list, and there are usually plenty of plants that are deer-resistant yet not on the lists. Still the following may be worthy of consideration.

Trees: Cedar, crape myrtle, cypress, Carolina silverbell, dogwood, ginkgo, Gordonia, hawthorn, American holly, Jerusalem thorn, Japanese magnolia, pine, pawpaw, southern magnolia, red maple, oak, palms, persimmon, pine, pomegranate, redbud, river birch, tulip poplar, and sweetgum.

Shrubs: Japanise anise, aucuba, banana shrub, barberry, boxwood, cepholataxus, cherry laurel, feijoa, gardenia, cornuta holly, dwarf yaupon holly, glossy abelia, juniper, leucothoe, ligustrum, mahonia, nandina, oleander, pyracantha, rose of Sharon, sago palm, spirea, tea olive, viburnum, yucca, and wax myrtle.

Flowers: Agapanthus, ageratum, amaryllis, bachelor's button or cornflower, butterfly bush, calendula, chrysanthemum, daffodil, dusty miller, elephant ears, gerbera daisy, iris, joepye weed, lantana, lobelia, marigold, narcissus, petunia, poppy, 'Goldsturm' rudbeckia, snapdragon, spiderwort, verbena, vinca, yarrow, and zinnia.

Groundcovers: Ajuga, aspidistra, holly fern, ivy, Christmas fern, cinnamon fern, Asiatic jasmine, Vinca major, and Vinca minor.

Vines: Flowering jessamine and allamanda.

Ornamental grasses: *Pennisetum* or fountaingrass, little bluestem, northern sea oats, pampas grass, and muhly grass.

Herbs: Most heavily scented herbs such as basil, mint, oregano, rosemary, thyme, scented geraniums, parsley, and Mexican mint marigold.

Sapsuckers: Rings of holes in the trunk of a tree is a sign of feeding from sapsuckers, a type of bird. People often mistake the holes for insect damage. But the straight lines of regularly spaced holes are characteristic of sapsuckers rather than insects. Unless the feeding is extremely heavy, though, over a long period of time, there is not significant damage. Temporarily, wrapping the trunk of an affected tree with a material such as burlap may break the feeding habit on that tree.

Fire Ants: Fire ants are more of a people problem than a plant problem. Fire ants, in case you haven't discovered the hard way, are the ants that make the large mounds and aggressively greet intruders with stings. Fire ants aren't especially large; they look like your typical ant. It's their habit of swarming in great numbers onto anything that disturbs their mound that makes them such a problem. Also, their large mounds can interfere with such routine operations as lawn mowing.

There are many new insecticides for fire ant control, http://www.aces.edu/pubs/docs/A/ANR-0175-A/ANR-0175-A.pdf Over 'N Out contains fipronil, and when broadcast as directed in spring, can give fire ant control from spring through summer, preventing formation of new colonies during that period. When you treat for fire ants, be sure to include the area around your air conditioning or heat pump units. Fire ants can nest in these units, causing considerable damage.

Squirrels: "Tree rats" is a suitable term for squirrels. I've known squirrels to eat everything in the garden from tomatoes, to apples, to patches out of St. Augustine grass lawns. They can be a real nuisance.

Unfortunately, there is no known control for squirrels. In some cases, gardeners have caged them out of prized plantings with small mesh wire. In other cases I've known gardeners to keep the local population down with a pellet gun or shotgun (this is a constant battle and the legality varies with locale). In some cases, traps can be used to remove the offenders. The bottom line is that there is no easy or very effective solution for the squirrel problem that so often exists in urban gardens.

Squirrels can be prevented from stealing pecans off pecan trees only if access to the tree is not available from adjacent trees or utility lines. A piece of smooth sheet metal or tin, wrapped around the trunk of the tree, about four feet off the ground, can prevent squirrels from climbing the trunk of a pecan tree. But, no limbs must hang low enough so the squirrels can reach the tree that way.

Birds: Birds can be pests of fruit crops such as figs, grapes, blueberries, or strawberries. Netting, to screen out birds, is available from many garden centers or mail-order catalogues. The netting is simply draped over the plant and secured at the corners. Sunlight can still reach the plant.

Yellowjackets: If you've ever stumbled onto the underground nest of these yellow and black wasp or bee-like insects, you'll remember.   When disturbed, yellowjackets swarm out of their underground nest in great numbers.   And, because the nest in sometimes in an area in which you want to work or play, you may wish to destroy it.

Be careful!   Many people are severely allergic to bee and wasp stings.   If you're one of these, call on a pest control company to eradicate the nest.

If you wish to tackle the job yourself, scout out the area during daylight hours.   Try to find all the entrance and exit holes to the nest.   There may be several. Also, map out an escape route which will enable you to run away quickly without tripping.

Then plan to go back after dark when all the yellowjackets should be home and there's not much in and out activity.   Dress as protectively as possible. Long sleeve coveralls are a great idea.   Tightly secure cuffs with rubber bands to prevent yellowjackects from flying up sleeves or legs.   A beekeeper's hat with veil would also be helpful.

For yellowjackets, you can use the hornet and wasp insecticides that come in an aerosol can (the kind that shoots a long stream of insecticide with knockdown power), but do this after dark.   Direct a strong and constant stream of spray into the main hole and don't stop until activity from the yellowjackets ceases or until they start escaping and force you to retreat.   I have used this method a number of times at night, after it's completely dark, and have never had a problem.

Weed control using glyphosate herbicides: Glyphosate is the active ingredient in several herbicides that give non-selective weed control. The first release and best-known brand is Roundup®, but there are various other brands of glyphosate herbicides now. They may vary in percentage of active ingredient, though, so always follow the label directions.

The beauty of glyphosate lies in its effectiveness and its safety.

Glyphosate is a systemic herbicide, meaning it is absorbed by green plant tissue (such as leaves, or green stems) and translocated to the root system. Because of this mode of action, it doesn't kill upon contact. But, because it affects the root system, glyphosate is usually one of our most effective herbicides.

Glyphosate is also fairly safe when used as directed. Its toxicity to you, the applicator, is not great. And, it does not remain viable in the soil. It is very quickly broken down by soil microorganisms. As soon as the weeds die, you can plant new plants in the area. There is one major precaution that must be heeded with glyphosate herbicides. In general, it will be absorbed by any green plant tissue. It doesn't distinguish between weeds and desirable plants. You have to be careful not to let even mist drift to other plants. And you need to be careful about spraying weeds in a bed, getting the glyphosate on your feet, and then walking out across the lawn while the wet material is on your shoes.

Glyphosate will not be very effective on slick-leafed plants such as smilax or greenbriar. More of the spray runs off than penetrates. Repeat aplications will be needed on plants with extensive or woody root systems.

All things considered, though, glyphosate can be a very helpful tool in the landscape. It can be used for spot weeding in beds, between shrubs, or beneath trees. It can be used for killing grass in cracks in walks or drives. It's very helpful in keeping grass away from young trees. (just be sure not to spray the bark of young trees with green bark, such as peaches or maples).

Glyphosate is especially useful in killing grass and weeds in an area a month prior to rototilling for a flower or vegetable garden. You'll have less problems with weeds coming back after tilling if you'll spray with glyphosate a month before.

All you need for application is a small pump-up type sprayer (or even just a spray bottle for small jobs). For some jobs, you may wish to make a hand-shield of cardboard or plywood to keep the spray off desirable plants. The mouth of a plastic milk jug or a funnel, fastened upside down over the spray nozzle, may also help reduce spray drift if you lower the funnel to the ground over the weed to be sprayed. Many backpack sprayers come with herbicide spray mist shields as an available option. These are very useful when spraying glyphosate in beds.

Brush Killers: These are herbicides that usually contain triclopyr as the active ingredient. They are non-selective herbicides that can be used on woody weeds and vines such as poison ivy. They can also be used to prevent stumps from resprouting. Let's say, for example, that you cut a mimosa or Chinese tallow tree that has sprouted up in your yard. Within a few minutes of making the cut, before the sap has had a chance to dry, use a paintbrush to paint the brush killer with triclopyr directly onto the cut stump. Take special care to make sure the herbicide saturates the outer edges of the trunk where the cambium layer lies. This should keep the trunk from resprouting growth later.

COMMON PESTS & POSSIBLE CONTROLS*

Azalea / camellia leaf galls: Pruning   out infected leaves and discard them. Change the mulch.

Aphids, whiteflies, lacebugs: Insecticidal soaps, insecticidal oils, acetamiprid, neem oil, azadirachtin, imidacloprid, bifenthrin, cyfluthrin, lambda-cyhalothrin.

Beetles: Carbaryl (Sevin®), imidacloprid, bifenthrin, cyfluthrin, lambda-cyhalothrin.

Caterpillars: *Bacillus thuringiensis* insecticides such as Dipel or Thurcide; Spinosad, carabyl (Sevin®), imidacloprid, bifenthrin, cyfluthrin, lambda-cyhalothrin.

Leafminers: Imidacloprid, cyfluthrin, azadirachtin, bifenthrin.

Leaf spot diseases: Fungicide depends on specific fungus

Mites: Insecticidal oils or soaps. Neem oil.

Pine bark beetles: Bifenthrin

Powdery mildew: Myclobutanil (Immunox), neem oil.

Scale insects / mealy bugs: Insecticidal oils, cyfluthrin, imidacloprid, bifenthrin, azadirachtin, lambda-cyhalothrin.

Slugs: Slug paste or other slug baits. Ammonia spray (see vegetable chapter).

Stem dieback / viruses: Pruning out the affected limbs to a point at least 6 inches below lowest symptoms of the stem.   Sterilize pruning instruments in between cuts.

*Pesticides can only be used on the sites and types of plants listed on their label. So before spraying your vegetable garden with just any pesticide off the shelf, make sure that the label specifies that it can be used on vegetables. Before using any pesticide, always read the pesticide label and follow the instructions and precautions carefully.   Never use a pesticide in a manner contrary to that specified on the label.   The label is the definitive authority.

IF ANY INFORMATION IN THIS BOOK CONFLICTS WITH INFORMATION ON THE PESTICIDE LABEL, FOLLOWTHE LABEL. ALWAYS TAKE THE TIME TO READ THE LABEL.

4

Trees

The basis of a comfortable garden or landscape

WHY TREES ARE SO IMPORTANT

We're all familiar with the benefits of the shade a nice shade tree casts. But, trees help on a global level by changing carbon dioxide into oxygen through photosynthesis.

According to the theories on global warming, the function of trees is more important than ever before because of the alarming rate with which carbon dioxide from the burning of fossil fuels is being trapped in our atmosphere. The buildup of carbon dioxide in our atmosphere prevents heat from escaping back into outer space. Many scientists say that it is this buildup of heat, sometimes called the greenhouse effect, that is having a noticeable effect on the earth's climate.

Present global temperatures are already the highest since records have been kept. No, it's not just your imagination. The American Forestry Association says that if current opportunities to improve tree growth were taken, the new growth would reduce atmospheric carbon dioxide by 450 million tons, offsetting a good portion of the carbon dioxide the United States releases annually from burning fossil fuels.

USING TREES TO SHADE YOUR HOME

By strategically positioning trees to cast shade on windows, walls, and glaring surfaces around your home, you can also reduce your utility bill by 20 to 30%. Keep in mind, though, when deciding where to plant trees in your landscape that sun position changes with both the time of day and the season of the year. So, it is important that you take time to accurately plan where to plant your trees to shade the appropriate spot at the appropriate time.

In the early morning and late afternoon hours, the sun is low in the sky, and trees will cast long shadows. At noon, the sun is high in the sky, and trees will cast short shadows. So, if you're concerned with shading a portion of your home during the middle of the day, the tree must be close to the area to be shaded.

Shadows also change direction with the time of day. A tree casting shade on an object at 1:00 p.m. on a summer afternoon will not shade the same object at 3:00 p.m., or even at 2:00 p.m., unless it is a very wide tree planted very close to the object to be shaded. The sun travels a great arc in the summer sky and with each passing hour makes a great change in position in the sky. But, during winter the sun travels in a much shorter arc in the sky. There is not as great a change in the position of the sun from hour to hour in the winter sky.

What all this means is that in order to shade your home in the summer, trees must be positioned fairly close to the home and must provide a wide angle of coverage. You'll very likely find that it takes several trees to provide the same width of shade coverage during the summer that one tree can provide during the winter. If you plant trees during the winter (a good time to plant trees), keep these factors in mind.

You can determine precisely where to place a shade tree to shade a particular part of your house. But to do this, you will have to carefully observe the shade patterns throughout the day at the time of year you wish to provide the shade.

 Deciduous trees are usually best for shading, because they will allow sunlight to warm the home in winter when heat is needed.

PROTECTING EXISTING TREES DURING CONSTRUCTION AND LANDSCAPING

We spend a lot of time and money trying to establish trees in the landscape. And, we must wait years for newly planted trees to begin providing shade. It's a shame that we are so careless during construction projects with the trees we already have.

Though trees can be magnificient figures in the landscape, they also can be sensitive creatures. Too often we view them as simply structural components in the landscape, much the same as we view utility sheds, swimming pools, or other structures.

We need to realize, however, that trees are living organisms. Large trees took years to grow to their size. It may take a lifetime to grow a replacement. But it only takes minutes to cause irreversible damage to a tree.

We've made a lot of progress in getting people to realize that bulldozer scars (or, on a smaller scale, lawnmower scars) harm trees. But, it's more difficult to convince people of the spread of a tree's root system and of the importance of minimizing damage to the root system.

It's a common belief that tree roots extend outward only as far as the tree branches extend. Yet, research has shown *that tree roots often extend three times or more as far out as the tree branches extend.* If we could only get those in the construction trades to understand this!

It's also a common belief that the shallow roots, those in the top foot or so of soil, are not vital to the health of the tree. But research has now shown that most of the roots that actually absorb nutrients, water, and oxygen are in the top two feet of soil. Furthermore, the roots in the top six inches of soil are much more important to the tree than ever thought before. Tap roots, those roots that extend downward like a large carrot, don't even exist in many cases. It's the shallower roots that really perform most of the functions so vital to the tree's health.

So, when shallow roots are scraped away during construction work, the tree suffers severely. Or, when six inches of clay fill is added over the delicate roots, restricting oxygen penetration, damage occurs. Even one pass of heavy equipment, such as a concrete truck, over tree roots can damage them through compaction, resulting in oxygen loss. Roots are lost in all cases, and the loss can result in dieback in the tree's top.

On this eroded site, you can easily see where the tree roots are... close to the soil surface.

Home buyers often pick a certain home because of the trees on the lot. Knowing this, builders may tend to leave a lot of trees on home lots. The problem is that they often abuse the trees during the construction process.

Very rarely do construction-damaged trees die before the home is sold. The home buyer buys a home with trees; they're just weakened trees. The trees may suffer a lot of limb dieback and limb drop in the following years. The trees often don't even totally die, at least not quickly. They just remain in a slow state of decline. The damaged, weak trees aren't nearly as attractive and full as they once were. Being weak, they're prone to pests. They don't have the root system they once did. So they suffer extremely during dry weather. Or they may even blow over in a thunderstorm. Or, they fall over after a heavy rain. Or, the homeowner, realizing that he has a lot of hazard trees on his property, with expensive targets (home, cars, etc.), ends up paying a tree service to remove the trees.

Most tree roots are in the upper 2 feet of soil and spread outwards 3 times the width of the canopy.

Protect your trees during the construction process and later as well. Try to keep any type of soil disturbance or compaction from damaging the root system. This not only means keeping the bulldozer from scraping around the tree roots. It even means not allowing parking or stockpiling heavy materials on the tree roots.

A tree protection barrier during construction should extend at least out as far as the tree branches. Photo from Governors Island blog, New York.

EVALUATING TREE HEALTH AROUND NEW HOMES

If you're considering buying a new home with trees on the site, spend some time evaluating the health of the trees. A little investigating may reveal some potential problems. Arborists, certified by the International Society of Arboriculture, may be helpful to you in this process. Or other professionals, such as a graduate urban forester, may also be hired.

Chances are that you didn't see the home during the construction phase. So you don't know what protection was provided the trees. Hopefully, there was minimal activity beneath the trees. Barricades should have been built, at least as far out as the branch tips, all the way around the trees. No clearing, construction activity, storage, or parking should have taken place inside these barricades.

Most home builders don't build such barricades, however, so root damage to trees on home sites is very common. It's such root damage that usually leads to decline of the trees after the house is sold. It is important that you learn to detect signs of possible root damage.

*Note the thin crown of this tree left in a parking lot.
It has had lots of root damage and is slowly declining.*

If there's a lawn or cleared soil right up to the tree, you know that the soil was scraped. And, because so many tree roots are in the top six inches of soil, it is inevitable that some root damage, probably a lot, occurred. It would have been much better if the natural leaf litter had been left around the tree and if the soil had not been scraped.

Whereas northern cool-season lawngrasses will grow under trees, most southern lawngrasses grow poorly under trees. Southern lawngrasses and trees just don't mix that well, not if you want to keep your trees healthy, have enough sun for the grass, and not have a maintenance nightmare mowing around trees. It's better to keep lawn areas open and let trees have the protection of their natural leaf litter as far out from their trunk as possible.

Environmentally-sensitive landscapes today retain some natural areas that a bulldozer has never touched. In such landscapes, the undergrowth was cleared away by hand or with the aid of glyphosate herbicides (such as Roundup®) without harm to the trees above. In some landscapes, much of the undergrowth is left for privacy screening. Wise home buyers are learning that using natural assets in a landscape is economically rewarding, too. Why scrape an area bare and then have to replant it? Properly managed native vegetation can be a positive asset.

If a tree is left sitting on a little mound of soil several inches above the surrounding soil level, you can tell that there has been considerable root damage during the clearing process. And, if you can determine that any soil has been added around the base of a tree, be assured that its roots have suffered. The degree of suffering depends on the depth and spread of soil added. A couple of inches of sand fill may not be that harmful. But, six inches of topsoil fill would kill some trees, and several feet of topsoil fill would slowly kill most trees by suffocating their roots.

Not all home builders are careless about soil and tree management when building. But, home buyers need to beware of potential problems before they buy a new home. Large trees cannot be replaced and may be very costly to remove.

DECIDING WHEN TO REMOVE TREES FROM YOUR LANDSCAPE

Sometimes trees are removed for arbitrary reasons such as to give more light to grow a lawn or because someone is tired of raking leaves. Removing a large tree for such arbitrary reasons, though, needs to be considered a serious step. There are alternatives.

Would it not be better to sacrifice a little lawn area and let the trees stay? And, rather than growing a lawn beneath the trees, why not just let the leaves accumulate to form a natural forest floor? You can control undergrowth if you wish with a couple of spot sprayings of glyphosate herbicide each year.

Trees require much fewer maintenance and energy inputs than does a lawn area. That's not to say that lawns don't still have their place. But, when water shortages and water pollution from runoff of lawn fertilizers and pesticides is a real problem, perhaps it is unethical to sacrifice healthy trees just because of the American infatuation with estate-sized lawns.

Of course, there can be good reasons for removing trees, too. If a tree has suffered irreversible construction blight or other significant decline so that it poses a safety hazard, it needs to come down. Dead or damaged trees or trees with a large portion of dead limbs hanging over your house or driveway are candidates for removal.

Storm Damage. Photo from Dickerson Landscaping

But, don't be in such a rush to remove a dead tree on the back of your lot that doesn't present a safety hazard. Woodpeckers, nuthatches, owls, bluebirds, and other desirable wildlife use such dead trees for homes. If you remove dead trees that don't present a safety hazard, you're needlessly removing the homes for such desirable wildlife.

Don't be overly alarmed about trees with cavities in their trunk. A hole in a tree doesn't signify that the tree is not healthy. The part of the trunk that sustains life is on the outside, just beneath the bark. The cavity matters only in terms of structural strength. If the cavity consumes most of the trunk, then, possibly there is a safety hazard, depending on the tree's location. But a tree with a cavity only part of the way through the trunk of the tree may stand for a long time. Don't equate cavities with declining trees.

So, yes, there are times it is wise to remove trees. But, let's consider removal of large trees prudently. Even dead or declining trees can have value.

CONSIDERATIONS WHEN ADDING NEW TREES TO THE LANDSCAPE
(ESPECIALLY IF YOU DON'T LIKE RAKING LEAVES)

As mentioned already, lawns and trees just don't mix that well. So, when adding new trees to the landscape, if possible, try to keep the two separate. Otherwise, there will be several problems.

First, the grass will offer competition to the young tree. Research even indicates that grass releases substances that are toxic to other plants. Secondly, in your efforts to keep grass away from the young tree, you may bump it with a lawnmower or girdle it with a weed-eater. Such a wound can provide entry for disease organisms and be the start of decline for the tree.

Finally, if the tree does survive, as it becomes larger, it will cause problems for the lawn grass. We just don't have any southern lawn grasses that are really very shade tolerant.   Some types of St. Augustine grass, once well established, will tolerate moderate shade, but even they will not tolerate dense shade. And, as trees mature, the shade beneath them becomes more and more dense, making it more and more difficult to grow lawngrass beneath them.

One other advantage to keeping trees and lawns separate is that it can greatly reduce the amount of raking required in the fall and winter. Just let the leaves fall where they may. If you have existing trees in a lawn now, you may consider letting the area revert to its natural state for this reason alone, especially if the lawn grass is doing poorly in that area anyway. The natural mulch will help the tree roots with better water and oxygen penetration through the soil.

The best approach is to plant your trees in beds rather than scatter them in the lawn area. The trend today is away from large lawn areas and toward larger natural areas and beds in the landscape. Lawn areas have become smaller and more functional.   Natural areas, groundcover beds, and mass plantings of shrubs are in style because such plantings require less maintenance than open lawn areas.

Research has also shown that trees in groups, rather than single trees, withstand storm-force winds such as hurricanes much better.

RECOMMENDED TREES

The following are among trees recommended for our area. A short description follows each name.   A distinction of which trees are native is not always made. Most of the trees are native, but non-natives included are considered worthy of planting also. The author feels that the important factor is selecting a tree suited for the intended site. Because sites to be landscaped are often no longer in their native condition, sometimes exotic plants are better suited than native plants. Some exotic species, though, are so aggressive as to crowd out native species. Such exotics, such as Chinese tallow are not listed.

Following this list of Recommended Trees are further breakdowns of trees for special purposes. The descriptions of the trees in those lists can usually be found in this list of Recommended Trees.

SMALL TREES

Japanese maples (Acer palmatum): Various cultivars are available. Generally, slow-growing small trees noted for their twisted, Oriental style form and lacy foliage. Foliage, varying with cultivars, is red in spring and fall, some cultivars all season. Avoid dry sites and full sun. Squirrels sometimes do bark damage.

Red buckeye (Aesculus pavia): Small native tree or large shrub. Needs a moist, fertile, good well-drained soil. Grows best in the shade of other trees. Showy red flowers in spring.

American hornbeam or blue beech (Carpinus caroliniana): Tolerant of all conditions except dry sites. Strong, attractive small native tree with smooth gray bark.

Redbud (Cercis canadensis): Early spring-flowering native tree with beautiful magenta-colored flowers. Tolerant of dry sites and poor growing conditions.

Fringe tree (Chionanthus virginicus): A small, native deciduous tree that flowers in mid-spring with flossy, white clouds of flowers. Many birds eat the fruit that follows on the female plants.

Chionanthus virginicus (Fringe tree)

Flowering dogwood (Cornus florida): Well-known but often mis-used small, spring-flowering native tree. Prefers good, fertile, moist, but well-drained site in the shade of other trees. Not best for street plantings and other hot, dry sites. Named cultivars, such a 'Weaver', 'Barton', etc. generally more showy than seedlings. 'Welch Junior Miss' is only pink dogwood for the Deep South and flowering will depend on winter cold.

Hawthorn (Crataegus spp.): Small spring-flowering native trees with white to pink flower clusters. Tolerant to wide range of soil conditions. Thorny branches. Leaves usually turn attractive red-orange in fall.

Loquat or Japanese plum (Eriobotrya japonica): Small evergreen tree tolerant of wide range of sites. If winter is not too extreme during flowering stage, edible fruit is produced in spring. Large, rich, dark green leaves.

Dahoon holly (Ilex cassine): Small to medium native evergreen holly tree. Will tolerate wet sites. Red berries in winter.

Deciduous holly or possumhaw (Ilex decidua): A small, deciduous native holly tolerating wet to dry sites. Spectacular show of berries after leaves drop.

Yaupon holly (Ilex vomitoria): Versatile small native tree or large shrub. Tolerant of wet to dry soils. Evergreen with attractive red berries on female plants. Very small leaves.

'East Palatka' holly (Ilex x 'East Palatka'): Hybrid pyramidal evergreen holly tree. One spine at tip of each leaf. Red fruit. Sun to shade. Tolerates wide range of soils.

'Savannah' holly (Ilex x 'Savannah'): Lots of red berries on pyramidal tree with dull green evergreen leaves. Tolerates wide range of soils. Sun to shade.

Crape myrtle (Lagerstroemia indica): Size depends on the cultivar selected. Some are dwarf, some are tall and spreading, others are narrow and upright in form... there's a crape myrtle for every site. Summer flowers of various pinks, reds, lavenders, and white. For sunny sites. Good fall leaf color. Attractive bark. Dry to wet sites. Use newer mildew resistant cultivars. Fast grower.

Ashe magnolia (Magnolia macrophylla **subspecies** *ashei):* Small native tree or large shrub-type magnolia with very large, almost tropical-looking deciduous leaves. White showy flowers. Needs fertile, moist, well-drained site in shade of other trees. Keep mulched. Bigleaf magnolia, the regular species, is also a good choice.

Southern crabapple (Malus angustifolia): Small native spring-flowering deciduous tree with pink flowers. Tolerates many soil types.

Wax myrtle (Myrica cerifera): Large fast-growing native shrub or small tree; evergreen. Tolerant of wide range of sites from wet. Females have gray berries that are attractive to birds.

Sourwood (Oxydendrum arboreum): Native tree that must have moist, fertile, but well-drained soil. Beautiful red to purplish color in fall. White, fragrant, showy flowers in summer.

American hophornbeam (Ostrya virginiana): Native, preferring normal to dry sites, not wet sites. Good urban tree, tolerant of adverse sites.

Jerusalem thorn (Parkinsonia aculeata): Small deciduous tree with very thin, almost fern-looking, leaves. Bright yellow flowers in summer. Grows well in all soils except poorly drained ones. Branches have thorns, so either avoid planting in areas of heavy traffic or remove lower limbs below head height. Will be injured by severe freezes.

Fevertree (Pinckneya pubens, P. bracteata): A small native tree that will tolerate wet sites as well as sites of normal moisture. When it blooms in early summer, the small, inconspicuous flowers are surrounded by rose-colored bracts similar to those of poinsettias. Full sun to partial shade. Difficult to find for sale.

Chinese pistache (Pistacia chinensis): Tolerant of adverse, dry sites. Noted for spectacular fall color of red-orange.

Chickasaw plum (Prunus angustifolia): Small native deciduous tree covered with clouds of white flowers in spring. Prefers moist but well-drained soils. Creates a thicket, as opposed to flatwoods plum (P. umbellata), which is also a good landscape plant but grows as a single specimen.

Cherry laurel (Prunus caroliniana): Large native shrub or small evergreen tree. Tolerates wide range of soils except the driest and wettest of sites. Birds will spread seeds and, therefore, can become somewhat weedy.

Taiwan cherry (Prunus serrulata): Small to medium size tree; blooming in very early spring or late winter. Very dark pink flowers. Seemingly the best Japanese flowering cherry for the deep South. One of our earliest flowering trees.

Bradford pear (Pyrus calleryana): The most popular cultivar of the callery pear. Small deciduous ornamental tree owing most of its popularity to attractive orange to red-orange fall color. Also attractive white spring flowers when grown far enough north (Atlanta or so) and sometimes even in deep South after cold winters. Flowers followed by very small fruit, not worthy of eating. Tolerant of wide range of soil conditions. Tough tree. Somewhat dense oval shape makes use as shade tree limited to small area beneath tree. Good tree for streetside plantings where uniformity is important and the dense, strong upright growth habit is wanted. Has narrow branch angles, resulting in some limb breakage as the tree ages.

Chapman oak (Quercus chapmanii): Small deciduous oak native to our sandy, poor soils. Good for landscaping on such sites. Young growth is yellowish-green. Brown leaves stay on tree until following spring. Slow-growing.

Bluejack oak (Quercus incana): A tough, small deciduous oak native to dry, sandy soils. Young, unfolding leaves in spring are pinkish on top and silvery white on undersides, fuzzy on both sides. Slow growing.

Myrtle oak (Quercus myrtifolia): A small, slow-growing, evergreen native oak, very tolerant of dry sites. Common on coastal sand dunes. Small, rounded leaves with curled margins.

Coastal plain willow (Salix caroliniana): Fast-growing native evergreen willow for wet sites or good moist soils.

Tree sparkleberry (Vaccinium arboreum): Native, semi-evergreen tree with small white flowers in spring. Tolerates wide range of soil types.

Chaste tree (Vitex agnus-castus): Attractive small deciduous tree with blue to purplish summer flowers, mildly fragrant. Fast-growing. Very adaptable to range of soil types and sites; tough tree. Foliage somewhat resembles marijuana.

Jujube (Ziziphus jujuba): Small date-like fruit bearing tree. Fruit ripens in late summer or fall. Tolerates dry sites but not wet sites. Deciduous.

MEDIUM TREES

Florida maple (Acer saccharum var. Floridanum or A. barbatum): The native sugar maple for the South. Great fall color, but dead leaves remain on tree in winter. Fairly tolerant of dry soils.

Red maple (Acer rubrum): Not tolerant of extremely dry sites, but great for most other sites. Red flowers and seeds in spring and red foliage in fall. Fast-growing native.

River birch (Betula nigra): Not tolerant of extremely dry sites, but an attractive multi-trunked tree for most other sites. White papery peeling bark is very attractive. Deciduous native.

Leyland cypress (Cupressocyparis leylandi): Tolerant of all but poorly drained or wet sites. Juniper-like evergreen foliage. Pyramidal, medium size. Can be affected by foliar diseases when there is poor air circulation because of planting too closely together.

Native persimmon (Diospyros virginiana): Tolerant of most sites except very poorly drained ones. The orange fruit is liked by wildlife, and once ripened by a fall frost, by many people. Fall webworms can be a problem for young trees. Oriental persimmons are more commonly grown for fruit and are smaller trees.

Cockspur coral tree (Erythrina crista-galli): This tree with unusual and showy red flower clusters is native to South America. Yet it will grow in Zone 8b and in Zones 9-10. In 8b it may be damaged by cold until it reaches a large enough size and has woody enough growth that cold damage is negligible. Can grow to 40-50 ft. Full sun.

The unusual flowers of Erythrina crista-galli

Water ash (Fraxinus caroliniana): Native ash good for wet sites. Wood is light and weak. Rounded top.

Ginkgo (Ginkgo biloba): Very slow-growing medium to large deciduous tree noted for fan-shaped leaves that turn beautiful yellow in fall and drop almost uniformly. Prefers good soils.

Honey locust (Gleditsia triacanthos var. inermis): Thornless variety of our native honey locust.

Very drought tolerant and tolerant of compacted urban conditions.

Loblolly bay (Gordonia lasianthus): Native broadleaf evergreen tree, native to swampy areas. Tolerant of wet sites. Showy and fragrant white flowers in summer.

Silverbell (Halesia caroliniana): Native, spring-flowering deciduous trees with white, drooping flowers. Needs fertile, moist well-drained soil. Prefers growing in the shade of other trees.

American holly (Ilex opaca): Small to medium native evergreen holly. Prefers well-drained but not dry soil. Traditional multi-spined holly leaves. Red berries on female plants.

Southern red cedar (Juniperus silicicola): Native needle-like leafed evergreen. Tolerant of all but wet sites. This and *Juniperus virginiana* are the cedars most of us know.

Goldenrain tree (Koelreuteria spp.): Small to medium deciduous tree with very showy yellow flowers in summer. Followed by showy reddish or salmon colored seed pods. Needs full sun to grow and flower well. Will tolerate dry sites but not poorly drained sites. Generates many seedlings nearby.

Japanese magnolia (Magnolia soulangiana): Small to medium tree with pink tulip or saucer-shaped flowers in late winter or early spring. Grow on good soils only, well-drained but not dry sites.

Sweetbay (Magnolia virginiana): Native evergreen magnolia tolerant of wet and poorly aerated soils. Leaves have silvery undersides. Showy, fragrant white flowers in early summer and at irregular intervals.

Water tupelo or black tupelo (Nyssa aquatica): Native tree, tolerating wet or good sites, but not dry sites. Good red or orange fall color.

Sand pine (Pinus clausa): Native pine, very tolerant of dry sites; not as large as most of the other pines. Needles are in bundles of two, about three inches long. Cones tend to persist on tree.

Sawtooth oak (Quercus acutissima): Very tough oak, good for most any type of site. Fall color is brown; brown leaves persist into winter. Sawtoothed leaves. Native to Korea, China, and Japan. Not especially better than the native oaks.

Bluff oak (Quercus austrina): Native deciduous oak with large, whiteoak-like leaves. For fertile, moist, but well-drained soils. Attractive shaggy bark that flakes into long strips.

Turkey oak (Quercus laevis): Native oak very tolerant of dry sites. Large, deeply cut leaves turn brilliant red in fall, then remain brown on tree until next spring.

Blackjack oak (Quercus marilandica): Native, deciduous oak with large paddle-shaped leaves which hang on the tree after browning. Not readily available in nurseries, but is tough, durable tree, tolerant of dry sites.

Chinquapin oak (Quercus muehlenbergii): Native, though not common, deciduous oak with large sharp-toothed leaves. Tolerant of most sites except compacted clays or wet sites. Sometimes good fall color.

Sassafras (Sassafras albidum): Good fast-growing native tree. Excellent fall color. Difficult to transplant; difficult to find in nurseries. Leaves can be oval-shaped or have one, two, or three lobes, all on same tree.

Basswood (Tilia floridana, T. caroliniana): Natives for fertile, moist, but well-drained sites. Deciduous, rounded leaves with single point at end. Inconspicuous flowers very attractive to bees. *T. floridana* larger than *T. caroliniana.*

Winged elm (Ulmus alata): Very tough, drought tolerant, native elm. An excellent street tree. Has corky, winged bark.

Florida elm (Ulmus americana floridana): Is a native form of the American elm. Not for dry or poor sites. Smooth, wingless twigs as opposed to winged elm.

Lacebark elm or Chinese elm (Ulmus parvifolia): Overused small shade tree, very popular because of fast growth rate, attractive bark, attractive weeping growth habit, and tolerance of wide range of extreme sites, including very dry sites and compacted soils. 'Drake' is popular cultivar. Seeds are messy on decks, porches, driveways, etc. Sometimes damaged by extreme winters.

LARGE TREES

Hickory (Carya spp.): Several species exist as native trees. Difficulty in transplanting prohibits wide nursery production.   Worthy of protecting existing trees on sites, though, for beautiful yellow fall color. Very sensitive to root disturbance. Mockernut hickory, *C. tomentosa*, has drought tolerance.

Deodar cedar (Cedrus deodara): Tolerant of all but poorly drained soils. Pyramidal, needle evergreentree. Medium size. Native to Himalayan Mountains, but grows rapidly here under good growing conditions.

Sugarberry (Celtis laevigata): Deciduous native with smooth bark except for prominent corky warts. Bears orange-red berries which attract birds. Best for fertile, moist soils but will tolerate somewhat drier soils.

American beech (Fagus grandiflora): A magnificent native tree, but a slow grower. Needs fertile, well-drained but moist woodlands type soil. Grass competition is detrimental. Beautiful smooth bark. Gold leaves in fall, persist as brown leaves in winter. Protect at all costs when existing on sites.

White ash (Fraxinus americana): Good native shade tree for sites with fertile, moist, but well-drained soil. Not for compacted soils. Will tolerate some wetness if not too heavy clay. Yellow to yellow-orange in fall.

Green ash (Fraxinus pennsylvanica): More tolerant of adverse sites than white ash, but neither is good on heavy clay soils. Faster grower than white ash. Typically has seven leaflets per leaf whereas white ash has nine or more.

Sweetgum (Liquidambar styraciflua): Native with strong upright growth habit as opposed to spreading crown. Not for extremely dry sites. Spiny burs can be minor nuisance in a lawn. Excellent yellow to red-orange fall color.

Tulip poplar or yellow poplar (Liriodendron tulipifera): Huge native tree needing large area. Not for dry sites or compacted soils. Somewhat brittle wood, and leaves drop sporadically throughout the season.

Southern magnolia (Magnolia grandiflora): Stately native broadleaf evergreen tree. Doesn't tolerate dry conditions well. Does not tolerate root disturbance. Best to leave low branches on tree to hide fallen leaves and protect against root damage. Beautiful fragrant white flowers in spring to mid-summer. Cone-shaped fruit ripen to expose red seeds in late summer to fall. Several improved cultivars available, including 'Little Gem', which only grows to 15-20 ft. tall with an 8-10 ft. spread. Southern magnolia is ensitive to magnesium deficiency, so young trees may benefit from applications of Epsom salts.

Flower of Magnolia grandiflora (Southern magnolia)

Black gum (Nyssa sylvatica): Native for wet to only moderately dry sites. Tolerates compacted soils well. Beautiful red or red-orange fall foliage.

Shortleaf pine (Pinus echinata): Native pine, tolerant of all soil types but the poorest drained of soils and very dry, sandy soils. Fast-growing, attractive pine with 3-5 inch needles, usually in bundles of two. Very small cones.

Slash pine (Pinus elliotti): Native pine with long, 7-12 inch, needles in bundles of two or three. Tolerates wet soils. Fast grower.

Spruce pine (Pinus glabra): One of the most attractive of the native pines; slender 3-inch needles, in bundles of two and attractive, shallowly furrowed bark. Retains limbs on lower part of tree, unlike most southern pines, therefore useful for screening. Tolerant of wide range of soils.

Longleaf pine (Pinus palustris): Native pine with long, 8-10 inch needles in bundles of three. Cones are very large, 6-10 inches long. Tolerates dry soils. Slow growing the first few years.

Pond pine (Pinus serotina): Native pine tolerant of high or fluctuating water levels. 6-11 inch needles in bundles of three, sometimes four. Cones are more rounded than those of most pines. Branches lower on trunk than most pines.

Loblolly pine (Pinus taeda): Native pine that will tolerate poorly drained soils, though will tolerate mildly dry conditions, too. Needles are 6-9 inches long, in bundles of three.

Sycamore (Platanus occidentalis): Huge native tree, requiring lots of room. Use only on large sites and moist, rich soils. Dieback disease and lacebugs can be a problem. Some people don't like the cleanup of the large deciduous leaves.

White oak (Quercus alba): Long-lived native oak with moderate growth rate, eventually becoming a stately tree. Large lobed leaves, sometimes turning dark red or orange-red in fall. Not for dry sites or compacted soils.

Southern red oak (Quercus falcata): Native oak tolerant of both dry and poorly drained soils. Fast grower. Fall color is usually just brown or yellow-brown.

Laurel oak (Quercus laurifolia): Native semi-evergreen oak tolerant of wide range of soil conditions. On dry, sandy, infertile soils eastern horn gall wasps make it unusable. Like water oak, not relatively long lived and somewhat spindly shape.

Swamp chestnut oak (Quercus michauxii): Deciduous oak native to good, fertile sites; not for dry sites. Attractive large chestnut-like leaves and large acorns.

Water oak (Quercus nigra): Fast-growing, large, semi-evergreen, native oak. Tolerant of wet sites and compacted soils. Not a highly desirable tree for planting, though, because of relatively short life span and somewhat spindly growth habit on many sites. May be worth saving when existing on sites, unless very close to the house, where it may eventually become a hazard. Leaves are somewhat paddle-shaped. No attractive fall color.

Willow oak (Quercus phellos): Deciduous oak with thin, willow-like leaves. Will not tolerate dry soils. Native to rich bottomlands.

Shumard oak (Quercus shumardii): A native deciduous oak that is excellent landscape tree. Tolerant of wide range of soil conditions.   Beautiful red to orange fall foliage. Large pointed red-oak type leaves.

Post oak (Quercus stellata): Native deciduous oak very tolerant of dry and adverse conditions. However, existing older trees will not tolerate much abuse in way of root damage or compaction.   Has broad lobed leaves with somewhat flat end on middle lobe.   Difficult to transplant, so not readily available in nurseries.

Live oak (Quercus virginiana): The native evergreen oak so popular in the deep South. Tolerant of wide range of soil conditions. Sand live oak is a subspecies that is smaller and more drought-tolerant. This is the live oak found in the coastal dunes.

Bald cypress and pond cypress (Taxodium spp.): Deciduous native cypresses that will tolerate but don't require excessive moisture.   Because of tolerance for poor aeration, will tolerate compacted, urban soils quite well. Will not tolerate extremely dry sites, though. Beautiful, lacy foliage that turns bronze in fall.

GOOD, FAST-GROWING SHADE TREES

Florida maple (*Acer floridanum or A. barbatum*)
Red maple (*Acer rubrum*)

River birch *(Betula nigra)*
Sugarberry *(Celtis laevigata)*
Sweetgum *(Liquidambar styraciflua)*
Tulip poplar *(Liriodendron tulipifera)*
Sawtooth oak *(Quercus acutissima)*
Laurel oak *(Quercus laurifolia)*
Water oak *(Quercus nigra)*
Sassafras *(Sassafras albidum)*
Chinese, Lacebark, or Drake elm *(Ulmus parvifolia 'Drake')*

TREES TOLERANT OF DRY SITES
Sugarberry *(Celtis laevigata)*
Redbud *(Cercis canadensis)*
Leyland cypress *(Cupressocyparis leylandi)*
Native persimmon *(Diospyros virginiana)*
Honey locust *(Gleditsia triacanthos var. inermis)*
Red cedar *(Juniperus virginiana)*
Goldenrain tree *(Koelreuteria spp.)*
Wax myrtle *(Myrica cerifera)*
Jerusalem thorn *(Parkinsonia aculeata)*
Sand pine *(Pinus clausa)*
Longleaf pine *(Pinus palustris)*
Chinese pistache *(Pistacia chinensis)*
Chickasaw plum *(Prunus angustifolia)*
Sawtooth oak *(Quercus acutissima)*
Bluejack oak *(Quercus incana)*
Turkey oak *(Quercus laevis)*
Chinquapin oak *(Quercus muehlenbergii)*
Myrtle oak *(Quercus myrtifolia)*
Post oak *(Quercus stellata)*

Live oak *(Quercus virginiana)*
Cypress *(Taxodium spp.)*
Winged elm *(Ulmus alata)*
Lacebark elm *(Ulmus parvifolia)*
Chaste tree *(Vitex agnus-castus)*
Jujube *(Ziziphus jujuba)*

TREES TOLERANT OF WET SITES
Red maple *(Acer rubrum)*
River birch *(Betula nigra)*
American hornbeam or blue beech *(Carpinus caroliniana)*
Loblolly bay *(Gordonia lasianthus)*
Dahoon holly *(Ilex cassine)*
Sweetgum *(Liquidambar styraciflua)*
Tulip poplar *(Liriodendron tulipifera)*
Wax myrtle *(Myrica cerifera)*
Southern magnolia *(Magnolia grandiflora)*
Sweetbay *(Magnolia virginiana)*
Water tupelo *(Nyssa aquatica)*
Black gum *(Nyssa sylvatica)*
Fevertree *(Pinckneya pubens, P. bracteata)*
Slash pine *(Pinus elliotti)*
Spruce pine *(Pinus glabra)*
Pond pine *(Pinus serotina)*
Loblolly pine *(Pinus taeda)*
Sycamore *(Platanus occidentalis)*
Willow oak *(Quercus phellos)*
Shumard oak *(Quercus shumardii)*
Live oak *(Quercus virginiana)*
Sabal or cabbage palm *(Sabal palmetto)*

Weeping willow *(Salix babylonica)*
Coastal plain willow *(Salix caroliniana)*
Bald cypress and pond cypress *(Taxodium spp.)*

EVERGREEN TREES
Deodar cedar *(Cedrus deodora)*
Leyland cypress *(Cupressocyparis leylandi)*
Loquat *(Eriobotrya japonica)*
Loblolly bay *(Gordonia lasianthus)*
Dahoon holly *(Ilex cassine)*
American holly *(Ilex opaca)*
Yaupon holly *(Ilex vomitoria)*
Red cedar *(Juniperus virginiana)*
Wax myrtle *(Myrica cerifera)*
Southern magnolia *(Magnolia grandiflora)*
Sweetbay *(Magnolia virginiana)*
Sand pine *(Pinus clausa)*
Slash pine *(Pinus elliotti)*
Spruce pine *(Pinus glabra)*
Longleaf pine *(Pinus palustris)*
Pond pine *(Pinus serotina)*
Loblolly pine *(Pinus taeda)*
Cherry laurel *(Prunus caroliniana)*
Laurel oak *(Quercus laurifolia)*
Myrtle oak *(Quercus myrtifolia)*
Live oak *(Quercus virginiana)*

PALMS
 Pindo palm (Butia capitata): Medium, 10-20 ft.,
palm with gray-green feathery leaves. Tolerant of wide

range of soil types and sites. Produces orange edible fruit, normally used in jellies rather than eaten fresh.

European fan palm (Chamaerops humilis): Small, 6-8 ft., palm that tolerates wide range of soil conditions. Salt tolerant. Fan-shaped leaves. Slow-growing.

Canary Island date palm (Phoenix canariensis): Large, 30-60 ft., stocky palm with feathery leaves. Not as tolerant of poor soils, especially poorly drained soils, as other palms. So large as to be out of scale with most homes.

Needle palm (Rhapidophyllum hystrix): Small, 3-5 ft., native palm that prefers fertile, moist soils and a little shade. Needle-like spines at the base. Extremely cold-hardy.

Sabal palm or cabbage palm (Sabal palmetto): Tall, 30-60 ft., slender native palm. Tolerates wide range of soil conditions once established. Fan-shaped leaves twisting on the stem. Extremely wind- and hurricane-tolerant. Salt tolerant.

Windmill palm (Trachycarpus fortunei): Slow-growing to 10-15 ft. Tolerant of many soils, but does best in a well-drained one. Very showy, fan-shaped leaves. Trunk is wrapped in a blackish, hair-like fiber. Tolerates moderate shade and low temperatures.

Mexican Washington palm (Washingtonia robusta): Tall, 60-80 ft., slender palm. Old leaves hang down the trunk just beneath the green fan-shaped foliage. Tolerant of wide range of soil types.

FLOWERING TREES

SEQUENCE OF BLOOM	FLOWER COLOR	TIME OF YEAR
Flowering cherries	Pinks, rose	Late winter
Japanese magnolias	White, pink, purple	Late winter-early spring
Red maple	Rusty red	Late winter-early spring
Redbud	Lavender, pinks	Late winter-early spring
Red buckeye	Red	Late winter-early spring
Chickasaw plum	White	Late winter-early spring
Crabapple	Pink	Early spring
Flowering dogwood	White	Early spring
'Welch Jr. Miss' dogwood	Pink	Early spring
Silverbell	White	Spring
Hawthorns	White	Spring
Tree sparkleberry	White	Spring
Fringetree	White	Spring
Ashe magnolia	White	Late spring
Jerusalem thorn	Yellow	Late spring, summer
Southern magnolia	White	Late spring-early summer
Goldenrain tree	Yellow	Summer-fall
Sourwood	White	Summer
Chaste tree	Blue	Summer
Crape myrtle	White, pink,	Summer

	lavender, red	

TREES WITH ATTRACTIVE FALL FOLIAGE

TREE	COLOR
American beech	Golden bronze
Black gum	Reds, oranges
Bald & pond cypress	Rusty color
'Bradford' pear	Reds, oranges
Chinese pistache	Orange to red
Crape myrtle	Orange, red, yellow
Dogwood	Red to burgundy
Florida maple	Red, orange
Ginkgo	Yellow to gold
Hickories	Yellow to gold
Japanese maples	Red, orange, burgundy
Redbud	Yellow
Sassafras	Red to red-orange
Sawtooth oak	Golden brown
Shumard oak	Red-orange
Sourwood	Red
Sweetgum	Orange, red, yellow
Tulip poplar	Yellow
Water tupelo	Orange to red
White oak	Red, orange
Willow oak	Light yellow
Winged elm	Light yellow

TREES WITH OTHER ATTRACTIVE FEATURES

American holly	Red berries

Chaste tree	Leaf shape and form
Chinese pistache	Good fall color, showy fruit
Crape myrtle	Attractive bark and form
Deciduous holly (possumhaw)	Bright red berries
Flowering dogwood	Red fruit, nice shape
Ginkgo	Unique leaf shape
Goldenrain tree	Pink fruit pods
Japanese maples	Leaf shape and branch form
Lacebark elm	Peeling bark
Loquat	Edible fruit, fragrant flowers
Red maple	Showy fruit in early spring
River birch	Peeling bark
Yaupon holly	Red berries
Southern magnolia	Limbs to the ground hide leaf litter
Sycamore	White bark

FERTILIZATION OF TREES

Don't over-fertilize trees or other plants. Plant nutrients are needed by plants. But many of those nutrients are already in sufficient amounts in the soil. It's best to use soil tests as a basis to determine if you need to apply more nutrients through fertilizer, and if so, which ones and how much. These soil tests can be run by your state's land grant university (University of Florida, University of Georgia, Auburn, Clemson, LSU, etc.). Contact your County Extension office of the university for more information.

The fertilizer rates given in this book are general guidelines. But a soil test can give you information tailored to your site. Too much fertilizer, especially if heaped around plants, can burn the plant roots.

Small and recently planted trees only several feet tall would require no more than about four tablespoons of a fertilizer such as 16-4-8 or 15-0-15. Apply the fertilizer in early March and then again in July. Spread the fertilizer on the soil surface extending out slightly beyond the branch tips of the tree. There's no need to remove mulch before spreading the fertilizer; just apply it over the top of the mulch and water it in.

For larger trees, apply one cup of the fertilizer per inch of trunk diameter as measured 4 feet above the ground. Apply in March and again in July. Spread the fertilizer over the root zone of the tree, starting several feet out from the trunk and extending beyond the branch tips of the tree. In fact, about 1/3 of the fertilizer should be applied beyond the branch tips, as many of the roots will be in that area.

Larger trees don't really need to be fertilized. If the trees are close to a lawn, the roots are in the lawn and they are receiving fertilizer when the lawn is fertilized. If the trees are in a mulched or natural area, the decomposition of the mulch and leaves recycles nutrients to the tree. Fertilizer just speeds up growth rate and doesn't normally make the tree any healthier if it is on the proper site.

If you have any palms in your landscape, you need to be careful about which fertilizers you use in your landscape. Palms are prone to potassium and magnesium deficiencies. University of Florida research has found that the best landscape fertilizer for landscapes which contain palms is 8-2-12 with 4% magnesium and with micronutrients. The fertilizer should have controlled release nitrogen, potassium (as sulfur-coated potassium sulfate), and magnesium (as prilled kieseite, which is a special form of magnesium sulfate. The micronutrients should be as follows: manganese in the sulfate, not oxide, form; iron in a chelate form; and boron in a slow release form such as Granubor. John Deere Landscapes and Graco Fertilizer Company are two companies that blend these fertilizers according to the formulation recommended by University of Florida. This fertilizer is suitable for use on all landscape plants. Use it at the rate of 12.5 pounds per 1,000 square feet of area.

5

Shrubs
Selecting the Right Ones for the site

Shrubs are used in the landscape for various purposes. They are used around the foundation of the house to hide less-than-attractive architectural features and to enhance the appearance of the house, more or less tying it to the ground visually. They are used in hedges to screen views. Shrub plantings are also useful in providing habitats and food for birds and other desirable wildlife. Sometimes single shrubs are used just because they're especially attractive, fragrant, or have some other desirable characteristic.

Just as there are numerous reasons for planting shrubs, there are numerous types of shrubs that you can plant. However, not all will perform any one function and not all will grow well on all sites. Some shrubs, because of their low height at maturity, are better for planting around a house's foundation or under windows than other shrubs. These same shrubs, though, probably wouldn't make a good screening hedge. Likewise, the shrubs that make a good hedge will probably outgrow the site quickly if used in a foundation planting next to the house.

Some shrubs will tolerate wet, poorly drained soils. Others will tolerate dry soils and full sun. Some shrubs that you may have grown in another part of the country may not even grow here.

It is important to select the right shrub for a given site and given use. Proper selection will save you many hours of headaches and maintenance for years after planting. The following lists were compiled to help you in your selections.

Of course, it's helpful to know what the plants on the list look like. So, use these lists in conjunction with image views through Google or a trip to your favorite nursery.

SMALL SHRUBS
(NORMALLY LESS THAN 4 FT.)

Sherwood abelia (Abelia x grandiflora 'Sherwoodii'): Dwarf form of abelia, an old summer-flowering favorite. White flowers, glossy evergreen leaves. Sun to light shade. Prefers fertile, moist soil.

'Confetti' abelia (Abelia x grandiflora 'Confetti'): Dwarf form of abeia with pink, white, and green variegated foliage. Evergreen. Grows to about 3 ft. tall and wide. Small white flowers in spring. Can be used in foundation plantings in mass, in containers, or as an accent plant. Full sun to part shade.

Crimson pigmy barberry (Berberis thunbergii 'Atropurpurea Nana'): Deciduous, red foliage. For sunny, well-drained sites.

Japanese boxwood (Buxus microphylla): Small evergreen leaves. Sun to shade. Not for extremely dry or poorly drained soils. Occasional problems with mites or nematodes. But, overall, is still a very low maintenance shrub.

Yewtopia plum yew (Cephalotaxus harringtonia Yewtopia): Drought-tolerant, heat-tolerant, deer-resistant, fine-textured plant for shade to part sun. Grows slowly to 3-4 ft. tall and wide.

Creeping euonymus (Euonymus fortunei): Evergreen, most cultivars variegated. Almost a groundcover. Sun to light shade. Tolerates a wide range of soil types. Green cultivars turn rich burgundy in winter.

Prostrate gardenia (Gardenia jasminoides 'Prostrata' or 'Radicans'): Miniature version of the evergreen shrub gardenia. White fragrant flowers. Very susceptible to whiteflies and nematodes. Short-lived. Prefers fairly good soil.

Carissa holly (Ilex cornuta 'Carissa'): Attractive small evergreen holly for sun to partial shade. Each leaf has one spine. Few if any berries. Tolerates all but the driest and the wettest of soils. Practically no pruning needed.

Dwarf Chinese holly (Ilex cornuta 'Rotunda'): Compact, dense, evergreen holly for sun to shade. Practically no pruning needed. Very good plant for wide range of sites. Interesting, coarse texture due to spiny leaves. Great for traffic control also.

Dwarf yaupon holly (Ilex vomitoria 'Nana'): This is a dwarf form of the very versatile native yaupon. Other dwarf cultivars include 'Stokes Dwarf' and 'Schillings'. Tolerant of wide range of soil conditions and sun to shade. No berries on the dwarf forms, but they serve as pollinators for other berry producing hollies. Practically no pruning needed. Very good plant.

'Compact Pfitzer' (Juniperus chinensis 'Compact Pfitzer'): Smaller version of the Pfitzer juniper, only reaching 3-4 ft. high and 6-8 ft. wide. For full sun. Will tolerate dry sites but not wet sites.

Shore juniper (Juniperus conferta): Grows to 2-3 ft. tall, good for mass planting as groundcover in full sun or light shade. Will tolerate all sites except wet, poorly drained ones. 'Blue Pacific' is a more compact, neater cultivar for most home landscapes.

Parsoni juniper (Juniperus davurica): One of the best low-growing junipers. For full sun to light shade. Feathery foliage. To about 2 ft. tall. Not for poorly drained soil.

Spreading juniper (Juniperus horizontalis): There are several cultivars, including 'Bar Harbor' or 'Blue Rug', which grows to 6-8 inches, and 'Plumosa' or Andorra, which grows to 1-2 ft. Are a groundcover type planting for full sun or light shade. Prefers dry conditions.

Dwarf crape myrtle (Lagerstroemia indica): Deciduous, flowering shrub for full sun. Various cultivars available. Tolerates wide range of soil conditions.

'Purple Pixie' loropetalum (Loropetalum chinense 'Purple Pixie'): A truly dwarf form of loropetalum, only reaching 1-2 ft. tall, and slowly growing to a spread of 4 ft. or so. With its cascading growth habit, is good for the front of beds, in containers, hanging over the edge of a wall, etc.

Evergreen burgundy foliage color holds year-round. Pink flowers in early spring or late winter.

In the foreground, Loropetalum 'Purple Pixie'

'Soft Caress' mahonia (Mahonia eurybracteata 'Soft Caress'): Narrow, dark green,   fine-textured leaves give a soft look to the garden. Grows to about 3 ft. tall and wide. For shade to part sun. Bright yellow flowers fall to winter.

Dwarf nandina (Nandina domestica): There are sterile cultivars (don't form berries and sprout seedlings everywhere) of dwarf nandinas such as 'Firepower', 'Gulf Stream, 'Harbour Dwarf', and 'Harbour Belle'. Some have excellent fall and winter red color. For sun to shade and tolerant of wide range of soil conditions. Give a soft, natural look to the landscape.

Nelson's Blue Bear Grass (Nolina nelsonii): Silvery blue-green foliage in typical bear grass form, growing 3-4 ft. tall. Very drought tolerant and salt tolerant. Full sun.

'Mojo' variegated pittosporum (Pittosporum tobira 'Mojo'): A very useful dwarf pittosporum only growing to 18-24 inches tall and 3-4 ft. wide. No pruning needed. More durable, tougher plant than 'Wheeler's Dwarf', below.

Mojo pittosporum

Wheeler's Dwarf pittosporum (Pittosporum tobira 'Wheeler's Dwarf): Excellent evergreen, compact plant for sun to shade. Practically no pruning needed. Will grow on wide range of sites. Stems are very brittle, so avoid planting in high traffic areas.

Wheeler's Dwarf pittosporum

Indian hawthorne (Raphiolepis indica): Some cultivars of Indian_hawthorne are small shrubs, making good substitute for small azaleas in sunny spots. Pink or white flowers in spring. More tolerant of dry sites than azaleas. Very popular in the West, becoming very widely used here, too. Subject to leaf spots on shaded sites.

Encore azalea (Rhododendron hybrid): Small, compact azaleas that bloom in spring, then again mid-summer to fall. For fertile, moist, but well-drained soil and sun to partial shade. Available in a range of azalea colors.

Gumpo azalea (Rhododendron eriocarpum): Small, compact, dense azalea. One of the Satsuki types. For fertile, moist, but well-drained sites. Partial shade best. Pink, white, or blush flowers in April or May.

Kurume azalea (Rhododendron obtusum): Hardy, mid-size azaleas, some over 4 ft. tall. Not for dry areas or poorly aerated areas. Our most common "dwarf" azaleas. Covered with masses of flowers in spring, ranging from white and soft pastels to vibrant reds and pinks. Normally bloom in March.

Satsuki azaleas (Rhododendron spp.): Group of April-May blooming azaleas. Not for dry, hot, or poorly aerated areas. Typically have strong horizontal growth habit and flowers larger than other "dwarf" azaleas.

Rosemary (Rosmarinus officinalis): This herb with fragrant foliage, very useful in the kitchen, makes a great shrub in the landscape, too. The fine-textured foliage is gray-green in color, so is a good contrast to darker green foliage. Needs full sun at least half the day. Don't overwater it; drought tolerant once established.

Bear grass or Adam's needle (Yucca filamentosa): Native to the southeast, bear grass is very drought-tolerant. Prefers full sun but will tolerate light shade. Are beautiful variegated forms also such as 'Color Guard'.

Yucca gloriosa 'Variegata'

Yucca gloriosa 'Variegata': Thick blue-green leaves with gold to cream-colored margins make this an attractive, drought-tolerant specimen plant.

Yucca 'Lone Star': Green-leafed yucca with dramatic foliage that has a strong horizontal orientation. Very attractive.

Yucca rostrata 'Sapphire Showers': Very striking powdery blue, thin leaves fan out to make this plant a showy drought-tolerant specimen.

Yucca smalliana 'Bright Edge': A little more compact than *Y. filamentosa* types. Attractive variegated foliage.

Coontie (Zamia pumila): Native cycad that grows to about 3 ft. tall and form a dense cluster of suckers about 5 ft. wide, but very slowly, over many years. Has shiny, dark green, fern-like foliage. Full sun to dense shade. All soils except poorly drained. Will tolerate a light salt spray but don't plant directly on beach. Drought tolerant once established. Scale insects sometimes a pest.

MEDIUM SHRUBS (4-8 FT.)

Abelia (Abelia grandiflora): White flowers all summer. Tough plant, tolerant of wide range of soil conditions. Good for hedges. Sun to part shade. 'Edward Goucher' not quite as tall and has pink flowers. Butterflies and bees love abelia.

Century plant (Agave americana): Striking accent plant with its gray-green foliage. Native to the arid regions of Mexico but does well in the humid southeast, too, as long as it has good drainage. Are also variegated forms such as 'Marginata', 'Mediopicta', and 'Striata'.

Aucuba (Aucuba japonica): For shade only. Has green or variegated (depending on cultivar) evergreen, glossy leaves. Tolerates wide range of soil conditions. Excellent plant as long as enough shade provided.

Japanese barberry (Berberis thunbergi): Deciduous. Depending on cultivar, red leaves through part or all of growing season. Spines on stems. For sun to part shade. Tolerant of most soils.

Beautyberry (Callicarpa americana): Deciduous native shrub. Bears bright purple berries in fall, attractive to wildlife. White-berried cultivar also available. Prefers light shade and fertile, moist soil.

Sweetshrub (Calycanthus florida): Deciduous native shrub with fragrant, though not particularly showy, spring flowers. Sun to shade. Not highly tolerant of dry sites.

Sasanqua camellia (Camellia sasanqua): Some cultivars such as 'Shishi gashira' are relatively low-growing; others would be considered large shrubs. Glossy, dark-green foliage year-round. Flowers in white or shades of pinks and reds from fall through February. Excellent plant for partial shade or filtered sunlight; fertile, moist, but well-drained soils.

European fan palm (Chamaerops humilis): Very slow-growing to 12 ft. Beautiful, clumping palm for sun to part shade, wide range of soil types. Tolerant of cold to about 10 degrees F. if not for extended period.

Sweet pepperbush (Clethra alnifolia): A spreading, deciduous shrub (4-6 ft. tall) that has fragrant white flowers in summer. Leaves turn yellow in fall. Is a pink form also. Prefers filtered sun but will grow in sun or shade. Needs acidic soil like azaleas. Grows naturally on poorly drained sites but will tolerate dry sites also. Spreads by sending up suckers.

Sago palm (Cycas revoluta): Palm-like, though not a true palm, very slowly growing to no more than 6 ft. Leaves killed by 10 degrees or below but plant will survive. Sun to shade, tolerant of wide range of sites. A good accent plant. Asian cycad scale is its major pest.

Sago palm

Fatsia (Fatsia japonica): Has large green, very tropical-like leaves. Needs shade or partial shade. Tolerant of all but very dry, hot sites.

Forsythia (Forsythia spp.): Deciduous shrub with brilliant yellow flowers in spring if enough cold received in winter. For sunny sites. Tolerates wide range of soil conditions except very dry ones.

Gardenia or cape jasmine (Gardenia jasminoides): Old Southern favorite, evergreen with very, very uniquely fragrant white summer flowers. Whiteflies are a major pest, with sooty mold resulting. Part shade to sun, well-drained, fertile, moist soils and good sites only.

Hydrangea (Hydrangea macrophylla): Deciduous shrub, producing pink or blue flower clusters in summer. Flower color depends on soil pH: acid soils produce blue flowers and basic or alkaline soils produce pink flowers. For shade or partial shade, moist, fertile, but well-drained soil.

Oakleaf hydrangea (Hydrangea quercifolia): Deciduous, native hydrangea producing white flower clusters in late spring. Red leaves in fall. For shade to partial shade, fertile, moist, well-drained soil.

Dwarf Burford holly (Ilex cornuta 'Burfordi compacta'): A versatile 6-10 ft. evergreen shrub with dark green glossy leaves. Only moderate berry production. Requires minimal pruning. For sun to moderate shade. Tolerant of wide range of soil conditions.

Dazzler holly (Ilex cornuta 'Dazzler'): Typically grows to 5-6 ft. Has large multi-spined evergreen leaves, clusters of large red berries. For sun to moderate shade. Tolerates wide range of soil conditions.

Gallberry or inkberry (Ilex glabra): A native evergreen with light green leaves. To 10 ft. tall. Has black berries during fall and winter. Sun to part shade. Moist, acid soils.

Blue Vase juniper (Juniperus chinensis 'Blue Vase'): 4-6 ft. tall evergreen with blue-green needle foliage. 4-6 ft. wide spread. For sun only, well-drained soils, tolerate dry sites. Give it plenty of room or it will look unnatural.

Pfitzer   juniper   (Juniperus   chinensis 'Pfitzeriana'): Needle-like foliage evergreen with rapid growth to 6 ft. tall and 10-12 ft. spread. Too large for most foundation plantings and many landscapes. For sunny sites and wide range of soil conditions with exception of poorly drained or wet soils.

Texas sage (Leucophyllum frutescens): Silvery-gray, evergreen foliage. Lavender to pink flowers. For dry, sunny sites. Adds interesting foliage color to the landscape and is good for dry sites, but is not particularly long-lived.

'Purple Diamond' loropetalum (Loropetalum chinense 'Purple Diamond): An intermediate-sized loropetalum that grows to 4-5 ft. tall. Evergreen burgundy foliage color holds all year. Pink flowers in spring or late winter.

Leatherleaf mahonia or Oregon grape holly (Mahonia bealei): Thick, spiny, evergreen leaves on canes; few branches. Leaves clustered at tips usually. Clusters of blue berries are especially attractive to mockingbirds. For partial shade to shade, best with a little morning sun. Tolerant of all but wet, poorly drained soils.

Fortune's mahonia (Mahonia fortunei): Deep evergreen somewhat fern-like foliage. For part shade to shade. Prefers fertile, moist, well-drained soils, good sites. Grows in an informal clump, with lanky stems sometimes falling over.

Indian hawthorne (Raphiolepis indica): Some cultivars are medium-sized shrubs, others are small. All are evergreen. Have either white or pink flowers. For sun to partial shade, well-drained soils. Prone to leaf spot disease, especially in shade.

Needle palm (Rhapidophyllum hystrix): Tough, versatile native shrubby palm. Very cold tolerant. Spines at base of plant give it the common name.

Partial sun to shade. Tolerant of wide range of soil conditions.

Needle Palm

Indica azaleas (Rhododendron indicum): The large azaleas of the deep South. Many colors available. Prefer shade to partial shade, moist, fertile, well-drained soils. Too large for use as a foundation planting for most buildings.

Low-maintenance roses (Rosa spp.): Though many types of roses, especially those grown for cut flowers, require high maintenance levels because of pest problems, some such as 'Knock Out' and 'Nearly Wild' require less. For full sun only. Perform best in fertile, moist, but well-drained soil. Bloom in cycles from March through November. See list at end of chapter.

Blue-stem palm (Sabal minor): This native palm grows naturally in moist wooded areas, ravines, and bottomlands from North Carolina to east Texas. It is cold-hardy in zones 8-10. There is a Louisiana form that's hardy to zone 7. It is slow-growing and stays low, but its bluish-gray leaves can be very large, making it a showy plant in the garden. Grows best with some protection from the harsh afternoon sun.

Saw palmetto (Serenoa repens): The dense native palmetto growth seen growing in pine woods across the coastal South. Fairly tolerant of wide range of growing conditions, from sun to partial shade. Drought tolerant. Grows to 4-6 ft. tall and wide. Are both yellow-green (more common) and silvery-blue leafed forms ('Silver Saw').

Spirea (Spiraea spp.): Several species of deciduous, white spring-flowering shrubs. Graceful, informal style. Sun to partial shade. Fertile, moist but well-drained soils are best. Beautiful when used as an informal hedge or shrub border as on many old rural homesites.

Sandankwa viburnum (Viburnum suspensum): Dark green leaves with slightly roughened upper surface. Evergreen. Sun to shade, tolerant of wide range of soil conditions.

Weigelia (Weigelia florida): Deciduous plant with arching form. White, red, pink, or purple spring flowers. Not that attractive rest of year. Sun to part shade. Flowers poorly if not enough winter chilling received.

Spanish dagger (Yucca gloriosa): A taller yucca, also native to the southeast, with pointed green leaves. Makes a dramatic statement in the landscape. Very drought-tolerant. Full sun to partial shade. There is also a variegated form.

LARGE SHRUBS (8 FT. AND LARGER)

Bottlebrush buckeye (Aesculus parviflora): Deciduous native shrub for full sun or partial shade and fertile, moist but well-drained soils. Showy white flower clusters in early summer.

Red buckeye (Aesculus pavia): Deciduous native shrub or small tree for full sun to shade and fertile, moist but well-drained soils. Red flowers in spring.

Florida leucothoe (Agarista populifolia): Native evergreen with somewhat of an irregular, weeping or arching growth habit. For shade to part shade only and fertile, moist, but well-drained soils.

Salt bush or groundsel tree (Baccharis halimifolia): Native, salt-tolerant plant that may be found naturally in wet areas, though is also moderately drought tolerant. Clouds of white flowers and fruiting structures in fall are showy, but plant is not particularly noteworthy during spring and summer. For full sun. Very tough. Especially suited for use around drainage areas and stormwater ponds. Not readily available in most nurseries but useful in the landscape where native.

Bottlebrush (Callistemon rigidus): Red, bottlebrush-like flowers on evergreen shrub. For full sun, well-drained soils. Sensitive to hard freezes.

Camellia (Camellia japonica): Evergreen shrub for part shade to shade and fertile, moist, but well-drained soils. Flowers various shades and combinations of pinks, red, and whites from fall through late winter, exact time depending on cultivar. Beautiful dark green, glossy foliage yearround.

Sasanqua camellia (Camellia sasanqua): Fall and winter blooming evergreen. For shade to partial shade. Size depends on cultivar, but generally smaller than regular camellias.   Some cultivars would be considered small to medium shrubs, particularly those with spreading form. Need fertile, moist, but well-drained soil. Typically blooms earlier than *Camellia japonica*.

Feijoa (Feijoa sellowiana): Gray-green evergreen foliage. For well-drained or even dry soils and sun or part shade. White, fragrant spring flowers with bright red stamens.   Followed by small, edible fruit. Good tough hedge plant, though not overly showy.

Althea or Rose of Sharon (Hibiscus syriacus): Very common deciduous, cold-hardy hibiscus. Many flower variations of white, red, to almost blue. Prefers full sun. Tolerant of wide range of soil types.

Burford holly (Ilex cornuta 'Burfordii): Rich, glossy evergreen leaves with red berries. Only one spine at tip of leaves. Rapid grower to 12-20 ft. For sun to shade. Best in fertile, moist, but well-drained soils.

Deciduous holly or possum haw (Ilex decidua): Deciduous holly with orange to scarlet fruits in fall persisting into winter for spectacular show once leaves drop. Attractive to birds. Partial shade to full sun and wet to dry soils.

Winterberry (Ilex verticillata): Deciduous holly similar to possumhaw. Steve Bender of *Southern Living* magazine says that possumhaw has silvery bark and leaves with rounded tips. But winterberry has brown to black bark and leaves with pointed tips. Also, he says, possumhaw will grow twice as large, up to 25 ft. tall and 15 feet across.

Yaupon holly (Ilex vomitoria): Large native evergreen shrub or, more typically, small tree, for sun to shade, wet or dry sites. Female provides small red berries for birds. 'Pendula' is a weeping form often used in landscaping.

Nellie R. Stevens holly (Ilex x 'Nellie R. Stevens'): Hybrid evergreen holly. Very durable and drought resistant. Tolerates wetter soils, too. Heavy red berry producer. Pyramidal growth habit.

Japanese anise (Illicium anisatum): Has light green, evergreen foliage with root beer smell when crushed. Unusual upright leaf orientation. Excellent hedge plant for part shade. Will tolerate shade or sun. Tolerant of most soils except extremely dry or extremely wet. Very cold hardy. Up to 15 ft.

Florida anise (Illicium floridanum): Native anise, grows up to 10 ft. Partial shade to shade and moist soils. Excellent large hedge plant for shaded areas or serves well as small specimen tree. Glossy evergreen leaves and small red flowers in spring. Flowers have somewhat unpleasant fish-like odor.

Yellow or Ocala anise (Illicium parviflorum): Excellent low-maintenance shrub for shade to sun. Grows to about 15 ft. tall and almost as wide. Stays full even without pruning. Good choice for a screening hedge. Or can be trained as a small tree by removing lower limbs. Foliage has fragrance of root beer when crushed.

Virginia sweetspire (Itea virginica): Airy, native deciduous shrub that has lightly fragrant white flowers in late spring. Good fall leaf color. Partial shade or partial sun.

Virginia sweetspire

Hetzi juniper (Juniperus chinensis 'Hetzi'): Rapidly growing evergreen with needle-like foliage. To 8-10 ft. tall and even wider. For full sun and well-drained soils. Tolerant of dry sites. Attractive bluish color.

Torulosa or Hollywood juniper (Juniperus chinensis 'Torulosa'): Twisting, slender upright juniper to 12 ft. or so. For full sun and well-drained soils. Tolerant of dry sites. Dramatic effect; don't overuse within a single landscape.

Japanese or waxleaf ligustrum (Ligustrum japonicum): Very tough, versatile, and rapidly growing shrub with waxy, green evergreen leaves. For sun to shade and wide range of sites and soil conditions. Fragrant white spring flowers.

Glossy ligustrum (Ligustrum lucidum): A larger ligustrum, very adaptable to a wide range of sites, sun or shade. Tends to be a heavy seeder and can become a problem sprouting up around the landscape. Leaves not as glossy as *L. japonicum*. Rapid grower. Attracts whiteflies, but they don't seem to injure it.

Loropetalum (Loropetalum chinense): There are white flowering forms, but the popular ones are the pink or red-flowering forms, especially those types that have red or burgundy colored foliage, too, such as 'Rubrum' and 'ZhuZhou'. Flowers come in late winter to early spring. Most forms get quite large, though 'Pixie' is a true dwarf, but very slow-growing. The larger types make a great 8-10 ft. hedge without any pruning.

Large loropetalum hedge, 10 ft. tall.

Banana shrub (Michelia fuscata): Evergreen with small yellow spring flowers having a strong banana-like scent that can be smelled from quite a distance. For sun to part shade. Needs fertile, moist, but well-drained soil. A southern classic. Gets scale but doesn't cause a major problem.

The very fragrant flowers of banana shrub.

Wax myrtle (Myrica cerifera): Versatile native evergreen shrub or small tree. For wet or dry sites, sun to partial shade. Allow it to become a small tree or prune it as a shrub. Suckers from the base. Female plants provide blue-gray berries for birds.

Oleander (Nerium oleander): Flowering, fast-growing, evergreen shrub. Leaves may brown during hard freezes. Flowers of pink, red, white, or yellow borne in summer. For full sun. Tolerant of variety of soil types. Very salt tolerant. All parts poisonous if eaten. Oleander caterpillars can defoliate it in summer if not controlled when they attack.

Fortunes osmanthus (Osmanthus fortunei): Evergreen with spiny leaves. Flowers are not noteworthy. For full sun or partial shade and fertile, moist, but well-drained soils.

Tea olive (Osmanthus fragrans): Evergreen with small, but very fragrant white flowers in fall and spring. For full sun or partial shade and fertile, moist, but well-drained soils. Very popular because of the long periods of fragrant flowers. A Southern favorite.

Chinese photinia (Photinia serrulata): A large photinia with large glossy leaves. New leaves have red tint. Showy white flowers in spring, but flowers have an unpleasant odor. For fertile, moist, but well-drained sites. This plant is best reserved for very large landscapes.

Redtop or Redtip photinia (Photinia x fraseri): Another large photinia, once widely planted for its brilliant burgundy new foliage. Very prone to a leafspot disease which can defoliate it, redtop is no longer widely produced or sold. If you wish to grow it, avoid frequent pruning and overhead irrigation. Both favor the disease. Best for full sun.

Pittosporum (Pittosporum tobira): Green or variegated forms, both having evergreen foliage. Variegated form not as large. For sun to shade and dry or wet soils. Very fragrant spring flowers. Good, versatile plants.

Yew podocarpus (Podocarpus macrophyllus): Evergreen shrub with very dark and slender foliage and columnar form. Easily shaped and controlled; versatile for a variety of uses. For sun to shade. Not for poorly drained soil. A favorite of aphids, but can tolerate high populations without damage.

Nagi podocarpus (Podocarpus nagi): A broader-leafed podocarpus, making a striking accent plant. For sun or shade. Not for poorly drained soils.

Cherry laurel (Prunus caroliniana): Vigorous, adaptable large native evergreen shrub or small tree. Commonly sprouts from seed spread by birds. Sun to part shade and moist, fertile, but well-drained soils.

Firethorn (Pyracantha coccinea): Evergreen noted for orange berries from fall through winter. Has thorns that can be quite painful. Somewhat rangy grower. Needs plenty of room to grow and cascade as natural growth habit. Very attractive where it has room to grow without over-pruning. For sun and well-drained soils. Mockingbirds love the berries.

Formosan firethorn (Pyracantha koidzumii): Pyracantha with red berries. Larger grower.

Florida azalea (Rhododentron austrinum): Decidious native azalea with fragrant, golden yellow flowers in late March or early April. Needs a good, moist, but well-drained acid soil and a partially shaded site shielded from harsh heat.

Piedmont azalea (Rhododentron canescens): Another common native, deciduous azalea. Depending on the particular plant, fragrant flowers range from pure white to deep pink. Blooms in late March or early April. Needs fertile, acidic but well-drained soil and a partially shaded site. Suckers prolifically.

Shining or winged sumac (Rhus copallina): A native deciduous plant, making a good small tree or large shrub. Brilliant red leaves in fall. Fruit, ripening in fall, attractive to birds. Tolerant of dry sites. For sun to partial shade. Has wings along stem of the leaves. Is not the same plant as poison sumac.   Suckers prolifically and spreads, so best for a large natural area.

Cleyera (Ternstroemia gymnathera): Cleyera is a versatile evergreen for sun to shade, moist, but well-drained soils. Rich, dark, glossy green foliage with colorful wine-red new growth. Naturally develops a good full form if you leave it unpruned and let it grow large. If you prune it to control height, it responds by sending up long shoots so it will require regular pruning.

Sweet viburnum (Viburnum odoratissimum): Evergreen shrub, tolerating most soils. For partial shade to sun, preferring partial shade. Very good hedge plant. Gets whiteflies but they don't seem to harm the plant. Clusters of fragrant, white flowers in the spring if the plant isn't pruned too severly. *V. odoratissimum* is cold-hardy to the mid-teens.

Sandanqua viburnum (Viburnum suspensum): Not as fast or large a grower as *V. odoratissimum.* Leaves have wrinkled appearance on surface.

SHRUBS FOR DRY, SUNNY SITES - TOLERANT OF DROUGHT
Abelia *(Abelia grandiflora)*
Agave species
Barberry *(Berberis spp.)*
Beautyberry *(Callicarpa americana)*

Bottlebrush *(Callistemon rigidus)*
Sago palm *(Cycas revoluta)*
Feijoa *(Feijoa sellowiana)*
Gallberry *(Ilex glabra)*
Yaupon *(Ilex vomitoria)*
Junipers *(Juniperus spp.)*
Ligustrums *(Ligustrum spp.)*
Wax myrtle *(Myrica cerifera)*
Oleander *(Nerium oleander)*
Photinia *(Photinia spp.)*
Pittosporum *(Pittosporum tobira)*
Yew podocarpus *(Podocarpus)*
Cherry laurel *(Prunus caroliniana)*
Pyracantha *(Pyracantha spp.)*
Indian hawthorne *(Raphiolepis spp.)*
Needle palm *(Rhapidophyllum hystrix)*
Sumac *(Rhus spp.)*
Saw palmetto *(Serenoa repens)*
Spiraea *(Spiraea spp.)*
Windmill palm *(Trachycarpus fortunei)*
Yucca species

SHRUBS FOR SHADED AREAS
Aucuba *(Aucuba japonica)*
Fatsia *(Fatsia japonica)*
Hydrangea *(Hydrangea macrophylla)*
Oakleaf hydrangea *(Hydrangea quercifolia)*
Florida leucothoe *(Leucothoe populifolia)*
Mahonia *(Mahonia spp.)*
Wax myrtle *(Myrica cerifera)*
Pittosporum *(Pittosporum tobira)*

Needle palm *(Rhapidophyllum hystrix)*
Azaleas *(Rhododendron spp.)*
Cleyera *(Ternstroemia gymnathera)*
Windmill palm *(Trachycarpus fortunei)*
Viburnum *(Viburnum spp.)*

SHRUBS FOR PARTIALLY SHADED AREAS
Abelia *(Abelia grandiflora)*
Boxwood *(Buxus spp.)*
Camellia *(Camellia spp.)*
European fan palm *(Chamaerops humilis)*
Eleagnus *(Eleagnus pungens)*
Fatsia *(Fatsia japonica)*
Feijoa *(Feijoa sellowiana)*
Gardenia *(Gardenia spp.)*
Hydrangea *(Hydrangea macrophylla)*
Oakleaf hydrangea *(Hydrangea quercifolia)*
Hollies *(Ilex spp.)*
Japanese anise *(Illicium anisatum)*
Florida leucothoe *(Leucothoe populifolia)*
Ligustrum *(Ligustrum spp.)*
Mahonia *(Mahonia spp.)*
Wax myrtle *(Myrica cerifera)*
Pittosporum *(Pittosporum tobira)*
Cherry laurel *(Prunus caroliniana)*
Indian hawthorne *(Raphiolepis indica)*
Needle palm *(Rhapidophyllum hystrix)*
Azaleas *(Rhododendron spp.)*
Cleyera *(Ternstroemia japonica)*
Windmill palm *(Trachycarpus fortunei)*
Viburnum *(Viburnum spp.)*

SHRUBS FOR WET SITES, POORLY DRAINED AREAS

Sweetshrub *(Calycanthus floridus)*
Oakleaf hydrangea *(Hydrangea quercifolia)*
Chinese hollies *(Ilex cornuta)*
Deciduous holly *(Ilex decidua)*
Inkberry or gallberry *(Ilex glabra)*
American holly *(Ilex opaca)*
Florida leucothoe *(Leucothoe populifolia)*
Ligustrum *(Ligustrum spp.)*
Wax myrtle *(Myrica cerifera)*
Oleander *(Nerium oleander)*
Tea olive *(Osmanthus fragrans)*
Cherry laurel *(Prunus caroliniana)*
Needle palm *(Rhapidophyllum hystrix)*
Windmill palm *(Trachycarpus fortunei)*

SALT-TOLERANT SHRUBS

Agave species
Salt bush *(Baccharis halimifolia)*
Bottlebrush *(Callistemon spp.)*
Sago palm *(Cycas revoluta)*
Fatsia *(Fatsia japonica)*
Feijoa *(Feijoa sellowiana)*
Althea *(Hibiscus syriacus)*
Burford holly *(Ilex cornuta 'Burfordii')*
Inkberry *(Ilex glabra)*
American holly *(Ilex opaca)*
Yaupon holly *(Ilex vomitoria)*
Dwarf yaupon holly *(Ilex vomitoria 'Nana')*

Chinese juniper *(Juniperus chinensis)*
Texas sage *(Leucophyllum frutescens)*
Ligustrum *(Ligustrum spp.)*
Leatherleaf mahonia *(Mahonia bealei)*
Wax myrtle *(Myrica cerifera)*
Oleander *(Nerium oleander)*
Pittosporum *(Pittosporum tobira)*
Broadleaf podocarpus *(Podocarpus nagi)*
Pyracantha *(Pyracantha spp.)*
Indian hawthorne *(Raphiolepis indica)*
Rose *(Rosa spp.)*
Sweet viburnum *(Viburnum odoratissimum)*
Sandankwa viburnum *(Viburnum suspensum)*
Yucca species

SHRUBS FOR HEDGES
Abelia
Anise
Indica azaleas
Boxwoods
Camellias
Sasanqua camellias
Cherry laurel
Cleyera
Feijoa
Hollies (esp. 'Burford' and 'Dwarf Burford')
Chinese junipers ('Hetzi' and 'Pfitzer')
Ligustrums
Loropetalums
Oleander
Photinia

Pittosporum
Podocarpus
Silverthorn (elaeagnus)
Spirea
Viburnums
Wax myrtle

SHRUBS, VINES, AND SMALL TREES FOR FRAGANCE
Sweet pepperbush *(Clethra alnifolia)*
Satsumas and oranges
Dogwood *(Cornus florida)*
Loquat *(Eribotrya japonica)*
Gardenia *(Gardenia jasminoides)*
Carolina Jessamine *(Gelsemium sempervirens)*
Banana Shrubs *(Michelia fuscata)*
Tea olive *(Osmanthus fragants)*
Pittolporum *(Pittosporum tobira)*
Florida azalea (*Rhododendron austrinum*)
Piedmont azalea *(Rhododendron canescens)*
Roses *(Rosa spp.)*
Confederate jasmine *(Trachelospermum jasminoides)*
Sweet viburnum *(Viburnum adoratissimum)*
Thryallis *(Galphimia glauca)*

LOW MAINTENANCE ROSES
Mrs. B.R. Cant
Marie Van Houtte
Duchesse de Brabant
Mons Tillier
Etoil de Lyon

Mme Scripion Cochet
Louis Philippe
Napoleon
Old Blush
Vincent Godrief
Archduke Charles
Souv de St. Anne`s
Levenson Gower
Souv de la Malmaison
Perle d'Or
Verdun
Mevrouw Nathalie Nypels
Marytje Cazant
Ballerina
Belinda's Dream
Prosperity
Clytemnestra
Cramoisi Superieur
Pink Perpetue
Knock Out
Drift
Carefree Beauty (Katy Road Pink)
Carefree Wonder
Cocktail
Sarah Van Fleet
Dortmund
Climbing Pinkie
Else Poulsen
The Fairy
Cecile Brunner
Caldwell Pink

Climbing Pinkie
Sea Foam

For more information on the Earth-Kind roses evaluated by the Texas AgriLife Extension Service, see http://aggie-horticulture.tamu.edu/earthkindroses/
But, remember that the humidity in Texas is different than the humidity in Florida or Georgia. So, though these are generally tough roses, susceptibility to black spot disease will vary some from Texas conditions.

Mrs. B.R. Cant rose

COLORFUL SHRUBS		
Shrub	**What is Colorful**	**Time of Year**
Abelia	White flowers; Confetti has colorful foliage	Summer flowers. Foliage all year.
Aucuba	leaves	Year round
Azaleas	various flower	spring

	colors	
Barberry	leaves	year round, winter
Beautyberry	purple fruit	fall
Bottlebrush	red flowers	late spring
Camellia	various flower colors	Fall -winter
Cherry laurel	white	spring
Chinese hollies	red berries	winter
Feijoa	white flowers, red stamens	spring
Forsythia	yellow flowers	spring
Gardenia	white flowers	spring
Hydrangea	blue-pink flowers	late spring-summer
Indian hawthorn	white-pink flowers	spring
Leatherleaf mahonia	grape-like berries	summer
Ligustrum	white flowers	spring
Loropetalum	white or pink flowers, burgundy foliage on many	spring flowers, ever-green foliage
Native azaleas	various flowers	spring
Oakleaf hydrangea	white flowers	late spring
Oleander	red, pink, peach, white flowers	late spring, summer
Pyracantha	orange berries	fall–winter
Redtop photinia	red young foliage	year-round
Sasanqua	various flower	fall-winter

camellias	colors	
Spirea	white flowers	spring
Sweet viburnum	white flowers	spring
Tea olive	white	fall, winter, spring
Texas sage	lavender flowers	summer
Weigelia	pink, red, white flowers	spring
Various hollies	red to orange berries	winter

PLANTING SHRUBS: SOME ADVICE

There's an adage that advises, "Don't plant a $10 plant in a 50-cent hole." You would be wise to heed that advice.

The hole in which you plant a shrub should be at least twice as wide as the root ball of the shrub. Three times wide, or even wider, would be better. Don't worry about digging a deep hole. The plant doesn't even need to be planted quite as deep as it was in the container. Just a tiny bit higher is better. Never plant too deeply.

Before putting the soil back into the hole around the plant, thoroughly break up all clumps. Then gradually fill back in around the shrub's root ball, gently firming the soil as you go. Mulch the plant when you finish. Water by hand, letting the water slowly soak into the soil directly over the root ball of the plant; that's where the roots are.

The exact time it will take for the plant's roots to

become established in the surrounding soil will vary with type of plant and environmental conditions. But, for the first year after planting, realize that the plant will still be relying largely on the roots in the original root ball. This limited root ball will be very susceptible to drying during periods of inadequate rainfall. So, it is important that you apply water whenever rainfall isn't adequate.

It is no longer recommended that soil amendments, such as peat, be mixed with the soil in individual planting holes. University research has shown no advantage to individually amending planting holes. Yet, there can be disadvantages in that water can stand in such amended holes, rotting roots. If you wish to use soil amendments, such as peat or compost, amend the entire planting bed, tilling the amendments in with the existing soil. But again, research has shown that amendments aren't necessary in most soils. What helps more than anything else is digging a wide planting hole.

DETERMINING SPACING BETWEEN SHRUBS

It's often difficult to know how far apart to space shrubs in a planting. But those tiny one-gallon plants can often become quite large with time. And, unless you know the ultimate size of the plants, you may overplant, waste money, and reduce the effective life of the planting by creating overcrowded growing conditions.

Below are listed some common types of shrubs and recommended planting spacings. This very useful information comes from an old University of Georgia Extension publication. You can use these spacings as recommendations for other similar shrubs, too.

Most spreading junipers: Space 3 ft. from walls, fences, or buildings. Space 3-4 ft. between centers of plants for groundcover uses. Space 3 ½ ft. from walks or drives.

Dwarf Japanese garden junipers: Space 3 ft. from walls, fences, or buildings. Space 2 - 2 ½ ft. from walks or drives. Space 3 ½ - 4 ½ ft. between centers for a mass effect.

Dwarf azaleas and other slow-growing small shrubs: Space 3 ft. from walls, fences, building, walks, or drives. Space 3 ft. between centers of plants.

Dwarf yaupons, rotunda hollies, boxwoods, nandina, mahonia, and other small to medium-size shrubs: Space 3 ft. from walls, fences, or buildings. Space 2 ft. from walks or drives. Space 3-4 ft. between centers for a mass planting effect. Space 5-6 ft. between centers if the appearance of individual plants is wanted.

Podocarpus, upright sasanqua cultivars, and other strongly upright-growing shrubs: Space 3 ft. from walls, fences, or buildings. Space 3 ½ - 4 ft. between centers for groupings, 2-3 ft. for hedges, and 4 ½ - 5 ft. where the appearance of individual specimens is wanted.

Cleyera, Sandankwa viburnum, and other fairly compact but large shrubs: Space 4-5 ft. from walls, fences, or buildings. Space 4 ft. between centers for clipped hedges, 4-5 ft. between centers in groupings, and 5-6 ft. between centers for the appearance of individual specimens.

Spirea, Indica azaleas, forsythia, and dwarf Burford hollies (medium to large, somewhat spreading shrubs): Space 3 ½ ft. from walls, fences, or buildings. Space 4-5 ft. between centers for a_mass planting and 6-8 ft. for the appearance of individual_specimens.

Pittosporum, Burford holly, camellia, and sasanqua (large, but not the largest of shrubs): Space 5-6 ft. from walls, fences, or buildings. Space 6-8 ft. between centers for a grouping effect; space 4-6 ft. for a clipped hedge.

Pyracantha and other large, unruly shrubs: Space 5 ½ - 6 ft. from walls, fences, or buildings. Space 8-10 ft. between centers in mass plantings. Space 10-12 ft. between centers for individual specimen effect.

Common tea olive, camellia, photinia, and other large shrubs/small trees: Space 8-12 ft. between centers in naturalized groupings. Space 7-8 ft. between centers for screening. Space 5-6_ft. between centers for a clipped hedge - probably not a good use for most plants in this group - they're just too naturally large to be maintained as a clipped hedge.

FERTILIZING SHRUBS:

To fertilize shrubs and small trees, use about two teaspoons of a_15-0-15, 16-4-8, or similar fertilizer (with half the nitrogen in slow-release form) per foot of plant height. Small shrubs, less than a foot tall, should receive no more than one level teaspoon.

Another way to figure fertilizer rates is on the basis of applying one pound of actual nitrogen per 1,000 sq. ft. To determine this rate, divide the percentage of nitrogen (the first number of the three   fertilizer numbers) in the fertilizer into 100. For example, apply 6 pounds of 16-4-8 per 1,000 sq. ft. Or, apply almost 7 pounds (6.66 lbs. to be exact) of a 15-0-15 fertilizer. Similar fertilizers may be used. Just be sure to adjust the rate on the basis of the amount of nitrogen in the fertilizer as discussed here.

There is no need to pull the mulch back before fertilizing.   When fertilizing shrubs and trees, just spread the fertilizer on the ground beneath the branch spread and slightly beyond. Water to wash it down through the mulch or grass.

Don't fertilize any more than necessary. All plants need nutrients.   But if you manage your landscape correctly, by the time your trees and shrubs are older, a nutrient recycling system should be in place. It's the new, young trees and shrubs in your landscape, which you want to grow faster, that will most benefit from the fertilizer.

When you're trying to encourage very young trees and shrubs to grow, you can fertilize up to four times a growing season (in March, May, July, and September). But moderate growth can be obtained with applications only in March and July.

Mature shrubs can often get by with only the March application. In fact, if you keep a 2-inch thick layer of pine straw or leaf mulch around the plants, mature shrubs may need no yearly fertilization. The nutrients released from the mulch breakdown is sometimes enough. Let the appearance of the shrubs guide you in determining the necessity and frequency of fertilization. You'll find that plants growing in sandy soils will require fertilization more often than those in heavier soils.

WATERING SHRUBS

Once shrubs become well established, you will find that you rarely need to water them. Only during very dry weather will rainfall not provide for their needs - if you have selected the proper shrubs for the site and have kept them mulched.

Some shrubs, such as azaleas or hydrangeas, will readily tell you with drooping leaves when they need water. Water stress may be more difficult to detect in shrubs with stiffer leaves. To check moisture needs of such shrubs during periods of longer-than-normal dry weather, develop the habit of occasionally monitoring the soil moisture level by digging in the soil with a garden trowel or with your hand. Be sure to check four inches or so down rather than just scratch the soil surface. If the soil is cool and moist enough to stick together when squeezed, there's probably adequate moisture.

When you do have to water, water deeply, applying at least half an inch of water if you can do so without it running off. Deep watering encourages deep rooting. And, deep rooting results in stronger, more drought tolerant plants. Frequent, shallow watering does just the opposite.

Of course, when you have just planted shrubs, and their roots are still restricted to the container root ball (they haven't ventured out, taking anchor in the surrounding soil yet), you will need to water more frequently. You may need to water as often as daily if it's summer and you've planted one-gallon plants. The key lies in not letting the roots dry out but not keeping them saturated either. You will simply have to feel the soil in the root ball to determine when to water. There is no hard and fast rule because there are too many variables such as soil type, time of year, size of plant, type of plant, etc.

Pay careful attention to watering for at least a complete year after planting. It takes that long, and sometimes longer, before new roots get well established in the surrounding soil. You may think a shrub or tree that you planted six months ago is well established. Yet if it goes too long without rain or watering, you can still lose a plant that long after planting.

WEED CONTROL AROUND SHRUBS

Most of your shrubs should be in groups with other shrubs. Minimize your plantings of individual shrubs out in the lawn and you'll greatly reduce the maintenance required. It's much easier to maintain a bed of shrubs than it is to maintain scattered shrubs here and there.

Maintain a mulch of pine straw, bark, or other organic material on the ground beneath the shrubs. If you have a hedge or other row of shrubs, don't simply mulch in little rings around each plant so that you still have to mow between plants. Rather, mulch the entire bed.

A generous 2-inch layer of mulch is your best method of weed control around shrubs. The mulch will also prevent the soil from packing and stunting the shrubs' growth. In addition, the mulch will moderate soil temperatures, conserve moisture, provide nutrients, and be attractive and neat.

Weeds that pop up through the mulch layer can be either hand pulled or spot treated with a herbicide containing glyphosate (such as Roundup®). Keep any herbicide mist whatsoever, though, off the foliage of the shrubs. Never spray when there is any wind. Weeds will be their worst the first 2-3 years after planting a new area. If you keep the area mulched, though, the weed problem will reduce drastically after several years.

The selection of selective herbicides (those that can be applied over the general area, killing the weed and not the desired plants) is very limited for use around shrubs. There are a couple that can be applied over the top of certain shrubs to kill existing weeds. But, these herbicides aren't approved for use on all types of shrubs.   Nor are they effective on all weeds. Consequently, they are rarely used in landscape situations.

There are a few pre-emergent herbicides (to be applied after weeds are hand pulled or spot-treated and before new ones emerge) available from garden centers. Again, these herbicides aren't approved for use on all shrubs; nor are they effective on all weeds. Read the label carefully before using any such herbicide.   Apply the herbicide exactly as the label specifies.

The bottom line is that there is no selective herbicide that will totally take the place of a good mulch used with occasional hand-pulling or spot-treating.

6

Lawns
Avoiding the Headaches

HOW LARGE SHOULD YOUR LAWN BE?

Many of us have a lawn, and some of us have more lawn than we need. Lawns do have many functional purposes. For example, lawns are great places for kids of all ages to play. And, lawns can be very attractive in themselves.

But lawns do require a fair amount of regular maintenance, at least if they are maintained to the standards most of us want. They usually must be fertilized, watered at times, and mowed regularly. At times they may even have to be sprayed for pests. Hundreds of millions of dollars, maybe even billions, are spent each year on lawn care in the United States.

What other plant do you fertilize, water, and baby along only to remove its new growth every week? Sounds kind of crazy when you think about it, doesn't it? Yet, most of us want at least a little bit of lawn in our landscape.

Lawns present another problem here in the South. The lawn grasses grown here will not tolerate shade very well. St. Augustine grass, our most shade-tolerant of southern lawn grasses, still needs a fair bit of sun to grow well. Yet so many of us want a lawn with trees in it. That just will not work well!

The types of grass we have in the lower South will only grow well in open areas where there are no trees.

For these reasons, you may want to think about decreasing the percentage of lawn area in your landscape. Grow a lawn where you really need it and really want it. But don't feel you need to have a huge lawn. And where the shade from trees makes it difficult to maintain a lawn, for goodness' sake, use alternatives there. Sometimes all you need to do is let the leaf mulch accumulate. And stop mowing where there is no grass. Or perhaps you want to incorporate groundcovers, shrubs, or understory trees in such shaded areas. The point is to not beat your head against the wall trying to grow a lawn where you have too much shade.

Leave natural leaf mulch or grow groundcovers in shaded areas under trees. The lawn will only grow well in the open areas where it receives sufficient sunlight.

WHAT'S THE BEST KIND OF LAWN GRASS?

There is no one perfect type of southern lawn grass. All the grasses have their problems and their strong points.

Centipede is a common grass in many areas, readily available as sod or seed. It is not salt tolerant and so shouldn't be planted where it will receive salt spray. It is not very tolerant of shade. It doesn't tolerate heavy foot traffic or other wear well. But, it doesn't require high levels of fertilizer. In fact, the best way to damage a centipede lawn is to over-fertilize it. Centipede only has to be mowed every 7-14 days. Nematodes can sometimes be a serious problem on centipede. And, centipede is subject to some fungus diseases.

St. Augustine is the grass most commonly planted along the coast because it is salt tolerant. It has wider leaf blades that give the lawn a coarser texture than centipede. But, it tolerates wear fairly well. St. Augustine grass cannot be started from seed. Nematodes are occasionally a problem for St. Augustine grass, but the most common pest is the chinch bug. St. Augustine is also commonly affected by some fungus diseases. Some types of St. Augustinegrass are more tolerant of shade than are our other lawngrasses. Seville, Delmar, and Captiva are the most shade-tolerant types.

Zoysia grass has become more popular in recent years. Old types of zoysia were slow to spread and slow to recover from damage. Meyer zoysia, heavily promoted in ads as a wonder grass, didn't do well under Florida conditions. Some of the zoysias had to be mowed with a reel mower rather than a rotary mower to prevent scalping. But newer zoysia types like El Toro and Empire grow faster and can be mowed higher.

UltimateFlora has a fine texture, similar to Meyer, but has performed better under Florida conditions. None of the zoysias are as good for shade as the shade-tolerant St. Augustines, though El Toro is better than most zoysias. And all zoysias are subject to pest problems, just as are all the lawngrasses. Most types of zoysia cannot be started from seed. Zoysia has good salt tolerance in general.

Bahia grass is excellent in terms of being tough as nails. It is extremely drought tolerant, has good wear tolerance, and doesn't require much fertilizer. But, bahia grass produces a tall Y-shaped seed head quickly during the growing season that requires it to be mowed every 5-7 days during the growing season for optimal appearance. Bahia grass can be seeded. It has very poor shade tolerance and salt tolerance. 'Argentine' bahia is preferred over 'Pensacola' bahia for lawns because seed heads are not as numerous.

Hybrid bermuda grasses will grow well in the South, but they are not used as often because of their high maintenance requirements.   They must be fertilized and mowed more often than the other warm-season lawn grasses.   And, they look much better if mowed with a reel-type mower.   Despite these high maintenance considerations, hybrid bermuda grasses have a high wear tolerance and quick recovery rate from damage.   Consequently, they're usually the grasses of choice for athletic fields and golf courses.

Common bermuda grass, often a weed in flower or shrub beds or the vegetable garden, is not often used as a lawn grass.   It is the only bermuda grass that can be started from seed, but it lacks the fine appearance of the hybrid bermudas. The required maintenance level for an attractive lawn is more or less the same as for the hybrid bermudas. Common bermuda is usually reserved for uses such as roadsides, etc., where toughness and rate of growth is more important than appearance.

Carpet grass is only suitable as a lawn grass in areas which stay constantly very wet. It is extremely intolerant of dry conditions and should not be used on most sites.

THE FOLLOWING LAWN CARE CAN PREVENT MANY PROBLEMS

Chances are that if you have a lawn you'll have problems with it from time to time. Most problems are related to care of the lawn. So, let's talk about lawn care and about potential problems.

THE NUMBER ONE LAWN PROBLEM- POOR SOIL CONDITIONS

Many lawn problems can be traced to the fact that the soil is too hard to allow good root growth. It pays to properly prepare the soil before planting your lawn. Thoroughly rototill the entire area before planting. Then rake the area to smooth it. Water the soil to settle it. If the site has been scraped of its topsoil, you may have to add topsoil or other soil amendments during the rototilling stage. Avoid the common mistake of planting sod on compacted soil that is too hard to invite good growth. It is impossible to totally correct the situation later.

Note the poor drainage in this compacted area of lawn. It will always be difficult to have a good lawn in such compacted soil conditions.

Construction activities tend to compact the soil on a home site. Before a lawn is planted on such a site, the soil needs to be tilled up and then smoothed out.

Short of starting over and properly tilling the area,

maybe adding some soil amendments, about all you can do to an existing lawn is call in a lawn service to aerate the area with a heavy-duty core type aerating machine. This will cultivate the soil by pulling plugs out, allowing better penetration of air, water, and fertilizer.

Don't forget that any type of frequent traffic, foot automobile, even dog traffic, will cause wear damage to the lawn and can compact the soil and cause poor grass growth.

Note the wilted drought-stressed streaks in this lawn where the soil is compacted.

Here is the cause of the compaction, two years earlier. The effects of compacting the soil are permanent.

ADEQUATE SUNLIGHT

Too often we try to grow grass in areas of inadequate sunlight. St. Augustine is our most shade-tolerant lawn grass, but even the shade-tolerant types of St. Augustine grass will tolerate only so much shade. If you insist on growing grass in a shaded area, I suggest plugging in St. Augustine (Seville, Delmar, or Captiva) and watering well. If your test plugs don't take off and grow within a month or so, you probably just have too much shade, provided you give the grass water, good soil, and other things it needs to grow. If it does grow well, then convert the area over from centipede or other present grass to St. Augustine grass.

Trees not only shade out lawngrasses, but the roots also compete with the grass. The solution for a bare site like this is to either mulch or plant groundcovers.

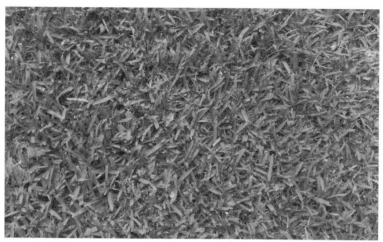

If there's not enough sunlight on a site to grow 'Seville' St. Augustine, then the site has too much shade for any of the lawngrasses.

WATERING

Lawn grasses usually require supplemental watering at times to grow well, and most people know that. Unfortunately, though, few people really water correctly and that contributes to many of our lawn problems.

Water an established lawn only when needed. Only when the grass begins to turn that wilted gray-green color should you water. But then, water deeply, applying ½ to ¾ inch of water so that the entire root zone will be wet. So often we don't water long enough, and a shallow grass root system is the result.

The only way to tell how long you should water is to place cups or rain gauges out in the sprinkler pattern to catch water for 15 minutes. Measure the amount of water in each cup and then take the average amount of water in the cups. Multiply that average amount by 4 to obtain the hourly watering rate. Suppose it is ¼ inch. Then you know you'll need to run the water 2 hours in that spot to apply ½ inch of water, the desired amount.

Apply approximately ½ inch
of water each time you water.

In summary, make sure you're watering long enough. But only water when it is really needed. Watering too shallowly and too frequently will lead to a multitude of problems. For instance, diseases are stimulated by a moist environment. Excess water also leads to excess growth which, in turn, leads to thatch problems.

Many of you have underground sprinkler systems complete with time-clocks. Turn the time-clock off for the most part. Rather, just set the clock to turn the system on those occasional nights it is needed. If you go on a vacation, set the time-clock to run the system every five days or so. And, by all means, take the time to measure the output from each zone of the system so you'll know how long each zone needs to run.

MOWING

Again, everyone thinks they know how to mow. But, so often, we mow the grass too low and weaken it. Think about it. You do everything you can to grow good grass. Then when it grows up you scalp it down. How devastating to the grass!

Measure the height of your mower blade from a flat surface such as the driveway. It should be a minimum of 1½ inches high for mowing centipede and 3 inches minimum for mowing St. Augustine grass. Mow bahia grass at 3-4 inches and zoysia at 1-2 inches. Bermuda grass should be mowed at ½-1 inch and mowed with a reel mower (not a rotary mower). Mow on the higher end of these ranges when the grass is stressed by shade or other factors.

Don't bag the clippings when you mow. They do not contribute to thatch. Over-fertilizing and over-watering do more to cause thatch, an accumulation of old grass runners, not clippings. Clippings, on the other hand, are good for the grass because they contain nutrients. You need to recycle them back into the lawn. Also, you'll save much time if you don't bag, even if you have to mow the lawn a little more often. Actually, you probably won't have to mow more often. Try it; I think you'll like it.

One last note on mowing: Sharpen that mower

blade every month. Not only will it make mowing easier, but it will make your grass look better and be healthier. Shredded leaf blades are an invitation for disease problems and give the entire lawn a brownish cast.

FERTILIZING

Your grass needs nutrients. But too rich of a supply leads to pest problems taking advantage of the lush growth. And, it means you'll have more of a mowing problem.

Use a fertilizer with slow-release nitrogen to avoid that fast rush of nitrogen availability and lush growth. Use 15-0-15, or a similar low-phosphorus ratio. The 8-2-12 with 4% magnesium recommended for palms in the tree chapter of this book would also be fine for lawns. Select a fertilizer with half of the nitrogen listed on the bag as water-insoluble. For example, in a 15-0-15 fertilizer, that would be 7.5% water-insoluble nitrogen. Also, it would be good to select a fertilizer with at least 2% iron.

Avoid fertilizers such as 29-3-3, 23-3-3, etc. They are too high in nitrogen (first number) in relation to the potassium, the last number. Unless you have had a soil test indicating that you need more phosphorus (the second number in the fertilizer), select a fertilizer with low phosphorus.

You'll pay more for a good fertilizer with water-insoluble nitrogen. But it will help you prevent problems in the long run.

*Use a 15-0-15 or similar low-phosphorus,
high potassium fertilizer.*

TOTAL NITROGEN (N) 15.00%*
    2.56%   Ammoniacal Nitrogen
    1.38%   Nitrate Nitrogen
    3.56%   Urea Nitrogen
    7.50%   Water Insoluble Nitrogen
SOLUBLE POTASH (K_2O) 15.00
CALCIUM (Ca) 7.50
TOTAL MAGNESIUM (Mg) 1.00
    1.00% Water Soluble Magnesium (Mg)
SULFUR (S) ....
    Combined Sulfur (S)

*Try to select a fertilizer that has ½ of its total
nitrogen in a water-insoluble or slow-release form.*

When to fertilize: DO NOT fertilize in the spring until three weeks after the grass greens up and not before mid-March when danger of frost is usually past. Otherwise, yellowing may result. Centipede grass can often get by on one fertilization annually, and even occasionally none if you're not bagging clippings and if your soil is not overly sandy. If you have a sandy soil, or if your grass is growing poorly, you may need to come back with a second application in August.

St. Augustine grass might also get by on one spring application, but it is probably more common to apply a second in August. Bermuda grass and zoysia grass, on the other hand, will require fertilizer applications 2-3 times over the growing season.

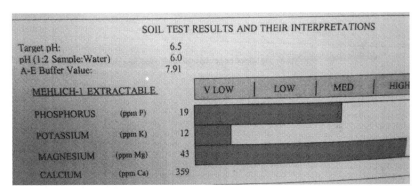

A soil test, done through your local county extension of your land-grant university, is a great tool for learning if you need to apply fertilizer, and what kind.

How much fertilizer? One pound of actual nitrogen per 1,000 sq. ft. per application. That means 6-7 lbs. of 15-0-15 or 12 lbs. of 8-2-12. Divide the percentage of nitrogen (the first number) into 100 to obtain the number of pounds of fertilizer you'll need per 1,000 sq. ft. If your fertilizer doesn't contain at least 1/3 of its nitrogen in a slow-release form, then reduce the amount of fertilizer per 1,000 sq. ft. by half.

You'll just have to calibrate your spreader by putting in a known weight of fertilizer, applying over a given area, and then re-weighing the spreader contents to determine amount applied over the given area. Adjust the spreader opening up or down accordingly. A broadcast spreader usually applies with less streaking than does a drop-type spreader.

What about "winterizer" fertilizers advertised in the fall? There is some truth to the claim that increased potassium (the third number in the fertilizer ratio, eg., 20 in 5-0-20) increases cold hardiness of lawn grasses. More accurately, it is an increased potassium to nitrogen ratio that gives the grass cold hardiness. But, many so-called winterizers on the market are too high in nitrogen. Nitrogen should not be applied at a rate greater than ½ lb. of actual nitrogen per 1,000 square feet after mid-September. If you apply a 5-0-20 winterizer, that would be 10 lbs. of fertilizer per 1,000 sq. ft. You shouldn't even use winterizers later than mid-October, though.

There's probably no need to apply a winterizer at all if you applied a fertilizer such as 15-0-15 as late as August.   Rather than applying the late summer fertilization of 15-0-15 or 8-2-12, you may prefer to use the 5-0-20 in September instead. Apply one or the other, but both are probably not needed.

THATCH AND SPONGY LAWNS

If your lawn seems very spongy when you walk across it, you have an accumulation of thatch. Essentially, thatch is just an accumulation of old grass growth, mostly stems and runners, that have not decomposed. Many people mistakenly think that the clippings from mowing contribute to thatch. However, clippings, being high in moisture content, decompose fairly rapidly and do not contribute significantly to thatch.

The problem with thatch is that the grass, as it grows, tends to root in the thatch layer rather than the soil. Consequently, the grass becomes shallow-rooted and is prone to drought damage, cold damage, and many other problems.

The key to keeping thatch from accumulating to troublesome levels is avoiding over-fertilizing and avoiding use of high water-soluble nitrogen fertilizers... and by not watering more often than absolutely necessary.

NEMATODE PESTS

Nematodes are tiny (have to use a microscope to see them) roundworms that live in the soil. Certain kinds are harmful to certain grasses because they puncture the roots to suck the plant juices from them. This results in stunted root growth, of course, results in thinning of the lawn.

Effective nematicides for home use are practically nonexistent. The key to dealing with nematodes lies in taking good care of your grass so that it can better tolerate the nematodes rather than trying to eliminate them. Sometimes you can use other tricks like switching to a different type of grass that the particular nematode doesn't prefer. That's the recommended solution, for example, if you have a ring nematode problem in centipede. You just switch to St. Augustine or any of the other grasses that aren't harmed by ring nematodes.

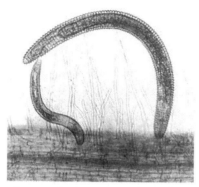

Microscopic view of ring nematodes feeding on a centipede grass root. Ring nematodes are only damaging to centipede grass. So the best solution is to simply plant a different type of grass.

The only way to find out how many nematodes and what kinds you have in your lawn is to have a laboratory sample run. If you suspect nematode damage to your lawn, your land-grant university extension service has a local county office which can provide you with information about sending a sample of your lawn for a lab check. Once you receive the results back from the lab, you will know what kind of nematodes your lawn has, whether the levels are considered damaging, and you will know more about your options for managing them.

DISEASES

There are three conditions that must be met in order for a plant disease to occur. First, there must be a host plant. Second, there must be a disease-causing pathogen.   Third,   there   must   be   favorable environmental conditions for the disease to develop.

In the case of lawn diseases, two of those conditions are always present.   The host plant, your lawn, is always there.   And, believe or not, in most cases, the fungal pathogen is always present, too – either in the soil or in the thatch layer. The only factor that remains to be provided is a favorable environment in terms of moisture   and   temperature.   Nature   controls   the temperature, and often the moisture. But when rains aren't frequent, you control the moisture. You also control the thatch level in the lawn. So, in some cases, you control whether that favorable environment is provided, and whether the fungus can start growing and parasitizing the lawn.

Most fungus diseases are favored by prolonged periods of moisture. Don't water the lawn more often than is necessary. And when you water, it's best to water early in the morning – so that the grass surface stays wet no longer than necessary. Set your sprinkler system to come on at 2:00 or 3:00 a.m. and go off about the time you get up. Or, if you're using a hose and sprinkler, try to start the water as soon as you get up and turn it off as you leave for work. Or, you can buy an inexpensive timer that will turn the water off for you.

As long as environmental conditions favor fungal spread, stopping a disease will be difficult, especially if the thatch layer in the lawn is thick. That's why it is so important to reduce thatch buildup by not over-fertilizing and over-watering.

Disease severity will be enhanced, too, if the grass is under stress from being mowed too low. So, be careful not to add this stress to your lawn. When a disease is active is the one time you should bag the clippings when you mow. Mow the diseased area last so as not track fungus spores to the other part of the lawn. And, use the bagger to catch the clippings from the diseased area.

Don't think that spraying a fungicide will eradicate a lawn disease and keep it from coming back. Fungicides don't kill the fungi that cause lawn diseases. They can only force the fungus into a state of temporary dormancy – provided you obtain good coverage, don't have too heavy a thatch layer, use the proper fungicide, and use proper timing. Repeat applications will be necessary to keep the fungus dormant long enough for the grass to recover. The long-term solution to managing lawn diseases, though, lies in keeping the grass healthy and not providing the ideal conditions for development of the fungus. Otherwise, spraying will only provide temporary relief.

When a fungus disease is active, it will usually spread fast. If you have a dead spot that stays the same size for weeks, it probably wasn't even caused by a fungus. If, on the other hand, the trouble spot is rapidly becoming larger over a period of a week or so, then it is a good possibility that you have an active fungus problem. Search for insect pests first, though, and rule them out. Sod webworms and chinch bugs also cause brown areas in lawns.

If you suspect a fungus disease in a damaged area of the lawn, carefully inspect the individual grass plants. If the grass easily pulls out from where the leaf sheath attaches to the stem, and if that attachment appears darkened and rotten, then it is very likely that a fungus disease is the cause of the problem.

You will find several fungicides for lawn diseases on your local garden center shelf. Read the label before buying the fungicide to make sure it is the one you need. Sprays are usually more effective than granular fungicides.

Many more lawn fungicides only come in larger packages and are for use only by licensed pest control operators. So, if you have a fungus problem that you cannot control with cultural controls and over-the-counter fungicides, you may need to call on the services of a licensed pest control company. Just be sure that the company has the necessary licensing and that the applicator has a card specifying licensure.

In summary, the key to disease control is providing the lawn with its basic needs but not over-watering and over-fertilizing.

INSECT PESTS

While there are normally always a few pest insects in any lawn, they aren't there in damaging numbers. The vast majority of insects in a lawn tend to be either harmless or beneficial.

To check for pest insects in a trouble spot in your lawn, get on your hands and knees and look closely near the soil line at the borders of the trouble spot. Remember, you're only concerned with pest insects; many of the others you see will be either harmless insects or even beneficial insects and spiders. If you don't easily see pests, you may try a soapy water flush that will drive many insects, good and bad, out of the thatch or soil. Mix an ounce of dishwashing detergent with two gallons of water. Slowly drench the mixture over a 2 x 2 ft. area on the border of the problem spot. Watch for several minutes.

Spittlebugs are small (about ¼ inch) dark brown to black insects with two orange stripes across their back. Their underside is also orange. They sometimes become a problem on lush centipede in mid to late summer as they suck on the grass plants and discolor them. Typically, they cause a yellow or red streaking of the grass blades. Other types of grasses aren't normally damaged. It takes a LOT of spittlebugs to cause enough damage to warrant spraying.

Chinch bugs are tiny black insects (about 1/16 to ⅛ inch) with white patches on the tops of their wing pads. The even tinier immatures are red. Chinch bugs stay near the soil line, sucking juices from the St. Augustine grass plants, usually in sunny areas of the lawn first. They do not affect the other types of lawn grasses; only St. Augustine grass is affected. And, they're not usually a problem in shaded areas, at least not first.

Chinch bug feeding results in yellowed areas of the lawn that turn straw-colored with time. A good way to check for chinch bugs in the lawn is to dig several clumps of sod from the perimeter of declining areas. Shake the grass over a white paper plate. If you shake well, and if chinch bugs are present, they should be more easily seen as they fall to the plate. Another handy trick is to use a hand vacuum to vacuum the affected area of the grass. Then examine the contents of the vacuum.

Chinch bug damage

Chinch bugs: eggs, nymphs, and adults. This is a greatly magnified image from UF-IFAS Extension.

Mole crickets are tan to brown insects with rounded heads and short, stubby legs for digging. They don't hop like field crickets, but rather crawl as they dig through the soil eating grass roots and making their slightly raised tunnels in the soil.

Sod webworm damage usually occurs in late summer to early fall. In early stages, a close examination will reveal that grass blades have been notched or chewed. If the damage becomes very severe (and it can - very rapidly), about all that remains will be grass runners. If you look very closely around the soil line you may find some of the quarter inch long caterpillars curled in a C-shape. The light green caterpillars are nocturnal and rest during the day, so they're often hard to find. You also may find small clumps of greenish or tan excrement if you look very closely. Often, the tan-colored adult moths can be seen flitting around the lawn during the day.

Just because you find a few of any of these insects does not mean that you have an insect problem in your lawn. Make sure that you have sufficient numbers to warrant treatment. You'll never completely eradicate any type of insects from your lawn and it is futile to try. Only when you have a large number causing visible damage in a spot is treatment necessary. And, then, you can often just treat the infested area and about a 15 ft. border around it.   Sometimes, though, the infestation will spread and the whole lawn will have to be treated. Monitor the infestation closely.

Be sure you use an insecticide that is labeled for the particular insect you are attempting to control. Ask the nursery or garden center personnel for recommendations. But take it on yourself to read the label before you leave the nursery to make sure the product is really the one you want. Some products you may wish to consider are Bayer Advanced Complete Insect Killer or Spectracide Triazicide Insect Killer.

SPRING LAWN PROBLEMS

Every spring many people complain of dead spots in their lawn. Fungus disease during the winter, drought during the winter, etc. can be factors, especially if compounded by a weak or shallow root system and a cold winter. Even a completely healthy lawn can sometimes be killed in spots by cold when that cold comes suddenly and the grass is green. Be sure to water your lawn during dry periods in the winter to prevent drought damage. The roots still need water. Don't let the soil become excessively dry.

Regardless of what caused the spots, unless they're huge, most will fill in given time. Centipede is especially very slow to take off in the spring. But be patient and you will usually find that by summer the lawn is all filled in again. St. Augustine lawns usually fill in much faster in the spring.

Don't try to fertilize the lawn too early in the spring. Wait until three weeks after the lawn greens up. This may very well be April.

If, after fertilizing, watering as needed, and giving the lawn some time, it still has dead areas, you may need to replant the larger dead areas which appear to have no live grass left in them. But, first, give time, the weather, fertilizer, and water a chance to help.

In summary, patience is the best remedy for many of the spring lawn problems. Given time and a little basic care such as mowing, fertilizing, and watering, chances are that your lawn will grow out of most of its spring patchiness. Spraying with pesticides in the early spring is not likely to help because there is usually no pest active then.

WEEDS IN THE LAWN

You'll always have a few weeds in your lawn. It's nothing to get overly alarmed about. If your lawn has good growing conditions, it will usually choke out most weeds. Most weeds are just opportunists. They grow where there's an open spot of soil. So focus on growing the grass so that it covers those bare spots rather than focusing on killing the weeds.

Many of the weeds are annual weeds. They only live for one season before going to seed and dying. They'll sprout back up the next fall or spring, depending on whether they're winter or summer annuals, and you'll not be troubled by them again until then.

You have several options for controlling these annual weeds. The best option is usually to apply a pre-emergence herbicide just before time for the seed to germinate (usually in late October for winter weeds or mid-March for summer weeds). If the pre-emergence herbicide doesn't stop the weeds, there are also post-emergent herbicides that can be applied to the young weeds after they emerge.

The problem with any herbicide application to lawns is that you are trying to kill one type of plant and leave the desirable plant(s) unharmed. If you apply the wrong herbicide, if you apply too much over a given area, or if you apply it when the environmental conditions are wrong, you can end up with damage to your lawn or other desirable plants. Believe me, it happens all the time!

It's best to leave herbicide application to professionals who have plenty of experience. Make sure that they are licensed by the state to perform lawn and ornamental pest control. Ask to see their card.

If you choose to apply a herbicide yourself, you'll probably only find a few lawn herbicides available for use on lawns by home gardeners. Some herbicide products containing the active ingredients atrazine or isoxaben can be used on centipede and St.

Augustinegrass for broadleaf weed control, primarily as pre-emergence herbicides. There are various post-emergence products containing combinations of the following ingredients: 2,4-D, dicamba, 2,4-DP, MCPA, and/or MCPP. However, these products should be used very carefully, and even then can cause some injury, particularly to St. Augustinegrass.

Before using any herbicide, read the herbicide label thoroughly and follow it to the letter. In fact, read the label before you even buy the herbicide to make sure you're buying the correct product for your type of lawn grass and the weeds involved. Don't blindly trust the sales person. No one herbicide can be used on all types of grasses.

Remember, it's best to focus on growing the lawn grass and not so much on killing the weeds.

PLANTING A NEW LAWN

Depending on the type of lawn, as mentioned at the beginning of this chapter, lawns can be started from seed, sod, sprigs, or plugs. Bahia and centipede are the only lawns you're likely to start from seed.

Most lawns will either be started from sod or plugs. **Sprigs**, which are individual stems or pieces of stem that have the potential to root, are not used that often, except for starting bermuda, and possibly zoysia, lawns. Sprigs are usually broadcast over a prepared soil and then pressed into the soil with a sod roller. An alternative method is to plant the sprigs end to end in furrows six to twelve inches apart. The sprigs are covered with an inch or two of soil, leaving part of each sprig exposed to the light. The furrow method is usually used for zoysia grass, whereas the broadcast method is usually used for bermuda grass.

Sodding, though appearing on the surface to be the way to an instant lawn, is not completely fool-proof. The sod pieces, having a thin root system, must regenerate a new, deep root system. Care of the sod during the period until new roots are formed is critical.

Before laying sod, thoroughly rototill the area and rake the soil surface clean. Thoroughly moisten the soil. Lay the sod pieces in a staggered brick-like pattern with the edges fitted tightly together to avoid any open cracks. If there are cracks, fill them with soil.

After the sod is laid, fertilize as you would an existing lawn. Water the sod until it is thoroughly moistened. Then roll the sod with a sod roller to ensure close contact with the soil.

Water the sod twice a day if it's summer when you put it out. Water in mid to late morning and again in mid afternoon with only enough water to thoroughly moisten the sod pieces and to begin to moisten the soil below. You don't want the sod to become sopping wet. But you must not allow the roots to dry out either.

Once the sod roots knit down into the soil below, you can reduce watering to an as needed basis. Still, don't allow the grass to become wilted for long periods. Once the grass turns the wilted gray-green color, turn on the water.

BUYING SOD

When you buy sod, naturally you will consider price.

But don't ignore other factors such as percentage of weeds contained, presence of pest insects, or diseases. Is the sod cut with a generous layer of soil and roots, or does it tear apart easily as you handle it because it is cut too thin? How long does the sod sit on the pallet after it is cut and before it is planted? Sod life on pallets during summer is less than 48 hours. Generally, how does the sod look? If it looks dry, weedy, or diseased before you plant it, don't expect it to get better. It may, but if it doesn't you will be stuck with it. When buying plants, and especially when buying sod, it's wise for the consumer to remember the old caveat emptor, let the buyer beware.

Other problems in establishing a lawn from sod are often attributable to the site selection, site preparation, or care of the sod after planting. The site may be too shaded to grow lawn grass. The soil may have been inadequately tilled and may be too compacted. The sod may have dried out for just one hot sunny day after planting. Or, as is sometimes the case, the sod may have been kept too saturated on a somewhat shaded site and a fungus disease began to rot it. Insect pests, too, can get started after the sod is laid, especially if it is in summer or fall.

There are just so many factors that can be involved in the failure of a lawn to establish successfully from sod that it is very difficult to pinpoint who is at fault. So, even if you feel that you have justifiably placed the blame of a sod failure on the sod vendor, you may have little recourse to force the vendor to refund your money or replace the sod.

You need to be an informed customer when buying sod. Be sure that the site on which you intend to plant the sod is sunny enough and properly prepared. If you have any doubts, the only way to assure that the site is suitable is to put out a small test patch of the grass first. Give it a month or so to see how it performs. Does the grass spread? Or does it look worse as time goes on. You may be impatient and feel confident in sodding the whole area without running such a test. But just be aware that it is your risk and yours alone.

A little extra effort and expense is involved in carefully shopping for sod, carefully preparing the site for planting, and giving it attentive care once planted. But considering the hundreds or thousands of dollars you're spending on the sod, it is well worth the effort and extra expense.

USING PLUGS TO PLANT A NEW LAWN OR REPAIR A DAMAGED LAWN

Using plugs to plant a lawn is not a new idea. People have been using plugs the hard way for years, cutting the plugs themselves from sod pieces. But the introduction of nursery-grown grass plugs some years back has made it easier than ever to plant from plugs. Nursery-grown plugs are especially useful in repairing small areas of damage in your lawn.

Nursery-grown plugs have several advantages over plugs cut from sod. First, you skip the dirty task of having to chop plugs from a piece of sod with a machete or hatchet. Instead, you simply pull the plugs out of a tray. The trays, by the way, are a lot less messy to haul home in the trunk of your car than is sod.

Plugs cut from sod have a shallow root system that was disrupted from the field when the sod was cut. But plugs grown in a tray at a nursery have a well-established root system, 2-3 inches deep, that is actively growing. The plugs go through no transplanting shock. Planting sod, or plugs from sod, is similar to transplanting a tree from one field site to another. There is a certain amount of transplant shock and a critical period of root regeneration.

If necessary, plugs in trays can be held for weeks before planting. In the summer, sod can normally be held no longer than 48 hours after it is cut from the sod field.

If your soil is soft and workable, it is easy to plant plugs. Basically, you just dig a hole and plant the plug as you would a flower plant or any other type of plant. Available at garden centers are even plugging tools that dig perfectly sized holes for the plugs. But, you I recommend that you use a shovel, especially if the soil is hard and compacted and needs a little cultivation. Space the plugs twelve to eighteen inches apart.

After planting, fertilize and water. Be sure that the plugs receive water, either from rain or irrigation, every day for about two weeks. Then reduce the frequency of watering to about every other day for a month. After this period, water only as needed.

Planting grass plugs is a good way to fill in damaged areas of the lawn without having to till up the whole area to plant sod. If the soil is very hard, though, it is advisable to till up the whole area, even when using plugs. Otherwise, the plugs will not easily spread over the hard soil.

Planting a few plugs in a shaded area where you wish to grow grass is an inexpensive way to see if the area receives enough sunlight to grow grass. If the plugs don't spread within a month or so, it could be a good indication that you shouldn't invest further money in grass for the area.

PLANTING RYEGRASS FOR WINTER COLOR OR EROSION CONTROL

During most winters the top growth of our permanent lawn grasses goes dormant and turns brown. To maintain a green lawn during the winter you can overseed your permanent lawn with a cool-season lawn grass. Annual, intermediate, and perennial (improved) rye grasses may be used, though annual rye grass is most commonly used.

The rye grass will grow through the winter and die in the heat of the following spring. It has to be reseeded each year.

Other than for aesthetics or erosion control in bare areas, there are no practical reasons for overseeding with rye grass. In fact, rye grass and your permanent grass will compete somewhat for nutrients, water, and sunlight in the early spring when the permanent grass is emerging but before the rye grass dies. To discourage this competition, and to hasten the transition from rye grass back to permanent grass, don't fertilize the rye grass after January. Water as infrequently as possible. Keep the ryegrass mowed closely during late winter and early spring.

When seeding rye grass in the fall, wait until daytime temperatures are consistently in the low 70's. This should be late October to November.

Mow your lawn closely, either bagging clippings or raking clippings after mowing. Spread the rye grass seed with a cyclone seed spreader. Overseed with annual or intermediate type rye grasses at 5-10 lbs. of seed per 1,000 square feet of lawn. Use 10-20 lbs. for perennial type rye grasses. When seeding bare ground with annual rye grass, use a rate of about 10 lbs. per 1,000 sq. ft.

Perennial ryes will not act as perennials in our climate. One of their advantages over annual rye is that they will die more quickly and evenly in the spring as the permanent grass is resuming growth, making for a smoother transition.

Water the lawn once or twice a day until the ryegrass seeds have germinated. Continue watering until the seedlings are well-established. Don't water so much as to cause puddles because they will wash the seed away. Also, overwatering will encourage disease development. Once the lawn is established, only water as needed.

Weekly mowing will be required. Don't fertilize until after the lawn has been mowed several times. Fertilize with 15-0-15 or similar fertilizer (containing 7.5% water-insoluble nitrogen) at the rate of 6 lbs. per 1,000 square feet.

You may decide overseeding with rye grass is not worth the trouble. Or, you may decide just to overseed a small highly visible area rather than overseed your entire lawn. The bright green lawn during the winter can be quite attractive.

7

Groundcovers
Alternatives to Lawn Grasses

Groundcovers are low-growing plants used to cover areas in the landscape much as a lawn is used. The primary advantage groundcovers have over a lawn, though, is that groundcovers are much easier to maintain once established. A properly selected groundcover doesn't require weekly mowing or frequent fertilization and watering.

An area, too shaded for lawngrass, that would be a good place for a shade-tolerant groundcover.

There are added advantages, too. Groundcovers are attractive because they add varying textures and colors to the landscape and reduce the boring sameness of too much lawn. Groundcovers will often grow in areas not suited for lawngrasses. For instance, there are many groundcovers suitable for shaded areas and groundcovers suited for areas too steep to be mowed.

Groundcovers, however, will not replace lawn areas intended for recreational purposes or widespread traffic. Restricted traffic can be handled in groundcover areas with the use of stepping stones or mulched paths. But groundcovers cannot replace a lawn for activities such as children's play.

Perennial or ornamental peanuts are a good groundcover for this sunny slope.

STARTING GROUNDCOVER PLANTINGS

The most difficult part of growing a groundcover is the establishment period. Cost of plants can be a problem. But cost can often be reduced by obtaining plants from friends with an established groundcover area in need of thinning or edging.

Planting a bed of groundcover can be tiring, too, because it often involves planting a large number of small plants. Sometimes it even involves dividing the plants to be planted into smaller divisions.

Before planting, rototill the whole area to be planted. If there are weeds present, ideally, one or two applications of Roundup® or other such glyphosate herbicide should be applied several weeks or several months before rototilling. This will give the herbicide time to work, and in the case of two applications, a chance to kill weeds that are likely to re-sprout from the first application.

If you rototill with live weeds still in the bed, you may or may not have significant future weed problems, depending on the type of weed present. Your best bet is to allow time to use the glyphosate herbicide if possible. Even doing so, you'll probably have to pull some weeds the first couple of years, until the groundcovers in the bed grow in full and thick. A mulch of pine straw or other such organic material during the establishment period will help reduce weed sprouting. Don't use landscape weed fabrics because they will interfere with the spread of your groundcover unless your groundcover is a type such as juniper that doesn't spread by runners or sprouts from roots.

Be patient during the establishment period. There's an old saying about groundcovers and vines... "The first year they sleep, the second year they creep, and the third year they leap." This means that it takes several years for the planting to really become established well. Water and fertilization, such as with a newly established lawn, will be important during the establishment period.

Weed control can also be a major consideration during the establishment period. Put down a good mulch of bark or wood chips before planting and the mulch will help hold down the weeds. Some hand-weeding will be required, though, as herbicides in garden centers for use by home gardeners for weed control in groundcovers are very limited. There are several available to professional pesticide applicators for use in liriope and Mondo grass. But most of the herbicides, with the exception of Image, are not available to the home gardener.

Once well-established, most groundcovers are fairly low in required maintenance. However, you may have to trim groundcovers such as Asiatic jasmine or ornamental peanuts to keep them from encroaching into lawns or onto sidewalks, etc.   In fact, Asiatic jasmine can be so aggressive that you may wish you hadn't planted it. Some groundcovers, such as liriope or ferns, may have old, spotted or dead leaves that need annual trimming before the spring growth emerges from the base. With liriope, simply remove the old growth at a point just above the newly emerging leaves in late winter or very early spring. In the case of ferns, you just cut off the dead leaves in late winter.

GROUNDCOVERS FOR SUN OR PARTIAL SHADE

Ornamental peanut (*Arachis glabrata*)

Aztec grass, variegated (*Liriope muscari* 'Aztec')

Clumping liriope, green forms (*Liriope muscari*)

Ajuga reptans

Daylily *(Hemerocallis spp.)*

Moss phlox *(Phlox subulata)*

Asiatic jasmine *(Trachelospermum asiaticum)*

Purple Queen *(Setcreasea pallida)*

Creeping fig *(Ficus pumila)*

GROUNDCOVERS FOR FULL SUN ONLY

Shore juniper *(Juniperus conferta)*

Creeping juniper *(Juniperus horizontalis):* includes 'Bar Harbour', 'Blue Rug',   etc.

Japanese garden juniper

(Juniperus procumbens)

Trailing lantana ((*L. montevidensis*)

GROUNDCOVERS FOR SHADE OR PARTIAL SHADE

Ajuga reptans

Creeping ardisia *(Ardisia japonica)*

Aspidistra or cast-iron plant *(Aspidistra elatior)*

Creeping plum yew (*Cephalotaxus harringtonia* var. Prostrata)

Goldenstar or green & *gold (Chrysogonum virginianum)*

Holly fern *(Crytomium falcatum)*

Florida native sword fern (*Nephrolepis exaltata*)

Arborvitae fern (*Selaginella braunii*)

Fox tail fern (*Asparagus densiflorus* 'Meyers')

Autumn fern (*Dryopteris erythrosora*)

Southern woods fern *(Thelypteris kunthii)*
Southern maidenhair fern (*Adiantum capillus veneris*)
Japanese painted fern *(Athyrium niponicum* variety *pictum)*
Dwarf gardenia *(Gardenia jasminoides 'Radicans' or 'Prostrata')*
Algerian ivy *(Hedera canariensis)*
English ivy *(Hedera helix)*
Hosta spp.
Clumping liriope (*Liriope muscari)* including the variegated forms
Partridge berry (*Mitchella repens*)
Creeping liriope (*Liriope spicata*)
Mondo grass, including dwarf Mondo grass *(Ophiopogon japonicus)*
Crystal Falls mondo grass (*Ophiopogon jaburan*)
Asiatic jasmine *(Trachelospermum asiaticum)*
Periwinkle *(Vinca minor and Vinca major)*
Blue phlox *(Phlox divaricata)*

FERTILIZING GROUNDCOVERS

Fertilization is important in the establishment period when you are trying to make the groundcover planting fill in. Once groundcovers are well established and healthy-looking, you can usually quit fertilizing them. Fertilizer may still sometimes be needed, though, in sandy soils or to help plantings recover from some type of damage. Use a general landscape fertilizer such as 15-0-15 or even a palm fertilizer such as 8-2-12 with

4% magnesium and with micronutrients. Apply the 15-0-15 at a rate of 6 lbs. per 1,000 sq. ft., or the 8-2-12 at the rate of 12 lbs. per 1,000 sq. ft.

8

Flowers & Colorful Foliage
Brighten the Landscape with Color

The use of colorful plants in home landscapes is more popular than ever before. Garden catalogs and magazines bombard us with new variety after new variety of flower. Never before have we had such choices of flowers and colorful foliage for our landscapes!

But all the choices can be more than a little confusing for even the experienced gardener. Which flowers will grow well in our area and which will not? And what's the correct timing for our area?

Though I certainly don't have all the answers, either, I have learned a lot over the years by experimenting with a variety of plants. Therefore this edition of this book has much more information in this chapter than previous editions. Here in the deep South, we have to contend with not only winter freezes but also brutally hot and humid summers. While the winter freezes set us apart from nearby places like south Florida, the summer heat and humidity, and the intensity of the sunlight set us apart from much of the rest of the country.

While I haven't finished learning and don't have all

the answers by any means, I pass along my findings in this chapter in hopes that they'll be helpful.

ANNUAL OR PERENNIAL?

We humans have the tendency to classify everything. So we typically classify plants as either annual or perennial. An annual completes its life cycle in one year, producing flowers, going to seed, and then dying. Next year's plants come from seed, or in the case of garden plants which are named cultivars or hybrids, from new plants we set out in the garden. A common example of an annual is impatiens. We plant them in the spring but we don't normally expect them to live through the winter. We must plant more the next year, or in the case of some impatiens, they will come back from seed.

A perennial, however, is a plant that lives over from year to year. In the case of flowers, a common perennial would be a daylily. It may die back in the winter, but it comes back from the root every year.

However, our classification of annual or perennial is complicated by location. Impatiens, for example, may not die back in Zone 9 some winters. So, are they then perennials? Or pentas, which is considered a perennial in Zones 9 and 10 probably won't come back from the ground in spring in Zone 8a. So is it an annual?

In the following sections, the plants are classified loosely as perennial or annual, primarily using Zone 8b as the location. But please be aware that whether the plant comes back in spring or not for you depends on your zone as well as the microclimate in your yard.

Zone refers to the USDA plant hardiness zones. Microclimate refers to areas in your yard that may be more protected than others. That is, a plant growing in a protected corner of your garden near the house may come back. But the same plant growing out in an open area may not.

PERENNIALS

Flowering maple (Abutilon 'Firefly'):
Interesting, orange, bell-shaped flowers hang from this shrubby plant which can grow to six feet tall and almost as wide each season after it has become well-established. Extremely easy to grow; full sun to light partial shade.

Joseph's coat (Acalypha 'Bourbon Street' and other species):
There are various cultivars of acalypha, but Bourbon Street is one of the best. Leaves are deep green bordered by orange to cream-colored margins. Can grow to 3 ft. or so tall and wide. Won't return after winter freeze so best to dig and overwinter in a pot, then put back in the garden again in spring. Acalypha 'Marginata Bronze' is somewhat similar, very attractive.

Acalypha 'Haleakala':
Large, deeply serrated leaves of a deep bronze color adorn this tall plant, giving it a distinct Oriental flair. This acalypha returned after several winters for us. Definitely worth growing. Full sun. 'Ceylon' is somewhat similar but has leaf margins variegated with pinkish-orange color.

Dwarf chenille or firetail (Acalypha reptans):
This acalypha can serve as a groundcover. Its fuzzy red

flowers cover the low-growing green foliage like cattails. Full sun to moderate shade. Will spread and the planting will gradually get wider and wider. Tends to stay green in winter.

Yarrow (Achillea millefolium): Fine-textured, fern-like foliage is attractive most of the year. The white flower clusters cover the plants in mass in summer.

Agapanthus or African lily (Agapanthus africanus): Clusters of blue flowers are borne atop tall stems during summer to fall. Perennial for sunny, well-drained sites.

Agastache 'Acapulco' and 'Tutti Frutti': Drought-tolerant flowering herbs. Acapulco has pink and coral bi-colored flowers. Tutti Frutti has lavender-pink flowers. For full sun. Attract hummingbirds and butterflies.

Bush allamanda (Allamanda neriifolia): Shrubby plant with glossy green leaves and mid-sized yellow allamanda flowers late spring through fall. Dies to the ground in winter but normally returns the following spring. Full sun.

Allamanda vine (Allamanda cathartica): Large yellow flowers from the time you plant it in spring until late fall. For full sun. Won't come back after winter in zone 8b. Should in 9b.

Soap aloe (Aloe saponaria): Thick succulent leaves typical of aloe, and in summer flower spikes of tubular orange flowers, attractive to hummingbirds. Normally overwinters okay in Zone 8b. Full sun to partial shade.

Variegated shell ginger (Alpinia zerumbet 'Variegata'): Showy lime-green and yellow variegated leaves on plant that grows to about 3 ft. tall. Winter freezes may burn back the foliage and stems, particularly on plants in the open. But comes back from the ground in spring. If growth not killed back, pendulous clusters of white flowers may form on second-year growth in the summer.

Variegated Shell Ginger

Alternanthera 'Brazilian Red Hots': Variegated burgundy-red and dark-pink leaves make this plant very showy from spring through fall, until the first hard freeze. Doesn't come back the next spring, but the long season of red-hot color makes it worthy of planting. For full sun, though color holds up best if shaded from the harsh afternoon summer sun.

Alternanthera 'Purple Knight': Very dark burgundy leaves on a large plant, growing to about 3 ft. tall and wide. Normally comes back the following spring.

Butterfly weed (Asclepias tuberosa): Drought-tolerant native perennial, often_seen among the grasses on roadsides. Orange flowers. Some cultivars available with yellow flowers. Flowers May-September.

Philippine violet (Barleria cristata):   An attractive perennial, reaching four feet or so over the course of the growing season. Beautiful purple flowers cover the plant in October and November. There is a white flowering form, too. The winter kills the plant to the ground, but it comes back next spring. Full sun to partial shade.

Red orchid bush (Bauhinia galpinii): Orange flowers from summer through fall, very attractive to butterflies. The plant is killed back somewhat during the winter but snaps back quickly in spring. Full sun. Grows to about 3 ft. tall and 8 ft. across.

Red Orchid Bush

Angel's trumpet (Brugmansia spp.):   Large, fragrant, trumpet-shaped flowers of salmon color or golden orange hang downward on a large shrub, about 6-8 ft. tall and wide. Dies to the ground in winter but resprouts readily in spring. Flowers summer through fall.

Brugmansia (Angel's Trumpet)

Yesterday-Today-and-Tomorrow   (Brunfelsia pauciflora): Shrub to about 6-8 ft. tall but very slowly. Flowers come out purple, fade to lavender, and then to white. All three colors are on the plant at the same time, thus giving its common name. Morning sun but protection from harsh afternoon sun is best. Can suffer a little cold damage in zone 8.

Butterfly bush (Buddleia spp.): A shrubby perennial reaching 10 ft. or so tall. Bears flower spikes in shades of purple, blue or pink, attractive to butterflies. For sun to light shade. Usually lives only a few years.

African bulbine (Bulbine frutescens): Are orange and yellow forms of this extremely drought-tolerant and cold-hardy perennial. Its flower clusters top the plants most of the growing season. Great choice for full sun where you can't water often.

Brunfelsia

Peacock flower, Pride of Barbados (Caesalpinia pulcherrima): Striking two-toned orange flowers in summer to fall on a shrubby plant that grows to about 5 ft. tall in one season. There is a yellow form, 'Flava', also. Dies to the ground in winter and usually returns in spring, though slowly. Full sun.

Caladium: Plants with colorful foliage from late spring until late fall. There are several leaf forms and various color combinations of red, pink, and white foliage. Shade to full sun, depending on the cultivar. 1-2 ft. tall.

White Caladiums

Calathea: Depending on the species and cultivar, various combinations of foliage variegated with green, burgundy, and cream colors. Most do best in shade and grow 12-18 inches tall. Die back in winter but return in spring.

Dwarf   red   powderpuff   (*Calliandra haematocephala 'Nana'*): Large red powderpuff-like flowers and flower buds that look like red raspberries make this small shrubby plant of 2-4 ft. tall attractive summer through fall. Comes back slowly in spring. Full sun.

Canna: Though most cannas are plagued by the leaf rollers which make holes in the leaves, 'Tropicana', both the orange and gold forms, and 'Bengal Tiger' are strikingly beautiful cannas because of their colorful foliage as well as their flowers. Full sun. Grow to about 3 ft. tall.

Orange cestrum (Cestrum aurantiacum): Large evergreen shrub (10 ft. tall and wide) with clusters of small yellow-orange flowers spring through fall. Full sun. Easy to grow.

Chrysanthemum   (Chrysanthemum   x morifolium): Fall-blooming perennial. Pinch until mid-August to induce bushiness. Various traditional fall colors of golds, oranges, yellows, etc. For sun.

Korean mum (Chrysanthemum hybrid): Pink-flowering fall chrysanthemum. Pinch until mid-August to induce bushiness. For sun.

Chrysanthemum x 'Mei-kyo': Small, one-inch flowers of dark rose with yellow centers in October. Keep pinched until mid-August to induce bushiness. Very vigorous grower and heavy flowerer. For sun.

Shasta daisy (Chrysanthemum x superbum): Old garden favorite. White flowers with yellow centers. 'May Queen' seems to be one particularly good cultivar. Flowers late spring to early summer. Sun.

Clytostoma callistegioides

Kaffir lily (Clivia spp.): Green, strap-like leaves and clusters of orange to yellow flowers in late spring. For shade to partial shade. Takes 4-6 years to come into bloom.

Argentine trumpet vine (Clytostoma callistegioides): A vigorous vine with lavender blue flowers in late spring. Spectacular when in bloom. Hardy down to about 20 degrees. Drought tolerant. Sun.

Taro or elephant ear (Colocasia esculenta): Cultivars such as 'Lime Zinger' and 'Elena' with chartreuse leaves. 'Black Magic' has deep burgundy, almost black leaves. Avoid the dark green-leafed forms because they will spread into the wild, especially in drainage ditches and waterways. Don't plant any taro near such an area. Size depends on cultivar, usually about 3 x 3 ft.

'Elena' Colocasia

Red Sensation cordyline (Cordyline australis):
Burgundy red, strap-shaped leaves emerge from a central stem. Is completely winter hardy. Will grow at least 5 ft or so tall after years. Full sun to partial shade. Needs good drainage and needs debris, such as falling tree leaves etc., to be kept from lodging in the crown of the plant.

'Red Sensation' Cordyline

Ti plant, (Cordyline terminalis): Wider *strap*-shaped leaves emerge from a central stem. Reddish-pink below and burgundy above. Does best where it receives some protection from harsh afternoon sun. Up to about 3 ft. tall in one season. Freezes kills it to the ground. Resprouts in spring in zone 8b.

Spiral or crepe ginger (Costus speciosus):
Large green or variegated leaves come off spiraling stems. In summer white crinkly crepe-paper-like

flowers emerge from red bracts. Partial to full sun. 3-4 ft. tall.

Crinum lily (Crinum spp):   Strap-shaped leaves emerge from central stem. Usually green but some forms have burgundy leaves. Flowers, summer through fall, in colors from white to pink to burgundy. Most are fragrant. Grand crinum lily reaches height up to 5 ft. Sun to light shade.

Grand Crinum Lily

Croton spp: 'Petra' is the most popular cultivar sold. Has the large multi-colored leaves of green, orange, yellow, and black. Won't survive winter freezes. But worth planting for easy color from April to late fall/early winter in Zone 8. Can be overwintered in a pot. In lower Zone 9, may overwinter okay. Sun to partial shade.

Mexican heather (Cuphea hyssopifolia): Tiny purple or white flowers cover this small bushy perennial all summer and until frost in the fall. Height typically reaches 1-2 ft. with a 2-3 ft. spread. Full sun.

Cigar flower (Cuphea micropetala):   This is a tough, drought-tolerant perennial that is covered with small yellow and orange, cigar-shaped flowers in the fall. Height typically reaches 3-4 ft. Full sun.

'Petra' Croton

Hidden ginger (Curcuma spp.): Flowers, color depends on species but many are pink, emerge in spring as the foliage also emerges. Very showy. The large leaves, some forms with some variegation, are attractive in themselves. Partial shade.

Dianthera nodosa 'Brazil': Relative of the shrimp plant (Justicia), this plant has pink flowers along the stem. Starts in late spring and flowers through summer. 1-2 ft. Prefers light shade.

Dianthus spp: There are several species of dianthus commonly sold. Your success with them as perennials will depend somewhat on your planting site and somewhat on the specific type of dianthus. Dianthus needs a well-drained, though not extremely dry, site. One of the best types as a perennial is a tall (18-24 inches) dianthus called 'First Love'. In mixed shades of pink and white, this dianthus has done wonderfully in local trials. Full sun. As dianthus prefers the cooler weather, best to plant it in the fall. It struggles through summer.

Blue ginger (Dichorisandra thyrsiflora): Not a true ginger, but a tropical relative of the wandering Jew, this plant grows to 4-5 ft. in zone 8b and has glossy green leaves and clusters of blue flowers during the summer. Partial shade.

Dicliptera suberecta

Hummingbird flower (Dicliptera suberecta): A spreading growth habit, even under dry conditions, and gray green foliage that stands about 12 inches tall are reason enough to plant this flower. But its bright orange flowers, attractive to hummingbirds, make it all the more attractive. Needs full sun to flower well. Very drought tolerant.

African iris (Dietes iridioides)- Clumps of strap-shaped , evergreen foliage to about 3 ft. tall make this plant a valuable filler in sunny areas of the landscape. But when the white flowers appear in summer, the plant is even more attractive. Spreads aggressively. The pale yellow form (*Dietes bicolor*) has narrower leaves and doesn't spread quite as aggressively. Very drought tolerant.

Duranta 'Gold Mound' and 'Cuban Gold': These two cultivars with chartreuse leaves really brighten up the garden. For sun to partial shade, these plants typically only reach 2-3 ft. in our area before winter freezes burn them back. They usually return the following spring, though somewhat slowly.

Purple coneflower (Echinacea purpurea): Pinkish-purple flowers with golden brown cone-shaped centers arise on 3-ft. stems from spring until frost. It is one of the easiest and most reliable of perennials to grown in sun to light shade.

Erythrina bidwillii

Coral bean tree (Erythrina bidwillii): Cross between South America's E. crista-galli and North America's E. herbacea (coral bean), this large shrub/small tree has showy red flowers in summer to fall. Full sun to part shade.

Pineapple lily (Eucomis 'Sparkling Burgundy'): Burgundy strap-shaped leaves stand upright to about 18 inches, making an attractive accent plant during the growing season. In the summer a flower stalk arises with a flower that looks like a small purple pineapple. Comes back reliably each spring. Morning sun and afternoon shade best.

Eucomis 'Sparkling Burgundy'

Caribbean copper plant (Euphorbia cotinifolia 'Burgundy Wine'): Beautiful rich burgundy foliage on a woody plant that can grow 5 ft or so tall and wide in one season. Full sun. Won't survive freezes, so pot it for the winter. The milky sap is a very strong skin and eye irritant. If you get it on you when pruning the plant, promptly wash off the skin or it can cause severe burn.

Euphorbia hypericifolia 'Silver Fog' or 'Diamond Frost': These euphorbias produce clouds of small white flowers constantly, giving the plants the appearance of Baby's Breath. But they are extremely tough landscape plants, being quite drought tolerant once established, and coming back well after winter cold. They work very well in containers combined with other plants also. Full to partial sun. Grow about 12 inches tall and 18-24 inches across. 'Breathless Blush' has red-tinged leaves.

Gaura lindheimeri: Small white, pink-tinged flowers arise on long wiry stems above the foliage in the spring and early summer. Prefers a well-drained, sunny site. Very drought-tolerant.

Bolivian sunset (Gloxinia sylvatica)

Bolivian sunset (Gloxinia sylvatica): Small clumping plant that grows about 12 inches tall and spreads. Flowers with bright orange, bell-shaped flowers in winter when little else is blooming. Sun to partial shade.

Rain lily (Habranthus robustus): Pink flowers arise spring to fall periodically after heavy rains, on 8-10 inch stems. Look similar to the *Zephyranthes* rain lily, but are different.

Firebush (Hamelia patens): This plant grows in shrub form to about 4-5 ft. in one growing season. Late spring through fall it is covered with tubular, bright orange flowers, very attractive to hummingbirds and butterflies. There is also a form of firebush that has pale orange flowers. This form tends to be smaller. Both need full sun to flower well. Comes back from the root every spring.

Butterfly ginger (Hedychium spp.): These are tall gingers with fragrant flowers. The stems, which emerge in spring, grow up to 5 ft. tall, die down again in late fall. Flowers in summer. White, peach, pink, or yellow, depending on type. Best in partial shade though will take full sun.

Swamp sunflower (Helianthus angustifolius): This plant will need pruning constantly until late summer to keep it from getting so tall that it falls over when it blooms in October. Still, it's likely it will reach 5 ft. tall. The flowers are brilliant yellow and very showy. Full sun.

Parakeet flower (Heliconia hirsuta): 'Costa Flores' and 'Peru' are two cultivars of this small-flowered *Heliconia* that flowers on first-year growth. Won't survive winter freezes in the ground, but if dug and potted before freeze can be carried over inside. Continues blooming and growing later into the fall than any other parakeet flower I've seen. Bloom from late spring until first winter freeze. Partial sun, not full sun, is best.

Heliconias

Parakeet   flower   (Heliconia   psittacorum): Cultivars such as 'Andromeda' and 'Lady Di' are available in garden centers. *H psittacorum* blooms on first year growth. So you can have flowers from late spring until late fall. Full sun. Won't survive winter freezes unless grown in pots and brought into a greenhouse for the cold weather. Hummingbirds love all the parakeet flowers.

Daylily (Hemerocallis spp.): One of the most versatile and adaptable of perennials, daylilies are available in a myriad of shades and sizes. Most bloom in late spring or early summer. Will tolerate full sun to partial shade and most soil types. Some varieties are evergreen; others die to the ground in winter.

Swamp mallow (Hibiscus coccineus): This native shrub grows to about 6 ft. Tolerates wet sites well. Large star-shaped red flowers in summer. Full sun.

Hardy hibiscus (Hibiscus moscheutos): There are various cultivars, with very large flowers, in colors of pink, red, burgundy, and white primarily. 'Southern Belle' (pink with burgundy center) is very popular. Zones 4-9. Die back in winter, return in spring. Flowers summer through fall. Full to partial sun.

Hibiscus moscheutos

***Tropical hibiscus (Hibiscus rosa-sinensis*):** Can be grown as an annual in Zone 8. Sometimes returns the following spring in Zone 8B. More likely in Zone 9.

Hosta spp.: For shade to partial shade and moist but well-drained soil, hostas can be an attractive groundcover. Some have attractive variegated leaves. Flowers mostly in white or lavender.

Amaryllis (Hippeastrum hybrids): Showy flower spikes of red, pink, coral, or white flowers in summer. Filtered sun to light shade best. Root-hardy in zone 8b.

Hydrangea macrophylla: Both the normal mophead flower form and the lacecap form (large petals surround a center of tiny, bud-like blooms) are attractive deciduous shrubs for the landscape. Flowers start in late spring and continue until fall with many new cultivars. Flowers are typically either blue or pink. Some cultivars have interesting leaves that are variegated or chartreuse. Shade to partial shade.

Oakleaf hydrangea (Hydrangea quercifolia): Native hydrangea with white flowers in late spring. Red foliage in fall.

Iochroma

Iochroma spp. These plants, though tender to cold, can grow quite large (5 ft. or so) in one growing season. Die to ground in winter and return in spring. Bloom in late summer through fall with clusters of tubular flowers in blue, purple, burgundy, red, or white, depending on type. Full sun.

Himalayan Indigo (*Indigofera gerardiana*): 4 ft. shrub that has purplish-pink blooms summer through fall. Full sun. Only suffers light cold damage; doesn't die all the way back normally.

Louisiana iris (*Iris x 'Louisiana'*): These are the easiest irises to grow in our area as they are bred from irises native to the South. Available in a tremendous color range. Tolerant of poor drainage. Full sun to partial shade.

Chicken Gizzard Plant or Bloodleaf (*Iresine herbstii*): 'Blazin Rose' as showy variegated leaves of dark burgundy and bright rose-red. Grows to about 3 ft. in full sun. Flea beetles chew holes in the leaves sometimes. There is also a lime green and cream variegated leaf form called 'Blazin Lime'.

Spicy jatropha (*Jatropha integerrima*): Glossy green leaves and lots of small cheery red flowers summer through fall make this shrub worth growing even in Zone 8a where it probably won't come back after winter freezes. It does return in Zone 8b and will probably stay evergreen in 9b. Full sun.

Shrimp plant (*Justicia brandegeana*): Reddish brown flowers resembling shrimp in spring through summer. For sun or partial shade. Reaches several feet in height.

Jacobinia (Justicia carnea): Native to South America, the most popular of this group of plants has terminal clusters of pink flowers on plants up to 2 ft. tall. For sun or shade but prefers filtered sun exposure.

Orange justicia, Mexican honeysuckle (Justicia spicigera): Small shrubby plant with orange flowers in late winter to early spring. Sun to partial sun.

Lantana (Lantana spp.): Vigorous, drought-tolerant, easy-to-grow perennials with aromatic foliage. Very attractive to butterflies. Clusters of flowers, color depending on species. Most are bi-or tri-colored mixtures of yellow, red, pink, white, or orange. Is also a lavender trailing form. For sun or partial shade. Don't use the types that set berries, as they can spread and be very invasive in natural areas. 'Sonset' is an example of a very good lantana that doesn't form seed.

Lion's ear, lion's tail (Leonotis Leonurus): Shrubby perennial that has clusters of orange flowers in the fall. Native to S. Africa, very drought-tolerant once established. Full sun to partial shade.

Variegated Tapioca (Manihot esculenta 'Variegata'

Variegated   tapioca   (Manihot   esculenta 'Variegata'): Large, tropical-looking green and yellow leaves held by red stems makes this a showy plant in the garden. Full sun. Treat as a large annual (4 ft.) in Zone 8b. Won't come back after winter freezes.

Dwarf   yellow   mussaenda   (Mussaenda   or Pseudomussaneda flava): Small (2-3 ft.) shrubby perennial with pale yellow bracts and darker yellow flowers all summer into fall. Usually returns in spring after winter freeze.

Daffodil (Narcissus spp.): Spring flowering bulbs in variations of yellow and white. Some fragrant. Plant in fall.

Firespike (Odontonema strictum): May reach 4 ft. tall. Tubular flowers of bright red in early fall are very attractive to hummingbirds. Prefers partial shade.

Blue phlox (Phlox divaricata): Early spring-blooming, low-growing phlox for use in shaded or partially shaded locations. Morning sun and afternoon shade is fine. Needs well-drained soil, but is not drought tolerant. Blooms about the time many spring bulbs bloom.

Border phlox (Phlox paniculata): The common 2-3 ft. tall phlox seen in many gardens. Summer and fall blooming. Primarily in pink, white, and red. For sun or partial shade. Good for the back of the perennial bed or border. All phlox plants seem to get powdery mildew on the leaves, but most seem to tolerate it without spraying.

Moss pink, sometimes called thrift in the South (Phlox subulata): A creeping phlox, only about six inches tall, that is covered with bright pink flowers in early spring for about a month. Mossy, fine textured foliage. Requires good drainage or will rot. Excellent rock garden plant.

Plumbago (Plumbago auriculata): In south Florida, plumbago is considered more of a shrub. But in our area, it is killed to the ground by freezes. It begins flowering about June and on through the summer with delicate blue flowers. Grows in full sun or partial shade and is very drought tolerant.

Low-maintenance roses: See Chapter 6 for more details. But low-maintenance roses make a good addition to the flower garden because there are many that bloom repeatedly from early spring through late fall. Full sun.

Black-eyed Susan, yellow coneflower, or orange coneflower (Rudbeckia fulgida): Blooms summer to fall with bright yellow flowers having dark centers. Needs full sun and good drainage. Popular cultivar is 'Goldsturm' as it is more compact, up to 2 ft., as opposed to parent which reaches 3 ft. tall.

Rudbeckia nitida 'Herbstonne': Taller *Rudbeckia* (3 ft. or so) which has large yellow blooms in late spring to summer. Full to partial sun.

Firecracker plant (Russelia equisetiformis): Long wiry, cascading stems with slender orange-red flowers from late spring through fall. Full sun to partial shade.

Scarlet sage (Salvia coccinea): Salvia with small, bright red flowers all summer. For full sun or partial shade. May best be treated as an annual except in milder winters.

Pineapple sage (Salvia elegans): Bright red flowers are heaviest in fall. Foliage has a pineapple scent useful for seasoning. Fast-growing, will die to ground in winter but come back in spring if roots well established and mulched. Easy to root. Sun, light shade.

Blue salvia or blue sage (Salvia farinacea): Widely used perennial salvia available in blue, purple or white-flowering forms. For sun or light shade. 'Victoria' is a blue-purple cultivar. 'Blue Bedder' is more blue. Prune back old flowers to keep the plant blooming its best. Also, may help to prune the whole plant back heavily in late summer. Can tolerate fairly dry conditions.

Salvia guaranitica: Medium blue flowers are intermittently produced on this 3-ft plant from June until frost. Spreads in a rather neat clump. Full sun to light shade.

Salvia x 'Indigo Spires':   Long indigo flowers spikes are produced from May until frost. Flower color is very intense in the fall. It's a vigorous grower and will require cutting back at least once during the growing season. It reaches 3-4 ft. tall and will become rather leggy unless cut back. Full sun.

Mexican bush sage (Salvia leucantha): Primarily a fall-blooming salvia with purple-and-white or purple flowers. Becomes rather lanky unless pinched back regularly until mid or late summer. Foliage is gray-green. Very drought-tolerant. Very attractive in fall when in full bloom. For full sun.

Forsythia salvia (Salvia madrensis): A large, fall-blooming salvia with yellow flowers. Grows rather rampantly. Full sun to light shade.

Sanchezia (Sanchezia nobilis or S. speciosa): This plant is grown primarily for its green foliage which is variegated with yellow. Can be grown in full sun but is most attractive when it receives a little protection from the afternoon sun. Grows 2-3 ft. tall in one season. Usually returns in spring after freezing to the ground in winter.

Sanchezia

Sedum 'Autumn Joy': Blooms in late summer to fall with pink or rusty red flowers resembling broccoli florets. Requires full sun and good drainage. Drought tolerant.

Winter cassia (Senna or Cassia bicapsularis): This shrub has clusters of small yellow flowers in late fall to winter when not much else is blooming. Hard freezes will knock it back, but it returns each year. Grows to 5-6 ft. with equal spread. Full sun.

Winter Cassia

Candlebrush (Senna alata), (Cassia alata): Spectacular spikes of bright yellow flower clusters arise from late summer through fall. The plant grows up to 8 ft. or so tall and even wider in one season. Killed to the ground in winter but plenty of seedlings usually emerge in spring. Full sun.

Hardy orange gloxinia (Sinnigia sellovii): Tall spikes hold red-orange bell-shaped flowers in summer.

Attractive to hummingbirds. Full sun to light shade. Can even be grown in Zone 7B.

Blue-eyed grass (Sisyrinchium angustifolium): Clumping native grass which grows about a foot wide and tall. In late spring to early summer, delicate light blue flowers cover the plant. Full sun to light shade.

Blue porterweed (Stachytarpheta jamaicensis): Winter hardy in zone 9b-10, the porterweeds are vigorous growers with tall flower stems (3-4 ft.) that strongly attract butterflies. Bloom spring through fall in zone 8. For full sun.

Coral porterweed (Stachytarpheta mutabilis): Coral-flowered version of the porterweed. Seems to offer the most chance of any of the porterweeds to return in spring in zone 8b.

Persian Shield (Strobilanthes dyerianus)

Red porterweed (Stachytarpheta sanguinea): Red-flowered porterweed.

Stoke's aster (Stokesia laevis): Native to the southeast, this early summer blooming perennial is well-adapted to well drained sunny or partially shaded sites. Flowers are blue or white.

Persian shield (Strobilanthes dyerianus): Attractive foliage of green and purple on about a 3 ft. plant. For shade to partial shade. Usually returns in spring.

Stromanthe sanguinea and S. sanguinea 'Tricolor': S. sanguinea has green foliage with burgundy undersides. 'Tricolor' has green and cream foliage with burgundy undersides. *S. sanguinea* tends to grow taller than 'Tricolor' (2-3 ft. as opposed to 18") and comes back much stronger after winter. Shade to partial shade.

Stromanthe sanguinea 'Tricolor'

Mexican mint marigold or Texas tarragon (Tagetes lucida):   Brilliant yellow flowers are produced in the fall.   The leaves have the typical tarragon fragrance and flavor and can be used similarly to French tarragon. Full sun.

Variegated Oyster plant (Tradescantia or Rhoeo spathacea): Attractive green, burgundy, and cream colored leaves. Forms a clumping groundcover. Full sun. Will freeze but should come back in spring from roots. The species is considered invasive in south Florida and so not recommended there.

Society garlic (Tulbaghia violacea): This small clumping perennial stays evergreen most years and forms small lavender flowers during the warm season. Full sun.

Verbena canadensis: Heavy flowering pink verbena that spreads rapidly to form a thick mat. For full sun and well-drained sites. Flowers all spring and summer, though flowers heaviest on the newest growth. Drought tolerant. Mite damage is the primary problem.

Verbena tenuisecta: Very drought tolerant verbena with violet flowers. Commonly seen as a roadside plant as some states' transportation departments have planted it as such. Leaves more finely dissected than *V. canadensis*. Flowers from spring until frost. Mites not as much a problem as with *V. canadensis*. Very tough plant. For sunny, well-drained sites. Will tolerate compacted soils, though.

Rain lily (Zephyranthes spp.): *Z. grandiflora* blooms periodically spring through fall after heavy rains. *Z. atamasca* blooms only in the spring, with white flowers. Both need full sun, moist but well drained soil. Are numerous other *Zephyranthes* species also.

Rain Lilies (Zephyranthes)

GROWING ANNUAL FLOWERS

Though many people like the idea of growing perennial flowers because they don't normally have to be replanted each year, many annuals can provide a lot of bang for the buck. For example, trailing torenias like Summer Wave or Catalina will bloom from spring until late fall in Zone 8b. After some mild winters they even come back the following spring.

Generally you should think of annuals as either being for the cool season or being for the warm season. Cool season annuals are those such as petunias and pansies that are best planted in the fall or early spring. Many cool season annuals will live through the winter just fine, but they won't survive the summer heat. They should be removed once the heat starts making them look bad. Warm season annuals, on the other hand, are those such as the torenias, that do fine in the summer heat but are killed a freeze. Of course, these are just broad categories into which we, as humans, place the plants. In reality, it's a little more complicated. Lobelia, for example, will tolerate neither our summers nor hard winter freezes. It is probably best used from early spring until summer.

Planting and removal times for annuals is probably best explained in a University of Florida IFAS Extension publication, "Gardening with Annuals in Florida", http://edis.ifas.ufl.edu/mg319 In the following pages also are some lists which group the annuals according to planting times.

STARTING ANNUALS

Most annuals in the landscape are started from small plants you'll purchase from the nursery. Some annuals can be started directly in the ground from seed, but seed establishment directly in the landscape is often not that easy because of moisture fluctuations, eroding rains, and other such environmental factors. There are some annuals, though, such as zinnias and cosmos, that are very easy to grow from seed. You're missing out on some fun if you're not growing them.

Some gardeners start seed indoors or in a greenhouse, later transplanting the young plants to the landscape. Though you can be quite successful with this technique after a little practice, most people simply don't have the room, patience, or time. So, the vast majority of gardeners just buy young annuals in cell packs from the nursery.

As with perennial flowers, good drainage is important for annual flowers. If you plant them in a soggy, poorly drained soil, chances are they won't live long.

Likewise, if you plant the little plants in a hard, barely cultivated soil, they probably won't fare very well. Take the time to loosen the soil up before planting.

Most annuals, as is the case with most perennials, prefer full sun. But, there are some annuals that will tolerate or even prefer moderate to light shade.

When you plant young annuals, often it is advantageous to pinch the terminal growth to make the plant become bushier. And, as the plant grows during the season, it may require further light pruning of the tips.

FERTILIZING, WATERING, AND SLUG CONTROL

Most annuals will benefit from monthly fertilization. The same 15-0-15 or similar fertilizer that you use on other landscape plants is fine. You will only need 6/10 of a pound of the fertilizer for 100 square feet (an area 10 x 10 feet). That's only about a cup of fertilizer.

Some annuals don't need monthly fertilization. Annuals such as Madagascar periwinkle (vinca) and portulaca actually prefer less fertile conditions. So, fertilize them less often.

Water often enough to keep your annuals from suffering drought stress, but don't overwater so as to cause root rot. Feel the soil and see when it's dry and learn to note early signs of wilting leaves.

Chewing damage on young flower plants is likely to be from slugs if you don't find insects present. Use a slug paste that you can buy from your garden center. Follow directions and precautions on the label.

ANNUALS TO PLANT IN THE SPRING (MARCH-APRIL)

Flower	Color
Ageratum	Blue or white
Alyssum 'Snow Princess'	White
Angelonia	Blue, lavender, pink, white
Begonias	Pink, red, and white (dark and green leafed types)
Browallia	Blue, purple, white, orange
Calibrachoa	Red, pink, yellow, orange, and blue
Celosia	Red, yellow, pink, orange, and peach
Cleome ('*Senorita Rosalita*' is good	Pink, lavender, and white

dwarf form)

Coleus	Multi-colored leaves of red, yellow, or green
Cosmos	Violet, pink, and white
Crossandra	Orange, yellow
Dianthus (Sometimes a perennial)	Pink, red, white, or burgundy
Diascia	All colors
Evolvolus (Blue Daze)	Blue
Gaillardia	Red and yellow
Geranium (Try heat resistant 'Caliente' & 'Calliope'	Red, pink, coral, lavender, white
Gomphrena (globe amaranth)	Violet, reddish, and white
Impatiens and SunPatiens	Pinks, red, violets, white, orange, and blue
Lobelia	Blue
Marguerite daisy	White, yellow, pink, blue
Marigolds	Various shades of yellow and orange
Melampodium	Yellow
Nemesia	All colors
Nicotiana	Red, pink, or white
Ornamental pepper	Red, yellow, orange, purple, black
Pentas	Red, white, pink, and lavender
Petunias	Pink, violet, red, white, blue, salmon

Portulaca	Pink, red, yellow, orange
Salvia	Red, white, salmon, or burgundy
Snapdragons	Red, white, pink, yellow, salmon
Torenia	Blues, pinks, white
Verbena	Violet, red, pink, blue, white, salmon
Vinca (Madagascar periwinkle)	Violet, pink, or white
Zinnia	Red, orange, violet, white, yellow, and salmon
Zinnia angustifolia	Orange-yellow, white
Zinnia 'Profusion'	White, orange, cherry, apricot

ANNUALS TO PLANT IN THE FALL (OCTOBER-NOVEMBER)

Bachelor buttons	Blue, violet, pink, and white
Calendulas	Yellow-orange
Chrysocephalum apiculatum	Yellow
Dianthus (Sometimes a perennial	Pink, red, white, burgundy
Diascia	All color
Dusty Miller	Silvery gray foliage
Erysimum 'Flambe Yellow' and 'Flambe Orange'	Yellow and orange

Flowering cabbage	Leaves of green and kale and or purple or green and white
Larkspur	Blue, pink, and white
Nemesia	All colors
Pansies	Blues, purples, orange, white, yellow
Petunias (including Supertunia 'Vista Bubblegum'	Pink, violet, red, white, blue, salmon
Poppies, California	Primarily oranges and yellows
Poppies, Iceland	Red, orange, yellow, pink, white
Poppies, Shirley	Red, orange, yellow, pink, white
Snapdragons	Red, white, pink, yellow, salmon
Sweet alyssum	White
Sweet peas	Red, pink, lavender, and white
Verbena	Purple, pink, red, and white
Violas (Johnny Jump-ups)	Purple, white, and yellow

ANNUALS THAT CAN BE PLANTED FOR THE SUMMER HEAT (MAY-SEPTEMBER)

Coleus	Multi-colored leaves

	of red, yellow, or green
Crossandra	Orange, yellow
Gomphrena (globe amaranth)	Violet, reddish, and white
Impatiens (for shade, except for Sunpatiens	Pinks, red, violets, white, orange, and blue
Marigold	Yellows and oranges
Melampodium	Yellow
Ornamental pepper	Red, yellow, orange, purple, black
Pentas	Red, white, pink, and lavender
Portulaca	Pink, red, yellow, orange
Salvia	Red, white, salmon, or burgundy
Torenia	Blue, purple, pink, yellow
Zinnia, common	All colors, except blue
Zinnia angustifolia	Orange-yellow, white
Zinnia 'Profusion'	White, orange, cherry, apricot

ANNUALS FOR SUNNY TO ONLY SLIGHTLY SHADED AREAS

Ageratum	Blue or white
Angelonia	Blue, lavender, pink, white
Bachelor buttons	Blue, violet, pink, and white
Begonias	Pink, red, and white (dark and green leafed types)
Browallia	Blue, purple, white, orange
Flowering cabbage	

or kale	Leaves of green and purple or green and white
Caladiums	Multi-colored leaves of green, pink, red, and white
Calendulas	Yellow-orange
Celosia	Red, yellow, pink, orange, and peach
Chrysocephalum	Yellow, orange
Cleome	Pink and white
Cosmos	Violet, pink, and white
Crossandra	Orange, yellow
Dianthus (Pinks or Sweet Williams)	Pink, red, white, and burgundy
Diascia	All colors
Dusty Miller	Grown for silvery gray foliage
Erysimum	Orange, yellow
Evolvolus (Blue Daze)	Blue
Gaillardia	Red and yellow
Gomphrena (globe amaranth)	Violet, reddish, and white
Impatiens	Pinks, red, violets, white, orange, and blue
Larkspur	Blue, purple, pink, and white
Lobelia	Blue
Marguerite daisy	Yellow
Marigolds	Various shades of yellow and orange
Melampodium	Yellow
Nemesia	All colors
Nicotiana	Red, pink, or white

Ornamental pepper	Red, orange, yellow, purple, black
Pansies	Blues, purples, orange, white, yellow
Pentas	Red, white, pink, and lavender
Petunias	Pink, violet, red, white, blue, salmon
Poppies, California	Primarily oranges and yellows
Poppies, Iceland	Red, orange,yellow, pink, white
Poppies, Mexican tulip	Yellow
Poppies, Shirley	Red, orange, yellow, pink, white
Portulaca	Pink, red, yellow, orange
Salvia	Red, white, salmon, or burgundy
Snapdragons	Red, white, pink, yellow, salmon
Sweet alyssum	White or pink
Sweet peas	Red, pink, lavender, and white
Torenia	Blues, pinks, white
Verbena	Violet, red, pink, blue, white, salmon
Vinca (Madagascar periwinkle)	Violet, pink, white
Zinnia	Red, orange, violet, yellow, white, and salmon
Zinnia angustifolia	Orange-yellow, white
Zinnia 'Profusion'	White, orange, cherry, apricot

ANNUALS TOLERANT OF A LITTLE MORE SHADE
(*most tolerant*)

Begonias*	Pink, red, and white (dark and green leafed types)
Caladiums*	Multi-colored leaves of green, pink, red, and white
Crossandra	Orange, yellow
Coleus*	Multi-colored leaves of red, yellow, or green
Evolvolus (Blue Daze)	Blue
Impatiens *	Pinks, red, violets, white, orange, and blue
Melampodium	Yellow
Salvia	Red, white, salmon, or burgundy
Torenia	Blues, whites, and pinks

ANNUALS FOR HOT, HARSH, DRY SUNNY AREAS

Gomphrena (globe amaranth)	Violet, reddish, white
Melampodium	Yellow
Portulaca	Pink, red, yellow, orange
Vinca (Madagascar periwinkle)	Violet, pink, white
Zinnia angustifolia	Orange-yellow, white

ANNUALS FOR CUT FLOWERS
Ageratum
Cosmos

Pentas
Angelonia
Dianthus
Poppies
Bachelor buttons
Gomphrena
Salvia
Calendula
Larkspur
Snapdragon
Celosia
Marigold
Sunflower
Cleome
Marguerite daisy
Sweetpeas
Coleus
Nasturtium

GOOD ANNUALS FOR CONTAINERS

Ageratum
Bacopa
Begonia
Browallia
Coleus
Dianthus
Geranium
Impatiens
Lobelia
Marigold
Melampodium

Nasturtium
Nicotiana
Pansies
Petunias
Phlox
Portulaca
Sweet alyssum
Torenia
Verbena
Vinca (Madagascar periwinkle)

ANNUALS FOR FRAGRANCE
Dianthus
 Nasturtium
 Nicotiana
 Petunia
 Sweet alyssum

SALT TOLERANT ANNUALS
Calendula
Cape daisy
Dusty Miller
Gaillardia
Gazania
Geranium
Kalanchoe
Portulaca
Ornamental cabbage and kale
Petunia
Snapdragon
Vinca

Wax begonia
Zinnia

ANNUALS THAT ARE EASY TO SEED INTO THE LANDSCAPE
Bachelor buttons
Cosmos
Larkspur
Nasturtiums
Poppies
Portulaca
Sweet peas
Sunflowers
Zinnias

PLANT SPRING-FLOWING BULBS IN FALL
One way to have color early next spring is to plant spring-flowering bulbs. Planted from October   onward through January, the bulbs usually flower sometime during the period from late February into May. Flowering time will depend on time of planting, kind of bulb, and weather.

Daffodils, or other types of narcissus bulbs (of which daffodil is one type), generally perform better in our climatic zone than most other types of spring-flowering bulbs. The Florida Daffodil Society has information on which daffodils will perform well in our area.   See   their   information   at http://www.profilingsolutions.com/FDS/

Most tulips and many of the other well-known spring flowering bulbs won't come back in our area.

They will come up and bloom the first year but not in subsequent years. The problem is our lack of sufficient winter chilling. You just have to treat many spring-flowering bulbs as annuals in our area. Anemones, ranunculuses, and hyacinths fall into the annual category. Chill tulips and hyacinths in the refrigerator before planting. And, soak anemone bulbs in water overnight before planting.

Your local garden center will have some spring-flowering bulbs that will come back each year and bloom. Spanish bluebell (*Hyacinthoides hispanica*) is one small bulb that does very well in our area. It's best planted in an area with a little afternoon shade. Snowflakes (*Leucojum aestivum*) also do very well here. There are even some types of tulips that can be grown in our area, though they may be difficult to find. The Southern Bulb Company http://www.southernbulbs.com/ is one source.

When planting any of the bulbs, be sure to select a well-drained site. The bulbs will rot in a soil that tends to stay too wet. The planting site also needs to be sunny or only lightly shaded.

The bulbs will perform best if the whole planting bed is tilled before planting. If you simply dig a single hole in the ground and stick in the bulb, root growth may be a struggle. Planting twice the depth of the bulb is a fairly widely accepted rule in our area.

OTHER FALL-PLANTED FLOWERS

Many chrysanthemums can be planted in fall for color. Cut them back after they bloom and they'll flower for you again next fall. You'll need to pinch them back occasionally next spring and summer (until late July) to keep them bushy.

Pansies are the most popular annual planted in fall. They'll provide color through fall, winter, and until the warm days of late spring. The coldest of freezes may nip them back but won't kill them. Plant in full sun and in a well-drained area. Erysimum is an excellent background plant for pansy plantings.

Plant snapdragons in fall so they'll be set to bloom early next spring. Petunias planted in fall will bloom in fall and then superbly next spring. Diascia and nemesia will bloom a little during the winter and will be spectacular in spring. Verbena planted in the fall will bloom through the fall and very likely survive the winter and bloom again in spring. All these flowers need full sun and well-drained soils.

Some *flower seeds* need to be planted in fall if the flowers are to be at the blooming stage next spring. Larkspur, bachelor buttons, sweet peas, and various poppies are examples. All are relatively easy to start, provided (you guessed it!) you pick a sunny, well-drained site.

Flowers planted in fall will require light monthly applications of fertilizer through the winter. Water them as needed.

9

Growing Fruit at Home
For Food and Beauty

THE REWARDS AND THE PROBLEMS

Growing fruit in the home landscape can be rewarding. One reward is, of course, the fresh fruit. There's just no comparison between peaches you buy in the grocery store and peaches you grow yourself. But there is an additional reward in the attractiveness of many of the fruit plants. Consider, for example, the pink flowers of a peach tree in spring or the orange fruit of a persimmon tree against a blue autumn sky.

But growing fruit at home can have its problems, too. Insect pests and fungus diseases like fresh fruit as much as people do. You'll have to protect some types of fruit from such pests if you are to be successful. Use one of the fruit tree sprays (combination insecticide/fungicide) available from garden centers. Follow label instructions carefully.

DIFFICULT-TO-GROW FRUIT

Don't lump all fruit into the difficult-to-grow category, though. Some types of fruit can be grown without a lot of spraying. First, lets quickly look at the fruit you may wish to avoid unless you have the time and discipline to stay on a regular preventative spray schedule.

Peaches are a good example. Unless you routinely spray peaches from the flower bud stage up until harvest, you'll find it extremely difficult to avoid a host of pests. Chances are you'll end up with wormy fruit if any fruit.

Nectarines and **plums** fall into the same category as peaches.   **Apples**, though not as troubled by pests as peaches, nectarines, and plums, sometimes tend to have their share of pests, too. So do **bunch grapes**. Muscadine grapes usually have fewer problems.

Pecans have their problems, too, especially if you select the wrong pecan variety. Plant a pecan for shade and be thankful for any nuts you may get in the home landscape situation.

Pecans fall prey to a number of problems, pecan scab disease being one of the most serious. Commercial pecan producers spray six or seven times a season with special pecan sprayers designed to reach the tops of the trees. Even with the proper spraying, production is sometimes limited due to the alternate year bearing habit of the pecan.

If you plant pecan trees at home, plant one of the varieties that has some degree of resistance to scab disease. Elliott, Curtis, Stuart, Desirable, and Moreland are the recommended varieties for plantings that will not be sprayed. Fertilize the pecan trees each February (50 lbs. of fertilizer for mature trees) and hope for the best. Pecan weevils, aphids, and rainy springs still can limit production, but spraying in the home garden is not feasible.

EASIER-TO-GROW FRUIT

Citrus, pears, figs, blueberries, blackberries, loquats, and muscadine grapes can be among the easiest of fruits to grow at home. But, with many of these, there are certain factors to consider. None are completely problem-free.

The **pear**'s biggest enemy is fire blight disease. Varieties recommended for the Deep South are generally fire blight resistant. Avoid varieties such as Bartlett that aren't resistant. If you further minimize possibility of fire blight problems by not over-fertilizing and not pruning excessively after establishment, you will probably have few problems growing pears.

Figs have been grown in home landscapes for years without any spraying. The fig's number one enemy is the nematode, a microscopic worm that feeds on its root system. But, by mulching the plant well and occasionally fertilizing, you can usually help the plant tolerate nematodes. There is no chemical treatment for nematodes anyway.

Rabbiteye blueberries are very picky about soil requirements. It's necessary that they have an acidic soil of pH not higher than about 5.2. But, provide the blueberries with their acidic soil and interplant them with the proper pollinator variety, and they'll usually have few problems. Beware; you can kill young plants by over-fertilizing.

To provide an acidic soil, don't plant blueberries within 20 feet of a house. Lime from the house foundation decreases soil acidity. Mix from ¼ to ½ cubic foot of Canadian peat with the planting soil. Keep the plants heavily mulched with pine straw, pine bark, or oak leaves. Don't use grass clipping as mulch.

Blackberries sometimes have a problem with fungus diseases. But, generally, if you'll do a thorough job of removing old canes immediately after harvest, you'll have less of a problem.

Muscadine grapes can have pest problems from time to time. But, you don't have to keep them on a preventative spray schedule in the home garden situation. The most important factor to remember when growing muscadine grapes is to prune heavily each year (remove everything but short spurs with 2-3 buds each on the two or four main arms). And be sure to interplant the proper pollinator variety.

Other types of fruit that don't have to be on a preventative spray program (but that may have to be sprayed occasionally) are **persimmons and citrus such as satsumas, kumquats, oranges, tangerines, tangelos, lemons, limes, grapefruit, and pummelos.**. Even apples may be grown sometimes without preventative sprays. But, peaches, nectarines, plums, and bunch grapes generally require sprays to prevent pest problems from overcoming them.

One final and very important word of advice on growing fruit: For most fruit, be sure to plant in a spot that receives full sun all day. Otherwise, fruit production will be poor. Some of the citrus will tolerate a little shade, but production is best in full sun.

PICKING THE RIGHT DECIDUOUS FRUIT VARIETIES FOR OUR AREA

Remember that we still don't have as much cold here as our friends further north. So we can't grow all the same kinds of deciduous fruit trees (ones that lose their leaves in winter) that they can grow.

Many types of deciduous fruit trees have a requirement for winter chilling. Unless that chilling requirement is met, the plant will not fruit well. So, despite the temptations of the mail-order catalogue pictures and the bargain prices in some of the discount stores, stick to fruit varieties known to perform well in your specific area. There will even be slight differences between what can be grown in Macon, Georgia and Tallahassee, Florida, though Macon is less than 200 miles north of Tallahassee.

Avoid fruits such as cherries that just don't grow here in the Deep South. And, though you may have fond memories of the taste of a particular apple or peach from your childhood in the north, don't try to grow it here.

The lists below have many of the deciduous fruit varieties that will grow in the Zone 8b. If you're in a different zone, consult with your local county extension office for a list of local variety recommendations. And, remember, there are always new varieties coming out. So don't restrict yourself to the varieties on this list. Just do your homework first to make sure the variety you are considering will work for your specific zone.

APPLES
Anna
Dorsett Golden (as
pollinator for Anna)
Tropic Sweet (plant with
Anna or Dorsett Golden)

BLUEBERRIES
Rabbiteye varieties; plant several
different varieties for pollination:
Aliceblue
Beckyblue
Climax
Bonita
Bluegem
Woodard
Brightwell
Delite
Tifblue
Choice
Briteblue
Southland
Alapaha
Austin
Bluebelle
Homebelle
Ochlockonee
Powderblue
Premier
Vernon
Chaucer

Southern highbush varieties:
Windsor
Primadonna
Star
Springhigh
Springwide
Sweetcrisp

BLACKBERRIES
Brazos
Cheyenne
Comanche
Cherokee
Arapaho
Navaho
Plant
Flordagrand &
Oklawaha together for pollination
Chickasaw
Choctaw
Kiowa
Ouachita
Rosborough

FIGS
Brown Turkey
Celeste
Green Ischia
Alma
Magnolia
Champagne

Hollier
Hunt
LSU Gold

PERSIMMONS
Non-astringent:
Fuyugaki
Hanafuyu
O'Gosho
Gwang Yang
Ichi-Ki-Kei-Jiro dwarf
Imoto Fuyu
Jiro
Maekawa-Jiro
Astringent:
Hachiya
Saijo
Tamopan
Tanenashi
Gailey (is required pollinator for Hachiya)

PLUMS
Gulfbeauty
Gulfblaze
Gulfrose
Excelsior
Mariposa
Early Bruce
Methley
Ozark Premier
Kelsey

(All require cross- pollination except Methley)

NECTARINES
Suncoast
Sundollar

PEACHES
Flordadawn
Flordaglobe
Flordacrest
FlordaRio
Gulf Crimson
Gulf King
La Feliciana
Sam Houston
TexRoyal
Rio Grande

PECANS (disease resistant)
Stuart
Elliott
Curtis
Desirable
Moreland

CHESTNUTS
Dunstan hybrids

PEARS
Softest:
Flordahome

Baldwin
Hood
Others:
Pineapple
Tenn
Ayres
Orient
Carnes
Leconte
For pollination,
plant Hood with
Pineapple or
Flordahome
Southern Bartlett

MUSCADINE GRAPES

Self fertile cultivars:
Jumbo
Summit
Supreme
Fry
Black Fry
Early Fry
Pam
Black Beauty
Sweet Jenny
Farrer
The following need pollination from a
self fertile cultivar:
Nesbitt
Ison

Granny Val
Polyanna
Pineapple
Late Fry
Florida Fry
Suwannee

COLD-HARDY CITRUS FRUITS

There are several kinds of citrus that can be grown in the warmer parts of the Deep South despite our cold spells during the winter. Satsuma, a citrus fruit very similar to a tangerine, and kumquat, a small citrus fruit which may be eaten peel and all, are the two most commonly grown cold-hardy citrus in our area.

The duration of freezing temperatures is more of a factor in causing freeze damage to citrus than is the actual temperature. For example, a brief drop to 24 degrees may cause no harm. But, several hours at 26 degrees may cause damage, particularly if the plant has had no previous exposure to freezing temperatures that season. As the days shorten and nights become cooler, plants slow top growth and attain a degree of winter hardiness. Satsumas might tolerate 15 degrees in January when they are completely dormant. But a prolonged temperature of 26 degrees might cause serious damage in mid-November.

So, regardless what type of citrus you plant in the lower South, there is always the possibility of cold damage. But, by selecting the most cold-hardy types, you greatly decrease the probability of damage.

Kumquats are undoubtedly the most cold tolerant of the commonly available citrus, tolerating temperatures down to 10 degrees when fully dormant. Active growth occurs only at relatively high temperatures, so the plants remain semi-dormant during late fall, winter, and early spring. They bloom later than other citrus and cease active growth earlier in the fall. So, they are better able to tolerate the winter's cold.

Kumquat trees rarely reach ten feet tall. As with all citrus in our area, kumquat trees are normally grown on trifoliate orange rootstock to impart cold hardiness. The trifoliate root stock further reduces the kumquat's natural height.

The kumquat fruit, produced in large numbers, are yellow to bright orange, and are generally no larger than 1 ¾ inches in diameter.

The fruit matures in the fall and holds well on the tree without much loss of quality. They may be eaten fresh, peel included, or may be preserved as marmalade or candied whole fruit.

'Nagami', 'Meiwa', and 'Marumi' are the three common kumquat varieties. 'Nagami' is more acidic than the others. 'Meiwa', which produces nearly round, sweet fruit, has become very popular for landscape use.

Satsumas are very similar to the tangerines you buy at the grocery store. Mature, dormant satsuma trees have survived 15 degree freezes without serious injury. Satsuma trees are medium to small in size. It's usually best to plant them in a sunny spot on the south side of the house where they will be shielded from north winds. Planted in such a spot, the northern winds often limit the tree's height to the height of the house.

Satsuma fruit matures in October to November but doesn't hold quality on the tree much longer than two weeks. They become puffy and lose flavor and juice content if left on the tree too long. Fruits become fully ripened for eating while the peel is still rather green. Not all fruit ripens at the same time.

'Meyer' *lemon*, though one of the most cold hardy lemon selections, is only cold hardy into the mid 20's. The fruit ripening period usually lasts for several months beginning in late summer. Good crops of large, practically seedless, juicy lemons are produced.

With care, and cooperation from Old Man Winter, some other types of citrus can be grown in Zone 8b. If you grow these other types of citrus, you need to have some method of protecting the plant during the hard, prolonged freezes. A plastic-covered frame, supplemented with a light bulb for heat, might work during freezes in the 20's. A wire cage, wrapped around the tree and stuffed with pine needles or hay to insulate the trunk, then covered with plastic, may be necessary during more severe freezes.

Try to always plant citrus on the south or southwestern side of the house in a sunny spot. Such an exposure, especially if close to the house, will provide the little bit of extra protection from the northern winds that can make the difference between life and death.

Oranges are grown by some in Zone 8b. Chinotto orange is as cold hardy as the satsuma. Other oranges, such as Hamlin, Parson Brown, and Pineapple are more sensitive to cold but are still grown successfully by some. So don't rule out oranges if you select varieties that ripen early and give the tree added protection during hard freezes.

In addition to the satsuma, some gardeners also grow other tangerines, such Dancy, Clementine, or Robinson. Some of these need to be pollinated by other citrus such as the Orlando tangelo, one of the most cold-tolerant tangelo varieties.

The limequat was developed from breeding the Mexican lime with kumquat. This resulted in a cold hardy lime that has fruit year round.

Grapefruit are grown by quite a few Zone 8b gardeners. Duncan and Marsh are white-fruited varieties, but red varieties such as Rio Red and Flame are grown also. If you want a super-large version of the grapefruit, grow the pummelo, the largest citrus of all, with some as large as basketballs. The pummelo is sweeter than the grapefruit and more cold hardy.

So, if you like citrus (and who doesn't?), you have some you can grow with no extra winter protection most years, and then some you will have to protect occasionally when it gets very cold.

PRUNING DECIDUOUS FRUIT TREES TO THE PROPER SHAPE STARTS AT PLANTING TIME

As soon as fruit trees such as pears or peaches are planted, they need to be pruned to begin training them to the proper shape. To severely prune a tree you may have just paid $20-$40 for is an emotional task. But, it must be done if the tree is to grow to the desired form. From then on, pruning needs to be done every year. It's generally done in January and early February.

Fruit trees are pruned for several reasons. It's desirable to keep the trees at a height that will facilitate easy harvesting. Pruning also removes excess leaf growth that will shade fruit and inhibit ripening. Probably most importantly, though, pruning creates and maintains a strong structure to bear and hold the fruit crop.

Pruning should always remove branches that interfere with the basic framework of the tree or branches that rub against each other. Try to select limbs that have a wide angle of attachment rather than a narrow angle which may split as the limbs grow larger, pushing against each other, and loading down with fruit.

Apple and pear trees, when purchased, are often unbranched sticks about 4 ft. tall. They should be cut back to about 3 ft. so that they will branch below that point the first growing season. Next winter when you prune, retain the central trunk and three or four spirally arranged branches around the trunk. The lowest branch should not be lower than 2 ft. from the ground.

The second winter after planting, the central stems or trunks of apple or pear trees need to be cut back to balance them with the other branches. You do not want any one branch to develop significant growth and height dominance over the others.

Mature apple and pear trees should not be heavily topped each year. Moderate annual pruning to remove dense inner growth, crossover branches, and some length is preferable to heavy pruning every three or four years. Heavy pruning upsets the balance of the tree, causing a proliferation of water sprouts.

Peach trees need to be cut back to about knee high at planting time. Leave several spirally arranged branches on the trunk. Reduce the length of the side branches so that only several buds remain on each branch. Remove all lower branches. The objective is to develop three or four primary framework branches and no central trunk.

Peach tree pruned after first year's growth.

Plum trees are pruned much the same as peach trees, but you may leave more than just three or four framework branches on a plum tree.

During the second winter after planting the peach, cut back each of the three or four selected framework branches to about 2/3 their length. The objective is to cause each of the framework limbs to branch into two more branches.   This will increase the number of framework branches from three or four to six or eight.

Plum trees tend to develop somewhat of an open center naturally without the hard pruning required on a peach.

Prune peach and plum trees every year.   Remove any crossing branches and those that are growing into the center.   Then shorten the tree considerably by cutting back limbs to outwardly facing buds.

Pecan or persimmon trees need to have the upper 1/3 of the young tree's main trunk removed at planting time.

In the second winter, remove all limbs within four feet of the ground from the trunk of the pecan tree. Remove persimmon branches closer than two feet to the ground.   If two limbs form a narrow angle of attachment, remove one of them. Otherwise, they will push against each other as they grow and may eventually split.

Mature pecan and persimmon trees require little pruning. Hopefully, you trained the trees in early years so that branches come off the trunk at wide angles rather than narrow angles.

Cut back **fig** plants to about half their height when planting.

The second winter after planting the fig, thin out dense growth and eliminate dead wood, Retain three to eight strong, upright sprouts at least 3-4 inches apart at the base.

Figs will need occasional shortening of the main branches to keep the bushes to a manageable height. Thin out weak growth and remove dead wood.

At planting time, the strongest, straightest cane of young **muscadine grape** vines is selected. This strongest cane is trained to a string or stake which rises to the lateral trellis wire. All other canes are removed and other shoots that may sprout off this main cane are kept trimmed off during the growing season. Only leaves growing directly from this main cane are allowed.

This main cane should reach the top wire of the trellis during the first growing season. If not, you'll have to select another cane and try again the second year. If, however, the selected cane does reach the top wire, cut it at that point the following winter so that a lateral will branch out to each side along the trellis wire. Be sure to leave at least one lateral shoot to grow each way on the bottom trellis wire, too, if you have a two wire trellis system.

When pruning in later year, you leave the main arms of the muscadine grape vines. But all the growth off these arms is cut back to a point so that only two or three buds per growth spur are left. Don't worry about sap that may bleed from the cuts; it's mostly just water.

Blueberry plants do not have to be pruned severely at planting time. But they should not be allowed to fruit the first season after planting. At planting time, prune or pick off the fruiting buds at the ends of the shoots.

The main objective in pruning blueberries is the promotion of strong new wood. If too little pruning is done, the plants are crowded with twiggy weak growth. Either remove or cut back old canes that have little strong new wood. Eliminate the twiggy growth in the top and outer areas of the bushes.

Blackberries and raspberries are pruned just after harvest by removing all old canes.

PRUNING OVERGROWN AND NEGLECTED FRUIT TREES

Most of us wouldn't make very good commercial fruit growers. Mostly out of fear of making a mistake, we're overly hesitant to prune our fruit trees. Yet, well thought out pruning can help a tree to bear more and better fruit.

If you're like most home gardeners, chances are you have a fruit tree or two that has hardly been pruned since it was planted. Now it's so thick and overgrown you just don't know where to start.

You begin by removing branches that cross over each other or that rub against each other. Basically, you want to remove most of the growth headed back toward the center of the tree. You are trying to open the tree and allow more light to enter. You try to select the outwardly headed limbs to keep.

Some trees, such as pears, and to a lesser degree, apples, naturally tend to shoot growth straight upward. You'll not have to do as much thinning on these trees as with a peach or nectarine tree. But, some thinning will be required.

If large limbs are allowed to grow toward the inside of the tree, soon they'll cross other branches. Soon those crossing branches become rubbing branches, causing injury to the branches they rub against. So, your first step is to thin the tree, removing such inwardly growing branches.

When thinning the tree, remove entire limbs. Don't merely shorten limbs. Cut the limb off back at the trunk or at the main limb from which it starts. Contrary to what you may have heard for years, don't paint the wound with pruning paint. Just make a good, clean cut. Don't leave a stub. But, don't cut so close, either, that you remove the little ridge of bark that connects the branch being removed with the trunk or main limb to which it is attached. That small ridge, called the branch bark ridge or collar, contains the cells from which callus tissue will begin to grow over and seal over the wound naturally. If you injure the collar, healing will not be complete.

Next, look at the outwardly growing branches. If two branches interfere with each other, you'll have to make a decision as to which branch to remove. They can't both stay. Keep the stronger, better placed limb.

After you've removed all the crossing and rubbing branches on the tree, then you still may need to do more thinning. Remove dead or diseased branches.

After doing so, sterilize your pruning tools with alcohol before cutting into healthy wood. Otherwise, you may spread the disease organism.

After removing dead or diseased branches, remove spindly growth and water sprouts. Such growth usually has no or few flowers and so will produce no fruit.

After you've thinned the tree so that more light can enter and so that branches aren't interfering with each other, you can consider reducing the size of the tree. Be careful, though. If you've let your tree grow unchecked for years, a drastic size reduction now will stimulate excessive vegetative growth at the expense of fruit production next season. Also, the succulent growth stimulated may be more susceptible to disease organisms, such as fire blight disease on pears and apples.

To reduce the size of the tree, you'll shorten limbs. When you shorten a limb, you destroy the dominance that limb's tip once had and establish the limbs just below the pruning cut as the new dominant growing points. So, when making your shortening cuts, cut back to outward growing limbs. If you cut back to an inward growing limb, it will become the new dominant growing point. But, because it's growing inward, you'll end up having to remove it later when it becomes a crossing or rubbing branch.

In a nutshell, that's all there is to pruning overgrown fruit trees. Of course, it's best not to let your trees become overgrown in the first place. Start pruning at the time you plant the young trees, training them to the proper shape. Then, each winter, make the necessary corrections and size reductions, keeping in mind that some trees will require more severe pruning than others.

FERTILIZING FRUIT TREES

Fruit trees generally need some fertilizer to obtain the nutrients necessary for plant growth. But, over-fertilization can result in vigorous growth that interferes with good fruit production.

There is no one particular fertilizer that has to be used. The general purpose fertilizers such as 20-20-20 are usually adequate. Better yet, do a soil test of the soil each winter and determine exactly what you need. You may find that you should use a fertilizer without phosphorus, the major fertilizer pollutant in our lakes. We shouldn't, therefore, use phosphorus when it's not needed.

When fertilizing, spread the fertilizer on the ground under the tree branches and slightly beyond. Water it in if possible. Never merely heap the fertilizer in one or two piles.

SPECIAL NOTE ON FERTILIZATION RECOMMENDATIONS

As mentioned in the following section on fertilization, some trees are very susceptible to over-fertilization. The fertilization recommendations given can be varied, and often need to be varied in accordance with the growth rate of your plants. But, always tend to vary in the direction of using less rather than more fertilizer.

Peaches, nectarines and plums: The March after the trees have been planted, apply half of a cup of 20-20-20 spread over an area 3 ft. in diameter. Each February thereafter, apply about 3/4 cup of 20-20-20 fertilizer for each year of age of the tree until a maximum of 5-7 cups is reached as the tree ages.

Apples: Fertilize the same as for peaches and plums. If you severely prune the apple tree, don't apply any fertilizer that year.   Similarly, if growth is excessive, stop fertilizing for a year or two until growth slows to a more normal rate (10-15 inches per year of terminal growth).

Pecans and Chinese chestnuts: Apply 3/4 cup of 20-20-20 fertilizer per tree the first season after planting in May. In succeeding years, apply one to 1-½ cups of fertilizer per year of age of a pecan tree in February. The maximum rate for mature pecans is 25 lbs. Chestnuts require about ½ cup for each year of age up to a maximum of 7.5 lbs. Pecans may also require zinc. If the fertilizer you use doesn't contain one unit of zinc, apply zinc as zinc oxide or zinc sulfate. On older trees, zinc oxide may be applied at the rate of 1- 1/3 cups per tree each year. Zinc sulfate may be applied at the rate of 5-1/3 cups per tree on mature trees. Zinc sulfate applications last 2-3 years.

Grapes: Before spring growth begins the first year grapes are planted, apply ⅛ cup of 20-20-20 around each plant. Spread the fertilizer, keeping it at least 6 inches from the vine. Repeat at monthly intervals until July. On two-year plants, use ¼ cup at each monthly application. Bearing vines will need about 1¼ cups of fertilizer per plant, applied in late February.

Blueberries: Never over-fertilize young blueberries; you can easily kill them! After new growth begins the first year, apply 2 ounces of acid azalea-camellia fertilizer (4-8-8) or ¾ ounce if the formulation is 12-4-8 or similar. In June, apply 1 ounce of ammonium sulfate per plant or 2 ounces of the 4-8-8 azalea-camellia fertilizer, or ¾

ounce of the 12-4-8 azalea-camellia fertilizer.   Don't apply the fertilizer within 6 inches of the trunk.

In late February of the second growing season, apply 3 ounces of the 4-8-8 azalea-camellia special or 1 ounce of the 12-4-8 azalea-camellia special. In June, apply 2 oz. of ammonium sulfate, 3 oz. of 4-8-8, or 1 oz. of 12-4-8 per plant.

For the third season and later, use a fertilizer, such as the 12-4-8 azalea-camellia special, high in nitrogen and low in phosphorus. In late February of the third growing season, apply 3 oz. per plant. After harvest, apply another 3 oz., being sure to keep the fertilizer away from the trunk.

Fertilization in future years should be done twice a year: in late February and immediately after harvest. Increase the amount of 12-4-8 applied by one ounce per year of plant age, not to exceed 6 oz. for the spring application on large plants. The post-harvest application should not exceed 5 oz. per plant.

Blackberries: About a month after planting, sprinkle 1/6 cup of 20-20-20 in a 24-inch circle around each plant. In June, sprinkle 1/6 cup of fertilizer over a

30-inch circle. Mature blackberry vines should receive three applications of $^1/_6$-$^1/_4$ cup of 20-20-20 per year. Make the first application in February, another shortly after harvest, and a third in late August.

Pears: Apply ½ cup of 20-20-20 per tree per year of age up to a maximum of 6 cups. Apply half of this amount in late February before growth begins and the other half after the fruit is set. Spread the fertilizer over the area beneath the branch spread of the tree and slightly beyond. If you don't get fruit set, omit the second application.

If the trees are heavily pruned, reduce the amount of fertilization for a year or two. Also, if shoot growth on trees exceeds 6 inches annually, reduce the rate of fertilization. Too much vegetative growth on pears can lead to fire blight disease.

Figs: In moderately fertile soils, figs may grow satisfactorily without fertilizer. But, in infertile, sandy soils, or where competition from other plants is heavy, fertilizer is needed.

For fertilizing 1-2 yr. old plants, apply 1/6 cup of 20-20-20 each month from March through the end of July. On older plants, apply fertilizer three times a year: late February, early June, and mid-July. Use 1/6 cup of fertilizer per foot of plant height at each application. If the fruit are not reaching maturity and ripening properly, excess fertilizer or drought may be the problem and fertilization should be reduced. Always keep a fig bush well mulched, preferably mulched all the way out to the tips of the branches. Spread your fertilizer over this mulch and water it in.

Persimmons: If your persimmon tree is in a lawn area, it will receive adequate fertilizer from that supplied to the lawn. Excess nitrogen will result in fruit drop. Trees are very likely to drop their fruit anyway during the early years of their life. Also, a heavy crop one year may result in a light crop the following year. To reduce this problem, thin the fruit to 6 inches apart on oriental persimmons within a month after bloom if a heavy crop is formed.

PEST CONTROL

As mentioned already at the beginning of this chapter under the section, "The Rewards and the Problems", fruit trees certainly have their share of pests. Some of these pest problems can be reduced by careful cultural management of the plants. But some will require preventative pesticide sprays.

If you have just a few fruit trees, the easiest way for you to approach pest control is to purchase what is normally referred to at garden centers as a "fruit tree spray" or "home orchard spray". Such pesticides are a combination of fungicide and insecticide formulated for use on home fruit trees. Buy one that has complete directions for the type of fruit you have. And spray religiously according to the directions.

For many fruits, you will need to start spraying before the flowers even open in the spring. The pesticide label should give you the correct timing for sprays. The key, though, is to start on a spray program early, before the growing season starts and well before the pest problem develops. Unfortunately, you must prevent most pest problems. You don't have the option of curing them once they develop.

WEED CONTROL

Practically all fruit trees need full sun in order to produce fruit. In planting, avoid shaded spots and areas where root competition from other plants is heavy. Keep grass away from the base of the tree or vine. Grass competition takes a heavy toll. Some plants, such as figs and blueberries need to be mulched. Use pine bark, pine straw, cypress mulch, leaves, or other organic material. Maintain a 2-3 inch thick mulch extending out to the branch tips.

Just as around landscape plants, glyphosate herbicides (such as Roundup^R and other brands) can be used around many fruit trees as directed sprays to kill emerged weeds. Refer to the herbicide label for specific recommendations and plant clearances. But, avoid getting any of the herbicide spray mixture on trunks of plants such as blueberries or young peaches, nectarines, or plums. The green tissue in such trunks will absorb the glyphosate, and damage or death of the plant can result. Always, follow the directions and precautions on the pesticide label carefully! They can save you much grief!

10

Vegetables & Herbs
For Freshness and Enjoyment

Growing vegetables in the home landscape is a popular hobby for several reasons. First, it can be profitable. The garden produce can save money in the family budget. Also, some vegetables, such as tomatoes, may be picked before they are fully ripe if they are to be sold in the grocery store. Home-grown tomatoes, on the other hand, can be left on the plant until they are ripe. Home-grown tomatoes are, indeed, tastier.

Finally, there is the enjoyment or therapy that comes from planting seed and nurturing it to maturity. Some people like to unwind at the end of a hard day by working in their rose garden; others prefer the sanctity of their vegetable garden.

You don't necessarily have to have a "vegetable garden", though, to grow vegetables. You can grow a few tomatoes, squash, cucumbers, peppers, or other such vegetables in small areas of your home landscape, maybe even tucked away between shrub or flower beds. Plants that are relatively compact and produce a lot of vegetables on one plant lend themselves well to such an arrangement. But, don't try to grow sweet corn, beans, or peas on a few plants mixed in with your shrubs and flowers. You'll never accumulate enough harvest at one time to make a meal.

Tomatoes, especially, can provide large harvests in small spaces. If you grow tomatoes in a raised bed of compost-like material, using lots of organic matter and fertilizer along with the soil, you can produce tremendous numbers of fruit.

THE SEASONS OF VEGETABLE GARDENING IN THE LOWER SOUTH

Vegetable gardening is pretty much a year-round thing in the lower South. The mid and late summer, because of the heat, will be the slowest season. Insects and diseases will be at their peak then, too, so many gardeners concentrate more on spring, fall, and winter gardens.

Spring garden: The spring garden is by far the most popular. It's really what is considered a summer garden a little further north.

Determining exactly when to plant the spring garden usually involves a little bit of gambling. You want to plant many of the seeds and plants as soon as possible after the last frost. The sooner you plant, the sooner you can harvest vegetables before the insects and diseases overwhelm the plants in the summer. But, if you plant too early, a late spring freeze may kill some of the tender seedlings. Mid to late March is normally the time to plant most of the plants for the spring garden. Some plants, being cool-season plants, need to be planted even earlier than March.

Here's a list of **warm-season vegetables** for the spring garden and when they should be planted. You'll note that some of the vegetables can be planted on through the summer, whereas others shouldn't be planted after March or April and not again until late summer or early fall for the fall garden.

Snap beans: March-April
Pole beans: March-April
Lima beans: March-August
Cantaloupes: March-May
Sweet corn: March-April
Cucumbers: March-April
Eggplant: March-July
Okra: April-July
Southern peas: March-August
Peppers: March-May
Sweet potatoes: March-June
Pumpkins: March-May
Summer squash: March-April
Winter squash: March
Tomatoes: March-April
Watermelons: March-April

Some cool-season vegetables can also be planted in the early spring
Here's a list and the timing for planting. Note that most of these can also be grown in the winter garden, planted in the fall. February or March is generally the latest you should plant most of these.

Beets: September-March

Broccoli: October-February
Cabbage: September-February
Carrots: September-March
Cauliflower: October-February
Celery: January-March
Chinese cabbage: October-January
Collards: February-March
Endive/escarole: February-March
Kohlrabi: March-April
Lettuce: October-March
Mustard: October-March
Bunching onions: August-March
Parsley: February-March
English peas: January-March
Irish potatoes: January-March
Radishes: September-March
Turnips: January-April

Summer Garden: A few of the warm-season vegetables will stand the summer heat. Still, insects and diseases will be a major problem during the summer. So, most likely you'll have to apply some form of insecticide. Here are the vegetables that you can plant for a summer garden and the dates they can be planted. Note that they're only part of the spring garden list:

Lima beans: March-August
Eggplant: March-July
Okra: March-July
Southern peas: March-August
Peppers: July-August

Sweet potatoes: March-June
Watermelons: July-August

Fall warm-season garden: In the late days of summer, you can begin planting your fall garden. The night temperatures begin to moderate a bit, so the plants will grow a little better again. And, there's still time to produce a warm-season crop before frost. Still, insect populations will be high. So, expect more trouble than with your spring garden. Here are some warm-season crops that could be included:

Snap beans: August-September
Pole beans: August-September
Lima beans: August
Sweet corn: August
Cucumbers: August-September
Southern peas: August
Peppers: August
Pumpkin: August
Summer squash: August-September
Tomatoes: August
Watermelons: August

Fall and Winter Cool-season garden: As nights begin cooling down a little in September, you can begin planting many of the cool-season vegetables again.

Beets: September-March
Bok choi, tatsoi, and mizuna: Oct.- Jan.
Broccoli: October-February
Cabbage: September-February
Carrots: September-March

Cauliflower: August-October and Jan.-Feb.
  Chinese cabbage: October-January
  Collards: August-November
  Endive/escarole: September
  Kohlrabi: October-November
  Lettuce: September
  Mustard: September-May
  Bulbing onions: September-December
  Radishes: September-March
  Spinach: October-November
  Strawberries: September-October
  Turnips: August-October

CONSIDERATIONS IN WHERE TO PLANT VEGETABLES

Where you plant your vegetables has a lot to do with how successful you'll be at producing a plentiful harvest.

Sunlight: Most vegetables need 6-8 hours of sunlight each day for maximum production. Some of the leafy crops such as collards, spinach, or broccoli can tolerate partial shade, but not complete shade.

Tree root competition: Don't plant near trees or large hedges. The vegetables will do poorly because of competition for moisture and nutrients.

Good drainage: Don't plant in a poorly drained area. The times you can cultivate the garden will be limited. And, root rots, stem rots, and other soil-borne diseases will likely be a problem.

Water supply: Vegetables need good drainage, but they also need water. You may produce a crop some years without any irrigation. But, most years there are dry periods when the ability to irrigate will be vital to the success of the garden.

SOIL TESTS AND LIMING

Before you intend to plant your vegetable garden, contact your local county extension service office for materials to send a soil sample to your state university soil testing lab. The lab test will tell you if you need to apply lime to the soil to raise the pH to a level more favorable for vegetables. If you find that you do, proceed with soil preparation, as given below, and mix in the required amount of lime to a depth of 6-8 inches. Do not lime unless a reliable soil test, such as from your University Extension lab, indicates the need; over liming could be just as bad or even worse for your garden.

If you don't get around to checking your soil pH well in advance of planting, you can still apply lime up to one or two weeks before planting. However, the lime will not fully lower the pH to the desired point until your vegetables are much further along. So, if possible, plan well ahead to check your soil pH and add lime if needed.

CULTIVATION AND INCORPORATION OF ORGANIC MATTER

Vegetable plants can benefit from a thoroughly worked soil. You can cultivate small areas with a shovel and hoe, but for larger plots you'll need a mechanical tiller. You may consider renting one for the garden preparation since it would be more cost effective than purchasing.

Cultivate the soil to a depth of about 8 inches a few weeks before planting time. The addition of organic soil amendments isn't absolutely necessary, but it certainly can help. Mix in organic matter well in advance of planting, preferably at least a month before seeding, unless it is well-composted. Well-composted materials can be applied at planting time. Animal manures, rotted leaves, compost, or cover crops all make good soil amendments. Mix them into the existing soil; don't merely spread them over the surface. Crimson clover, rye, or vetch are common winter cover crops that can be tilled into the soil when preparing the spring garden.

FERTILIZING BEFORE PLANTING

Even if you use organic materials for amendment you may still need to use some commercial fertilizer in your vegetable garden. Grades such as 15-0-15, 10-10-10, 20-20-20, 6-12-12, or 5-10-15 have proven to give good results with most vegetable crops. But the best thing to do is to have a soil test before you plant so that you will know exactly what fertilizer to use. If the soil pH is above 6.3, select a fertilizer that contains micronutrients.

A week or so before planting, spread (broadcast) the fertilizer over the entire vegetable garden at a rate of 2-4 lbs. of 8-8-8 or 10-10-10 per 100 sq. ft. If you use 15-0-15 or 20-20-20, use only 1-2 lbs. of fertilizer per 100 sq. ft.   At planting time, band 1-2 lbs. of fertilizer per 100 ft. of row in one or two bands each two to three inches to the side and one to two inches below the seed level or plant row. One pint of the average mixed fertilizer weighs about one pound.

FERTILIZING DURING THE GROWING SEASON

During the growing season it may be necessary to sidedress two or three times with fertilizer at half the initial banded rate. Sidedressing refers to the practice of placing fertilizer in the soil beside your plants. To sidedress, make a 1-2 inch deep furrow down both sides of the row, 4-5 inches away from the plants. Uniformly distribute your fertilizer in the furrow and then cover the furrow with an inch or two of soil.

For plants such as watermelons, cantaloupes, cucumbers, and pumpkins, which are planted in widely spaced hills, sidedress in a circular furrow around the plants rather than down the rows.

Different vegetables differ in their fertilizer requirements. Some such as beans and southern peas are *light feeders* and may require no sidedressing. *Medium feeders* may require one or two sidedressings during their growth. Medium feeders include beets, cantaloupes, carrots, cucumber, eggplant, greens (kale, collards, mustard, turnips, broccoli, cauliflower, and spinach), herbs, okra, English peas, peppers, pumpkins, radishes, rhubarb, Swiss chard, and watermelon. *Heavy feeders* may require 2-3 sidedressings. Heavy feeders include cabbage, celery, Irish potato, lettuce, onion, sweet potato, corn and tomatoes.

WATERING

When plants are young they need to be watered more frequently but in smaller amounts and as they get older the frequency lessens and the amount increases.

Your vegetables need about 1 to 1½ inches of water per week during the warm growing season. The type of soil also influences the frequency and amount of water. On soils with high clay content, one application of an inch of water any week that no rainfall is received should be adequate. On sandy soils, 2-3 applications of ½ inch each may be needed weekly.

Any watering practice that wets the foliage favors disease development. Consider using soaker hoses or drip irrigation rather than overhead sprinklers to keep the water off the foliage. If you do use sprinklers, water in the morning. There's a type of black soaker hose that has thousands of tiny pores per inch of hose. It's more expensive than the traditional flat soaker hose that squirts water out of pin-sized holes. But, the hose (sometimes called "leaky pipe") can be shallowly buried in the row and then lifted at the end of the season, to be used again the next season, season after season. Using this type of soaker hose is similar to using drip irrigation; the foliage will not be wet at all.

VARIETIES OF VEGETABLES

There are many different varieties of each type of vegetable (too many to list here). And, selecting the proper varieties can make a big difference. Look for recommendations from your local state university extension service on the web. For example, University of Florida's recommendations are at http://edis.ifas.ufl.edu/pdffiles/VH/VH02100.pdf and University of Georgia's at http://www.caes.uga.edu/applications/publications/files/html/C963/C963VegeChart.pdf

Stick with proven varieties for large plantings and experiment with new varieties on a small scale until you learn how they perform.

SPACING OF VEGETABLES

Obviously, different types of plants require different spacings in the garden. The University of Florida guide just mentioned also has spacing recommendations for various vegetables. Such charts usually tell you how many seeds or plants will be needed to plant a given area of garden.

POLLINATION

Bees are very important in pollinating plants in the vegetable garden. Because bees are most active in the morning, apply any needed pesticides in the late afternoon or early evening. Use sprays rather than dusts, because the sprays, once dry, are less hazardous to the bees.

NEMATODE CONTROL

Nematodes are microscopic worms, some of which feed on plant roots. Most soils contain some plant parasitic nematodes, but populations are not always high enough to cause significant plant damage.

Nematode damage is less likely in soils with high levels of organic matter. So, continue to add available organic matter to your garden each year.

Nematode damage is also less likely in gardens where crops are rotated so that members of the same plant family are not planted in the same area of the garden year after year. For example, avoid planting tomatoes, eggplants, or peppers in the same spot of the garden in successive years. All these plants are in the Solanaceae family and may be hosts to the same kinds of nematodes.

When nematode populations do become excessive, you have two major options. The first is soil solarization. This involves thoroughly cultivating the affected area in mid or late summer, removing clumps of plant debris, moistening the soil and then covering it with clear plastic. The edges of the plastic should be buried to seal in the hot air. If the plastic is left on for 6-8 weeks, the temperature beneath it will build to a level high enough to significantly reduce the nematode population.

Another option is bio-fumigation. In this practice mustard is planted as a cover crop in the garden area and tilled into the soil before it seeds. Research indicates that the decaying mustard plants give off a gas which helps to kill nematodes, fungi, bacteria, and other   microorganisms.
http://www.ghorganics.com/Mustard%20for%20Pest%20Control%20Not%20for%20Your%20Sandwich.htm

INSECT PEST CONTROL

Realize that not all insects you see in the garden are harmful. Many are harmless; others are actually beneficial pollinators or predators of pest insects.

You should check the garden closely for insect damage twice a week. If the damage is excessive you may spray with an approved insecticide. There are many to choose from these days. Follow pesticide label directions and precautions carefully.

Bacillus thuringiensis formulations such as Dipel^R or Thuricide^R can be used to control cabbage worms, tomato fruitworms, hornworms, pinworms, and squash vineborers. Commercial soap pesticide formulations, such as Safer^R Soap, can be used to control aphids, spider mites, thrips, or whiteflies. Both these products, the soap and the B.T., are environmentally safe and good choices for the pests they control.

Malathion will control many insects: aphids, cabbageworms, cucumber beetles, leafhoppers, leafrollers, Mexican bean beetles, pea weevils, spider mites, stink bugs, and thrips.

Carbaryl (Sevin) will control: armyworms, budworms, cabbageworms, Colorado potato beetles, cucumber beetles, corn earworms, flea beetles, fruitworms, hornworms, pinworms, leafhoppers, pickleworms, melonworms, Mexican bean beetles, pea weevils, stink bugs, and thrips. Carbaryl is deadly to bees, so take care not to spray when bees are active. Also, use the liquid formulation of carbaryl rather than dusts to further safeguard bees. Once a spray dries, bees aren't likely to be poisoned by it. But carbaryl dust can get on the bee days later and poison not only the one bee but many more if he makes it back to the hive.

Spinosad is a microbial insecticide that is also effective against many caterpillars. It is available under such tradenames as Green Light Spinosad Lawn & Garden Spray or Monterey Garden Insect Spray. It also controls thrips, leaf miners, and Colorado potato beetles.

Neem Oil, a product extracted from the seed of the neem tree is another botanical product. It is useful against aphids, mites, and whiteflies. It is labeled for use on most vegetables and is sold under tradenames such as Monterey 70% Neem Oil or Fertilome Rose, Flower, & Vegetable Spray. Thorough coverage of the pest is necessary for good control.

Azadirachtin is also extracted from the seed of the neem tree but is different from neem oil. It works as a natural insect growth disruptor. It also acts as repellent/feeding inhibitor to many insects. It's labeled for use on most vegetable crops as well as herbs. It is especially good for whiteflies and aphids, and it provides some control of small caterpillars as well as a variety of other insect pests. Gordon's Garden Guard Liquid Insecticide and AzaMax are two such products for use in the home vegetable garden.

Acetamiprid is sold as a ready-to-use spray under the trade name Ortho Max Flower, Fruit, and Vegetable Insect killer.   It is one of the best controls for whiteflies.

Pyrethrin and Pyrethrum are botanical insecticides favored by organic gardeners. They provide a rapid knockdown of insects, but not a thorough kill. So piperonyl butoxide is often mixed with pyrethrin to provide better results in products such as Bonide Pyrethrin Garden Insect Spray Concentrate. But piperonyl butoxide is not accepted in organic gardening. So organic gardeners prefer products such as Safer Brand Yard and Garden Insect Killer, a combination of pyrethrin and insecticidal soap. All the pyrethrin products can be used close to harvest date, but because they don't have a long residual, their effectiveness is limited also.

Pyrethroids are a group of synthetic insecticides that are modeled after the natural plant-derived pyrethrum. Pyrethroids are used at very low rates and are effective against a wide range of insects. The following five pyrethroid insecticides are currently labeled for use in the home vegetable garden.

Permethrin: Permethrin, the oldest of the pyrethroid insecticides, is available under names such as Bonide Eight Vegetable, Fruit & Flower Spray and Hi-Yield Indoor/Outdoor Broad Use Insecticide. Because permethrin controls so many different insect pests and is labeled on most vegetables, it is one of the most useful insecticides for home vegetable gardeners to keep on hand. Permethrin is one of the best treatments for control
of stink bugs and leaf-footed plant bugs, and it also works well against tomato fruitworms and hornworms. But be aware that permethrin often causes populations

explosions of those pests that it doesn't control (spider mites, aphids, whiteflies, loopers).

Cyhalothrin: Lambda cyhalothrin is one of the newer pyrethroid insecticides (Spectracide's Triazicide Insect Killer Once & Done Concentrate is the most common brand name). It is very effective against a number of different insect pests, including stink bugs, but is labeled for use
on only a few vegetable crops.

Cyfluthrin: Cyfluthrin is another relatively new pyrethroid insecticide. It is sold under the brand name Bayer Advanced Garden Power Force Multi-Insect Killer Concentrate. Like cyhalothrin, it is very effective against a number of different insect pests, including stink bugs, but is only labeled for use on a few vegetable crops.

Esfenvalerate: Esfenvalerate is another of the older pyrethroid insecticides. It is labeled for use on a number of different vegetables and controls a wide range of insect pests. Monterey Bug Buster is an example.

Bifenthrin: Bifenthrin is an effective pyrethroid for control of stink bugs, leaf-footed bugs, tomato fruitworms, and a variety of other insect pests. However, it is labeled for use on only a few vegetables, including tomatoes and many cucurbits. Ortho Bug-B-Gon Max Lawn and Garden Insect Killer is one example of a bifenthrin product.

MITE CONTROL

There are currently no effective miticides that are labeled for use in home vegetable gardens. Because of the lack of an effective miticide, it is very important to avoid unnecessary insecticide sprays. Such sprays can cause mite populations to rise rapidly because the predators of the mites are killed.

When it is necessary to treat for spider mites, you will have to rely on products such as insecticidal soaps, neem oil, or summer weight horticultural oils. Spraying undersides of infested leaves with a fine mist of water can also help reduce mite numbers.

SLUG CONTROL

(Thanks to W.S. Cranshaw, Colorado State University Extension entomologist and professor, bioagricultural sciences and pest management for this information.)

Pesticides effective against slugs and snails are known as molluscicides. These often are different chemicals than those used to control insects and other garden pests. Slugs are not susceptible to poisoning by most insecticides.

Metaldehyde is the most commonly used and effective molluscicide. However, it cannot be used among vegetables and edible crops. An alternative slug bait that recently has become available includes iron phosphate (ferric phosphate) as the active ingredient. Trade names include Sluggo, Slug Magic, Garden Safe Slug & Snail Bait, and Escar-Go!, among others. Data suggest iron phosphate generally is comparable in effectiveness to metaldehyde. Furthermore, iron phosphate products can be used around edible crops and do not pose special hazards to dogs.

Ammonia sprays make excellent contact molluscicides, but must be applied directly to exposed slugs. These sprays aren't harmful to most foliage, but it's best to do a test on a limited area first to make sure you won't get burn.

Because slugs normally feed at night, limit treatments to an overcast evening that follows a late, afternoon rain shower. Household ammonia, diluted to a 5 percent to 10 percent concentration, is effective for this purpose.

DISEASE CONTROL

You're likely to always have some plant disease problems in the vegetable garden. But, you can reduce the incidence of disease problems by following some basic guidelines.

Plant only disease-free, healthy plants in the garden. There's no need in introducing diseases into the garden on diseased plants!

Rotate the spot where you plant your garden each year if possible. If this isn't possible, at least try to rotate the spots where you plant specific types of vegetables in the garden. If you can't rotate, and if you had a problem with a particular soil-borne disease or a nematode in an area last year, use either soil solarization or bio-fumigation as mentioned earlier under nematode control.

Monitor your garden on a regular basis, at least twice a week. Remove diseased leaves or plants as they first show up. You can greatly slow disease spread.

Choose varieties resistant or tolerant to diseases when possible. Tomato varieties marked with the letters VFN mean that variety is resistant to verticillium wilt, fusarium wilt and root- knot nematode. Remember, that resistance is not infallible.

Plant fungicide-treated seed. Such seed is usually colored with a dye to indicate treatment.

Treat seed with hot water. Placing seeds in hot water helps eliminate bacterial diseases that can come in with the seed. This treatment is suggested for seeds of eggplant, pepper, tomato, carrot, spinach, lettuce, celery, cabbage, turnip, radish, and other crucifers. Seeds of cucurbits (squash, gourds, pumpkins, watermelons, etc.) can be damaged by hot water and should not be so treated. The hot water treatment has to be done carefully to be effective and to not damage the seed. This Ohio State University Extension site http://ohioline.osu.edu/hyg-fact/3000/3085.html gives the details.

When a foliar disease starts in the garden, pick off affected leaves early. Sometimes you can stop the disease by doing so. You cannot cure a diseased plant but you can prevent the disease from spreading to healthy leaves and plants. But, often you'll have to resort to fungicide sprays so that you can prevent the rapid spread of the disease to other plants of the same type. For example, if a disease starts on beans, spray all the beans in that general area. The principle behind fungicide use is providing a protective coating on healthy leaves to prevent the spores of the disease from germinating and infecting them.   Therefore, it pays to start the fungicide sprays before the disease becomes severe.

Fungicide sprays are generally more effective than dusts. Follow the fungicide labels completely. The label will tell on which plants you can use the fungicide, directions for mixing and applying, how soon you need to re-apply, how soon you can eat the vegetables after application, etc.

Chlorothalonil is a fungicide that can be used for control of anthracnose, Botrytis, downy mildew, early blight, fruit rots, fungal leaf spots and blights, gummy stem blight, late blight, powdery mildew, and rust. Some products with chlorothalonil as the active ingredient include Fertilome Broad Spectrum Liquid Fungicide, Gordon's Multi-purpose Fungicide, and Hi-Yield Vegetable, Flower, Fruit and Ornamental Fungicide.

Copper fungicide is used for control of anthracnose, bacterial leaf spots and blights, downy mildew, early blight, fungal leaf spots and blights, gummy stem blight, late blight, powdery mildew, scab, white rust, and white mold. Copper fungicides include Bonide Liquid Copper Fungicide.

Neem oil fungicides include Concern Garden Defense Multi-purpose Spray; Ferti-lome Rose, Flower & Vegetable Spray; Gardens Alive! Shield-All II, and Green Light Neem Concentrate. Neem oil controls anthracnose, downy mildew, fungal leaf spots and blights, gray mold, powdery mildew, and rust and scab.

Phosphorous acid (mono- & dipotassium salts) is the active ingredient in Monterey Agri-Fos Systemic Fungicide. It is useful in control of root, crown and fruit rots caused by *Phytophthora* and *Pythium* as well as in control of downy mildew and late blight.

Mancozeb can be used on some vegetables in control of anthracnose, downy mildew, early blight, fungal leaf spots and blights, gummy stem blight, late blight, and rust. It is available as Bonide Mancozeb Flowable with Zinc or Southern Ag Dithane M-45.

Maneb helps control anthracnose, downy mildew, early blight, fruit rots, fungal leaf spots and blights, gummy stem blight, late blight, and rust. It is the active ingredient in Gordon's Maneb Tomato & Vegetable Fungicide and Hi-Yield Maneb Garden Fungicide.

Be sure to only use formulations of any of these fungicides which are labeled for use in vegetable gardens and on the particular types of vegetables you wish to spray. Follow all label directions and precautions very carefully. Never use a pesticide in any manner contrary to that specified on the label. If the pesticide label contradicts information in this book, follow the label information.

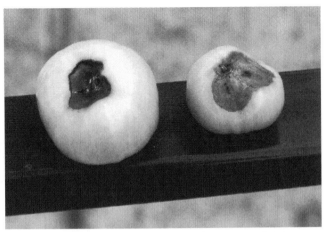

Blossom end rot of tomatoes is caused by a calcium imbalance. Fluctuations in moisture tend to bring it on. Try to keep moisture levels of tomatoes consistent.

HERBS

Herbs can be grown by everyone, even those who live in apartments. It doesn't take much space, for example, to grow a few plants of basil and fennel in containers. Even rosemary can be grown in a container.

All you need is a container with drainage, a well-drained soil mix, and a spot that receives full sun for at least part of the day.

Here are a few herbs you may wish to try:

Warm-season
Basil
Fennel
Anise hyssop

Cool-season
Arugula

Dill
Cilantro
Parsley
French sorrel
Salad burnet
Sage
Thyme

Year-round
Rosemary
Garlic chives
Mint
Greek oregano
Ginger

11

Birds & Other Wildlife
Add a New Dimension to Your Landscape

Some of my most vivid childhood memories are of the birds, butterflies, bees, and other wildlife in the gardens around our home. I spent countless hours out in the yard catching butterflies and bees. I was fascinated with these little colorful creatures that could fly so well and that stayed so busy going from flower to flower.

I learned to identify all the birds in the garden. I just about wore out the pages of the encyclopedias with the color photos of the birds.

A garden full of birds, butterflies, and bees gives your child a rich and colorful world that will help them to begin to appreciate nature and its beauty at an early age. It's an opportunity that should be provided for every child whenever possible. And even to us adults, the activity of birds singing and moving about helps to make our home landscapes seem more like home. Yet, we can't take birds or other wildlife for granted. If we want them around, we must provide food, water, shelter, and cover for them in our yards.

You may think that you can just put out a bird feeder and attract all the birds you want. It's not that simple, though. The birds want cover, shelter, and water also. For cover they need a mixture of trees, shrubs, and plants of various sizes.

Think about it from the bird's view. You wouldn't hang around where there are not plenty of places to hide from hawks or other predators. Nor, if you're a small bird, would you even want to hang out where you have to share your perch sites with larger more raucous birds such as blue jays. Rather, you would want plenty of trees and shrubs around with room enough for everyone. Then, whenever the coast was clear, you could dart over to the bird feeder for a few seed or to the bird bath for a drink of water.

It would also be great if there were some other sources of food, such as berries or seed on plants, besides the bird feeder. If you're a ground feeder, such as a towhee or a brown thrasher, you don't even care about the bird feeder. You want a good mulch of leaves, pine straw, or other organic material at the base of shrub beds so that you can forage for food and be reasonably well hidden.

And, finally from the bird's view, you must have a nesting site nearby if you're to make this home. Depending on the type of bird you are, the nesting site could be anything from a large shrub or small tree to a cavity in an old dead pine tree.

If you wish to encourage a diversity of birds in your yard, then you must have a diversity of food, nesting sites, and cover. A homesite with a large lawn, a few small tightly clipped shrubs, and a couple of large shade trees won't attract that many birds. But a homesite with a diversity of large trees, some understory trees, evergreen and deciduous trees, neat but not tightly sheared medium to large hedges and shrubs, and a not-so-large lawn is much more likely to attract a diversity of birds.

Many of the plants that are attractive to birds are also attractive to other small animals such as raccoons, opossums, foxes, and, of course, squirrels. So, there is the added benefit of being able to watch these animals, too.

SOME LANDSCAPE PLANTS TO ATTRACT BIRDS

SHRUBS AND SMALL TO MEDIUM TREES

Red buckeye (Aesculus pavia): A small native deciduous shrub that blooms in the spring with red tubular flowers liked by hummingbirds. Needs partial shade.

American beautyberry (Calicarpa americana): This small native deciduous shrub produces bright purple berries in clusters on the stem, ripening in the late summer to fall. If pruned a little during the early growing season to make it a little bushier, it can be an attractive landscape addition as a small shrub. Many birds such as mockingbirds, woodpeckers, and cardinals like the berries.

Hackberry or Sugarberry (Celtis laevigata): Medium to large deciduous native tree. Many birds eat the fruit.

Fringe tree (Chionanthus virginicus): A small, native deciduous tree that flowers in mid-spring with flossy, white clouds of flowers. Many birds eat the fruit that follows on the female plants.

Flowering dogwood (Cornus florida): One of our most favored and attractive of small deciduous native trees. Beautiful spring flowers, great fall leaf color, and bright red berries which are loved by many birds in winter!

Hawthorn (Crataegus spp.): Small thorny, deciduous tree. Beautiful flowers in spring; often great fall color. Fruit eaten by some birds. Native.

Dahoon holly (Ilex cassine): Another evergreen native holly with red berries liked by birds. Leaves usually spineless.

Possumhaw (Ilex decidua): Small, native deciduous holly. Attractive red berries on female plants are attractive food for many birds.

American holly (Ilex opaca): Somewhat slender, upright native evergreen tree. Females produce typical red holly berries eaten by many birds. There are several hybrids of American holly, including 'Savannah' and 'East Palatka'.

Yaupon (Ilex vomitoria): A small, evergreen native holly tree. Females produce small red berries attractive to birds. Buy only plants specified in the nursery as female. There is a weeping cultivar available, too, but it probably wouldn't be as inviting to birds because of branch structure.

Southern red cedar (Juniperus silicicola): Evergreen native tree, producing small blue fruit attractive to many birds. The density of the cedar makes it a good nest site for many birds and a good screening plant for landscape purposes. Relatively fast-growing. Medium in size.

Oregon grape holly (Mahonia bealei): Medium evergreen shrub with thick, spiny leaves. Clusters of blue berries are especially attractive to mockingbirds. For shade to sun.

Crabapple (Malus angustifolia): Attractive small, flowering, deciduous tree with fruit attractive to several birds.

Wax myrtle (Myrica cerifera): Be sure to buy only plants specified as female plants; only they produce the berries eaten by many birds. Yellow-rumped warblers, ruby-crowned kinglets, and others like the waxy gray berries. I enjoyed watching cardinals nest in a wax myrtle by my home office window for years. Wax myrtles can be trained as hedges, small trees, or large shrubs, reaching 10 ft. or so in height if desired. Though some people aren't excited by wax myrtles (they're such a common native), they're a most adaptable and versatile landscape plant.

American hornbeam (Ostrya virginiana): Small deciduous native tree. Nuts eaten by some birds.

Cherry laurel (Prunus caroliniana): Fast-growing, shiny-leafed evergreen small tree that makes a good hedge or an attractive single plant. Many birds attracted to the fruit in winter. Native. Biggest drawback is that it sprouts easily wherever birds spread the seeds.

Black cherry or wild cherry (Prunus serotina): The black fruit from this slender, medium-size native deciduous tree provides food for many birds in the summer. Eastern tent caterpillar webs infest the tree most every spring but do not cause permanent damage. The leaves grow back, and the caterpillars provide food for the yellow-billed cuckoo.

Pyracantha (Pyracantha spp.): A non-native, cascading shrub with thorns and beautiful orange berries in the fall. Needs plenty of room and full sun. Mockingbirds love the berries and tend to stake out territory in pyracantha bushes.

Blackberry (Rubus spp.): Another fruit that both you and the birds can enjoy. Cut back old canes just after harvest season to keep them productive and neat. Need full sun. The new named varieties offer larger berries than our wild berries.

Elderberry (Sambucus canadensis): Though not usually thought of as a landscape plant, this large native shrub, producing clusters of cream-colored flowers in spring and berries following, is attractive to many birds. Could be useful in the landscape.

Sassafras (Sassafras albidum): Medium-sized native deciduous tree. Females have dark blue fruit attractive to birds. Good purplish red fall leaf color. Attractive tree that should be planted more.

Winged elm (Ulmus alata): Good small to medium native shade tree. Deciduous. Seed liked by many birds.

Blueberry (Vaccinium spp.): The blueberry can make an attractive hedge, though it is deciduous (losing its leaves in winter). It will provide fruit for you and many birds. See the chapter on fruit for more information on selecting blueberry cultivars. Needs full sun.

LARGER TREES

Maples, red and Florida (Acer rubrum and A. saccharum var. Floridanum or A. barbatum): Winged seeds eaten by some birds. Red maple has bright red seeds in spring. Both red maple and Florida sugar maple have attractive fall color. Natives.

Hickory (Carya spp.): Nuts eaten by blue jays, woodpeckers, and crows. These stately deciduous trees have the most striking gold foliage! Natives.

Persimmon (Diospyros virginiana): The native persimmon gets quite large with time, unlike the Oriental persimmons we often plant for fruit. Fruit of the native persimmon are smaller and very astringent until quite ripe. Are attractive to birds and other wildlife.

American beech (Fagus grandifolia): Nuts liked by many birds. Magnificent large native tree with beautiful whitish bark. Gold fall foliage. Brown leaves hang on tree into winter.

Sweetgum (Liquidambar styraciflua): Tall, slender deciduous tree with very attractive fall color. Seeds borne in the spiny sweetgum balls liked by many birds. Native. Becomes quite tall with time.

Southern magnolia (Magnolia grandiflora): Birds like the red seeds. Good cover for birds, too. Evergreen native. White flowers in early summer.

Red mulberry (Morus rubra): The berries of the female trees attract many types of birds. Fruit can be messy, so don't plant overhanging roof, patio, driveway, etc. Native.

Black gum (Nyssa sylvatica): Blue fruit eaten by birds such as woodpeckers, cardinals, blue jays, etc. Hollows in old trees make nest sites for some birds. Red to orange fall leaf color on this native.

Pines (Pinus spp.): Including natives loblolly, spruce, shortleaf, longleaf, pond, slash, and sand pines. All are evergreen. Seeds provide food for many birds. Trees provide cover and nest sites.

Oaks (Quercus spp.): Includes natives live oaks, white oaks, laurel oaks, water oaks, Shumard oaks, southern red oaks, and others. All are deciduous except live and laurel oaks. Acorns provide food. Trees provide cover, nest sites, and insects for food.

Sabal palm or cabbage palm (Sabal palmetto): The black berries serve as food for a variety of birds. One of the more cold-hardy palms. Native to much of our region.

VINES

Trumpet vine (Campsis radicans): The orange flowers of this deciduous native vine are very attractive to hummingbirds.

Coral honeysuckle (Lonicera sempervirens): Red flowers of this deciduous native vine attract hummingbirds.

Virginia creeper (Parthenocissus quinquefolia): Small dark berries of this deciduous native vine serve as food for many birds. This vine is often confused with poison ivy, but Virginia creeper has five leaflets, not three as does poison ivy. Turns a beautiful red in fall. Poison ivy, incidentally, also has berries eaten by many birds.

BIRD FEEDERS IN THE LANDSCAPE

Obviously, bird feeders attract birds. Some birds can even be drawn into relatively barren areas when you supply them with preferred food on a regular basis. But, bird feeders work best when you also provide the other aspects of the birds' preferred habit. The cover, nesting sites, water, and feed are all important if you wish to permanently increase the diversity of birds around your landscape.

You can enjoy feeding birds year-round. You'll find different birds there during different seasons of the year. Don't worry, though, if you don't have food in the feeders all the time. Though the birds will become accustomed to finding feed in your feeders, rarely is there a shortage of feed in the wild this far south, even in inclement weather. So the birds can survive even without your feed.

Your bird feeder should protect the seed from getting wet. Wet seed will spoil quickly and can be harmful to the birds.

Place the feeder so that there is cover to escape predators within 10-20 ft. from the feeder. But don't place the feeder right in the midst of thick shrubbery or other such cover where a cat could sneak up unseen.

It's best not to mix different kinds of seed in one feeder. The birds will pick out their favorites and the rest will fall to the ground where it sprouts and becomes weedy. So avoid most commercial seed mixtures.

Sunflower seeds are a favorite of many birds. Cardinals, goldfinches, purple finches, woodpeckers, titmice, chickadees, blue jays, doves, and even wrens, will visit feeders with sunflower seeds.

You may reduce visits by less desirable or nuisance species to your feeder if you keep their favorite foods out of the feeder. For instance, wheat is preferred by house sparrows.

Squirrels can be a nuisance also. The most effective 'squirrel-proof' feeder I've found is a metal pole with the wide saucer-shaped squirrel baffle/feeding platform that fits around it. A perch feeder mounts on top of the pole over the squirrel baffle/feeding platform. Even this type of feeder has to be in an open spot out of jumping distance of squirrels (8-10 ft.).

There are also squirrel baffles available for hanging feeders. And there are poles with sliding spring-loaded sections designed to keep squirrels from climbing them. If you live in an urban area and don't want to share the bird seed with squirrels, you'll have to use one of the squirrel-proof mechanisms.

A rather recent addition is the availability of seed treated with hot pepper sauce. It doesn't affect the birds, but the squirrels hate it. Cole's Wild Bird Seed is one company that makes such products, http://www.coleswildbird.com/no-squirrels-allowed.php

A **suet feeder** will attract some birds that may not come to a seed feeder. For example, mockingbirds will come to a suet feeder. Raw suet (beef fat) will become rancid quickly, so either buy suet cakes from a store that sells them for bird-feeding, or you can make your own.

To make suet cakes, melt a cup of ground suet in a saucepan. Blend in a cup of smooth peanut butter. In a separate bowl, mix together 2-3 cups of yellow corn meal and 1/2 cup of enriched or whole wheat flour. When the suet/peanut butter mixture has cooled and started thickening, blend in the dry ingredients. Pour the mixture into a flat cake pan and cut into cakes when hardened. Or, pour the mixture into muffin tins. Use the suet cakes in suet feeders. Or, an alternative would be to stuff the thickened suet mixture into pine cones for hardening there. The cones could then be used as suet feeders. (Note: If squirrels are a problem, you may wish to delete the peanut butter from the recipe.)

Hummingbird feeders are typically used to attract hummingbirds. Of course, many flowers are useful in attracting hummingbird, too. But the feeders, which you fill with sugar water and hang so that the red color of the feeders are visible, often attract quite a few hummingbirds.

Be sure to buy a hummingbird feeder that can easily be cleaned with vinegar water each week. It's important to keep the feeders clean. Try not to place the feeders in direct sun.

To mix the feeder solution for the feeders, dissolve one quarter cup of white granulated sugar per cup of hot water. Let the solution cool to room temperature (or put in the refrigerator to cool it more quickly) before filling the feeders. Don't add red food color to the solution. It hasn't proven definitely that it causes health problems for the hummingbirds, but there is a possibility.   And it isn't needed to attract the birds. The red color of the feeder is sufficient attraction. So, leave out the food color to play it safe.

Hummingbirds migrate to the tropics for the winter. So, you may only have hummingbirds during the spring, summer and early fall. Or, if you leave the feeders out for the winter, you may be surprised by some hummers that do stay around.

WATER

There's more to supplying water for birds than just buying a bird-bath and occasionally filling it.

First, be picky about the birdbath you buy; if the sides are too steep, the birds won't use it for bathing. The water needs to gradually slope out to its deepest point of 2-3 inches so that the birds can wade in.

The birds prefer a shaded spot, protected, about 15 feet from shrubbery and 3 feet off the ground.

The sound of dripping or misting water will help insure that the birds find the water. Consider rigging up a mist of water that shoots up into an overhanging tree and drips back into the birdbath. Birds are most active from sunrise to 10:00 a.m. and from late afternoon to shortly after sunset. You could install a timer at the hose outlet to turn the mister on and off at those times.

Finally, keep the water clean. This will benefit both the birds and you, too, as mosquitoes will breed in unchanged birdbaths. And, make sure that water's always there on a dependable basis. Mosquito dunks are available that you can put in the water to prevent mosquitos from breeding, but you should be changing the water often enough anyway to keep the mosquitos dumped. Maybe just use the mosquito dunks when you know you will be away for a week or more, or if you find you're too forgetful to change the water.

BIRD HOUSES

Birds that nest in cavities in trees, branches, or fence posts often have a difficult time finding enough nest sites in developed urban areas. Bird houses can provide such birds with nest sites.

When building or buying a bird house, make sure it is properly designed for the particular species of bird you wish to attract. Birds are picky about their nest sites.

Bluebirds prefer houses with a floor of about 5x5 inches. The walls should be about 8 inches high. And, the entrance hole should be 1½ inches in diameter and 6 inches above the floor. The house should be positioned 5-10 ft. above the ground.

If you live in an urban area without any wide-open fields, you probably won't get bluebirds, though. But, you can attract birds such as Carolina wrens, purple martins, chickadees, and woodpeckers with appropriately designed houses.

A house for a red-bellied or red-headed woodpecker, though, obviously needs to be larger than a bluebird house. Build the floor 6x6 inches, the walls 15 inches tall, and the entrance hole two inches in diameter and nine inches above the floor. Put 3-4 inches of sawdust in the box and position it 8-20 ft. above the ground.

Bluebird house with predator guard
above and snake guard below.

When building bird houses, it's wise to slant the top to provide better rain runoff. And, design the back or top so that it will hinge open for cleaning in between nestings. Otherwise, mites can become a problem for the birds.

Build bird houses of ¾ inch durable woods such as cypress, western cedar, or exterior-grade plywood. Use rough-cut lumber; it will give the birds a foothold when they are entering and exiting. Never use metal or plastic; they absorb heat and may kill the young birds. An exception to this is in the case of the anodized aluminum purple martin houses. These houses are properly ventilated to allow cooling. Any good bird house should have a gap or ventilation holes under the roof overhang. The house should also have drainage holes.

BUTTERFLIES

At some time or another most of us have paused to appreciate the beauty of a butterfly as it flits through the garden from flower to flower. If you would like to see more butterflies in your garden, then it helps to provide food for both the butterflies (the adult stage of the lifecycle) and the caterpillars (the larval stage of the lifecycle). It's also a good idea to provide water in the garden for butterflies.

It's not absolutely critical that you have food plants for the caterpillars in your garden. But it does help. Different types of butterfly caterpillars have different types of preferred food plants. So if you're going to see that type of butterfly flitting through your garden, there have to be food plants for the caterpillar somewhere reasonably nearby.

The University of Florida extension publication, *Butterfly Gardening in Florida*, http://edis.ifas.ufl.edu/pdffiles/UW/UW05700.pdf has information on food or host plants for various types of butterfly larvae or caterpillars.

If you have bare soil in your garden, butterflies can drink water from the soil when it is wet. Or, you can make a water station for the butterflies by taking a clay tray, filling it with sand, and placing a rock in the center. Put the tray in an area frequented by the butterflies and moisten the sand. Don't add so much water, though, that it completely covers the sand.

Most butterflies feed on the nectar from flowers. The following are some nectar plants for your butterfly garden that you, too, will find attractive. You will find a little more detail on most of them in the chapter on flowers.

Purple coneflower (*Echinacea purpurea*)
Beach sunflower (*Helianthus debilis*)
Swamp hibiscus (*Hibiscus coccineus*)
Firebush (*Hamelia patens*)
Black-eyed Susan (*Rudbeckia hirta*)
Yellow coneflower (*Ratibida pinnata*)
Cut-leaved coneflower (*Rudbeckia laciniata*)
Salvia (various species, such as *coccinea*, *leucantha*, and *elegans* as well as crosses such as 'Wendy's Wish')
Stoke's aster (*Stokesia laevis*)
Blue porterweed (*Stachytarpheta jamaicensis*)
Coral porterweed *(Stachytarpheta mutabilis)*
Red orchid bush (*Bauhinia galpinii*)
Butterfly bush (*Buddleia spp.*)
Cape honeysuckle (*Tecomaria capensis*)
Spicy jatropha (*Jatropha integerrima*)
Princess flower (*Tibouchina urvilleana*)
Pentas (*Pentas lanceolata*)

Mexican heather (*Cuphea hyssopifolia*)
Cigar flower (*Cuphea micropetala*)
Cigarette or firecracker plant (*Cuphea ignea*)
Indian blanketflower (*Gaillardia pulchella*)
Lantana (plant the ones that don't set seed)
Plumbago (*Plumbago auriculata*)
Zinnia
Abutilon
Red powderpuff (*Calliandra haematocephala*)
Ixora
Firespike (*Odontonema strictum*)
Peacock flower or Pride-of-Barbados (*Caesalpinia pulcherrima*)
Butterfly weed (*Asclepias tuberosa*)
Butterfly ginger (*Hedychium coronarium*)
Swamp sunflower (*Helianthus angustifolius*)
Firecracker plant *(Russelia equisetiformis)*

OTHER WILDLIFE IN THE GARDEN

There are likely other types of wildlife that visit your garden too. In fact, some of these may even live in your landscape, especially if you have a wooded landscape of some size.

Most of these types of wildlife are nocturnal, mainly active at night. There is probably a lot more wildlife action in your yard each night than you realize. Foxes, for example, are very common, even in urban areas. You're not that likely to see them, except possibly just before dark. But you may hear them at night if you know what to listen for. Here's one site on the internet with various fox sounds: http://www.angelfire.com/ar2/thefoxden/sounds.html Some of the sounds will probably surprise you.

Raccoons and opossums are quite common, too, and may visit your garden quite regularly at night. In dry weather they may even be visiting your bird bath •for water every night.

Barred owls are not unusual, even in urban areas. You've probably heard their call at night... http://www.youtube.com/watch?v=fppKGJD3Y6c Sometimes their conversations can get pretty rowdy, especially if it's 3:00 a.m. and you're trying to sleep... https://www.youtube.com/watch?v=DzhSxhhAYbE&feature=related

Many of you have deer coming into your garden and eating some of your plants. And in parts of the South armadillos are regular night visitors. Rabbits and squirrels, though fun to watch, can also cause some problems in the garden. Squirrels, of course, are active in the day, not at night.

You may, or may not, want some of these various forms of wildlife in your yard. But most of them, with the exception of the armadillos, are a part of the natural environment and they're just doing their best to survive our encroachment on their habitat.

So whether you like the wildlife and want to encourage it, or whether you just wish it would stay out of your yard, the answer is the same. We need to give the wildlife more of its natural habitat. Wooded areas and areas with some underbrush, especially corridors of such areas that run some distance through a number of properties, all give the wildlife space where they can live and travel. Dead tree snags and brush piles also benefit wildlife by providing shelter and in some cases, food.

What you don't want to do is feed the wildlife. If we have enough natural areas, the wildlife will find more nutritious natural food in the wild. Feeding also concentrates animals together unnaturally, sometimes causing problems such as spread of disease. And feeding the animals may cause some loss of their natural instincts.

SOME ADDED SOURCES OF INFORMATION
North American Bluebird Society
http://www.nabluebirdsociety.org/
Hummingbirds of Florida
http://edis.ifas.ufl.edu/pdffiles/UW/UW05900.pdf
Florida Hummingbirds
http://floridahummingbirds.net/1511.html
Georgia Hummers
http://www.gahummer.org/
Georgia's Wintering Hummingbirds
http://georgiawildlife.com/node/502
Plant a Garden for Hummingbirds
http://agr.georgia.gov/plant-a-garden-for-hummingbirds.aspx
Landscaping for Florida's Wildlife
http://www.amazon.com/Landscaping-Floridas-Wildlife-Re-creating-Ecosystems/dp/0813015715
Garden for Wildlife

http://www.nwf.org/Get-Outside/Outdoor-Activities/Garden-for-Wildlife.aspx
Native Nurseries: The Store for Nature Lovers
http://www.nativenurseries.com/

12

Pruning
Why, When and How

Pruning is an important part of landscape maintenance. Yet, it is the most misunderstood part of landscape maintenance. Consequently, it is often either neglected or done wrong.

WHEN TO PRUNE

Just before spring growth begins is an excellent time to do most pruning. The major exception is with *spring-flowering plants* such as azaleas or loropetalums. Wait until they finish blooming to prune them so that you don't prune off the long-awaited flowers that have formed on last year's growth.

Summer-flowering plants, on the other hand, need to be pruned in late winter or early spring if you're going to prune them. They'll form flower buds on the new growth that pops out in early spring. Oleander and crape myrtle are good examples.

Deciduous shade trees, if and when they need pruning, are usually pruned during the late fall or winter after they drop their leaves. Fruit trees, as already discussed in the chapter on fruit trees, are pruned in January or February.

PRUNING STEP-BY-STEP

There can be various reasons for pruning a plant. And the reason for pruning determines how you prune.

The first step in pruning any plant is to **remove wood that is dead, weak, damaged, diseased or insect-infested**. Next, you need to **remove branches that are rubbing against each other. Third, you need to remove branches that are growing in the wrong direction** (such as branches growing toward each other and that will soon be rubbing branches).

With multi-stemmed shrubs you sometimes need to **remove tired old branches and allow new ones to grow** (nandina is a good example).

Another reason for pruning is when you wish to **train a plant into a certain shape or form**. Training a formal boxwood hedge or training a peach tree to an open center are examples.

Sometimes you prune just to **maintain a plant at a certain size**. It's best to plant the type of plant that will achieve the desired size with the least amount of pruning. But sometimes pruning is needed for size control.

HOW DIFFERENT TYPES OF PRUNING CUTS ACHIEVE DIFFERENT RESULTS

Regardless of all the reasons for pruning, there are basically only two types of pruning cuts you can make. But which of these two types of pruning cuts you use determines the result achieved. If you use the wrong type of cut, you will not accomplish the desired result. In fact, you may achieve just the opposite.

The first major type of pruning cut is the ***thinning cut***. A thinning cut is when you remove an entire limb all the way back to the main trunk or to another major limb. No new growth results from a thinning cut. When you make a thinning cut you achieve your objective instantly.

Thinning cut, entirely removing a limb back to another limb. This cut was a little ragged. It appears that too small a pruning tool was used. Try to make clean cuts. But you can see the cut was made just outside the branch bark ridge.

The other major type of pruning cut is what is often referred to as a ***'heading-back' cut***. When 'heading back', you cut back just part of a small branch. This destroys the apical dominance of the cut branch and causes buds or limbs behind the cut to begin growing. A 'heading-back' cut, therefore, thickens the plant. But the effects aren't instant. It's not until after the new growth pops out and fills in that you see the results.

Result of heading back cuts on crape myrtle.
Will require a lot of followup thinning cuts.

You may be thinking, then, that a heading-back cut is good because it thickens the plant. Sometimes it is good; sometimes it's not. For example, if you're trying to reduce the size of a plant and you use all heading-back cuts, the effect is immediate in that it does reduce the size of the plant, but not long lasting because all the growth that pops out just below the cut will soon be growing upward, usually at a fast rate. If you've ever topped a crape myrtle, for instance, have you ever noticed how fast the sprouts shoot up from just below the point of the cuts? Soon you have a new problem, an over-abundance of shoots that will need thinning.

Heading-back cuts result in a proliferation of fast growth from just behind the cut. Over time, if you continue to prune with nothing but heading-back cuts, the plant will become very thick on the surface... so thick that no light can reach the interior. So if some limbs ever die back on the surface, the plant is left with a big ugly hole.   Such a plant can benefit from thinning so that light can reach further into the plant. Too much thickness also results in a lot of cross-over and rubbing branches, which also are undesirable.

This is a bad pruning job. Heading-back cuts should not have been used to keep these limbs from growing into the building. Appropriate thinning cuts, strategically removing some of the limbs, would have given much better results.

Heading-back cuts should not be used on large limbs. Don't use heading back cuts when the lateral limbs are not at least one-third the size of the limb being headed back.

WHEN TO HEAD-BACK AND WHEN TO THIN

So, there are times to head-back and times to thin. Suppose, for instance, you're trying to get a new hedge with tall, lanky growth to fill in. You may head-back growth frequently (after each new flush of growth hardens off) in order to make the hedge fuller. At the same time, though, you need to make some thinning cuts to remove branches that will soon become crossing or rubbing branches.

Another bad pruning job. All heading-back cuts were used on a tree. Thinning cuts should have been used in most cases.

Let's go back to the example of a crape myrtle. Personally I don't like to top crape myrtles. I think it destroys the naturally beautiful form of the plant. But some people do like to top them. If you do, you will need to follow up after the new growth shoots out, with some thinning cuts to remove the branches that are growing inward or that are too close together and that will soon create a mass of tangled branches.

Properly thinned crapemyrtle

Most older plants of all types could benefit tremendously from some judicious thinning. In fact, most older plants really need little heading-back. One of the major reasons for heading-back growth on an older plant is to reduce its size. So, if you planted the plant in a spot where it has plenty of room to grow, most of your pruning cuts will be thinning cuts. The common error that most people make in pruning is using too many indiscriminate heading-back cuts.

MAKING THE PRUNING CUT... AND, SHOULD YOU USE PRUNING PAINT?

For years horticulturists and arborists encouraged the use of pruning paints or tree dressings to cover pruning cuts larger than the size of a quarter. The most recent research, however, shows no advantage to covering pruning wounds with such a material. They don't seal out fungi or bacteria.

On the contrary, such pruning paints and dressings could even seal in moisture, making conditions more favorable for disease organisms. The current recommendation is just that you make a good, clean pruning cut so that the plant can quickly seal off the wound itself.

Never leave stubs like this when pruning.

If you're removing a limb, never, never leave a long stub off the trunk when you make your pruning cut. Instead, cut back to just outside the ridge of bark that attaches the limb to the trunk or larger limb. Your cut should not be so flush to the trunk that no protrusion at all is left. Yet, neither should a long stub be left.

Similarly, if you're cutting back a limb to a point where a lateral limb branches off, be sure to cut the main limb back fairly close to the point where the lateral limb branches off. Don't leave a long stub extending beyond the lateral branch.

HEDGE SHEARING

Hedge shearing involves primarily all heading-back cuts. Hedge shearing is permissible on certain small-leafed plants, such as a boxwood hedge, where a formal appearance is desired. But, shearing is an unwise and overused practice on many other shrubs. Frequent shearing results in dense growth on the surface of the plant. But the interior of the plant often develops into a tangled mess of crossing and rubbing bare branches with few leaves. If injury ever occurs to a portion of the surface leaves, a gaping hole is left in the plant.

Try to use a combination of thinning and heading-back cuts on most plants. The results will usually be a more feathery, natural-looking plant and a healthier plant. And, you'll have to prune much less often than if you had sheared the planting into a formal hedge.

Formal hedges require monthly or bi-monthly pruning to keep them formal.

These dwarf yaupons were continually sheared, resulting in very dense growth on the surface but no interior foliage. So after they suffered some dieback from disease, ugly holes were left in the hedge. If some thinning cuts had been used occasionally, to allow more light into the shrubs, this could have been prevented.

PRUNING OVERGROWN SHRUBS

The ideal situation is to plant the proper plant for a given spot... a plant that will never outgrow its site and will only require light pruning to keep it in shape. In reality, though, we often have shrubs that outgrow their spot and that begin hiding windows or crowding entrances. How do you prune such plants?

Often home gardeners try to solve the problem by cutting the shrubs back to about half their size. The result, though, is often oddly shaped plants which usually grow back to their original height by the end of the first growing season.

More severe pruning is usually a better solution. Many overgrown shrubs can be rejuvenated by cutting them back to within 6-12 inches of the ground. This is one case in which it is acceptable to use heading back cuts on large limbs.

Burford holly that had been repeatedly sheared, and as a result, had the "bare bottom" syndrome.

Most broadleaf shrubs, such as azaleas, Chinese and Japanese hollies, camellias, pittosporums, gardenias, nandinas, and abelias, respond okay to such drastic pruning if their root system is healthy and vigorous. Provided you prune at the proper time, a healthy plant has about a 90 percent chance of recovery. Weak, diseased plants often die as a result of severe pruning.

Late February to mid-March, before new growth begins, is the best time for severe pruning.

Rejuvenation pruning of the Burford holly in the previous photo. Note that some thinning was done of the headed-back limbs, to select the best ones, properly spaced.

Some types of plants will not tolerate such severe pruning. Boxwoods, for example, recover extremely slowly from drastic pruning, taking years if they recover at all.

Narrow-leaf or needle evergreens, such as junipers, should not be pruned drastically. Such plants have few dormant buds beneath the bark of old wood and will usually die from severe pruning. It is best to remove such overgrown plants.

On those plants you can rejuvenate by severe pruning, use clean cuts. A pruning saw is usually

Rejuvenated Burford holly from the previous photo.

needed to cut the large limbs at their base. Sterilize the pruning tools with alcohol frequently to prevent the spread of disease organisms from diseased to healthy wood.

After pruning back an overgrown plant, be sure to give it the best of care if you expect it to recover. Water plants weekly during dry weather. Make sure there is a 2-inch layer of mulch, such as pine straw, extending well beyond the base of the plant. Fertilize at a normal rate for the original plant size (Two teaspoons of 15-0-15 per foot of original plant height in March, May, and July).

Growth will be slow at first. It may take 4-6 weeks before the new buds break through the bark. But, after that, growth will come quickly, provided there are ample nutrients and moisture for the plant.

As the new shoots elongate, you may find that they are very long and lanky. You will need to tip-prune shoots when they become 6-12 inches long so that side branches will develop. Do this several times during the growing season so that a more compact plant is formed.   At the same time, you will need to thin out many of the new shoots to prevent overcrowding.

This is another way to handle an overgrown shrub. This Burford holly was trimmed into a tree form. Thinning cuts were the principal cuts used, to remove the lower limbs and the crossing or crowded limbs.

PRUNING ROSES

If you have rose bushes in your landscape, January or February is the time to bring out the pruning tools and give the roses their heavy annual pruning. Pruning is necessary to get the best flowering performance from your plants the following flowering season.

Thinning cuts were first used on this rose, to remove weak or diseased stems completely. Then heading-back cuts were used to shorten the rose to the desired height. The new growth will sprout out just below the cuts on the shortened stems.

Before you do any cutting, you should remove the mulch around the base of the bush and look at the overall condition of the plant. If the overall bush is not very vigorous and the base of the plant is severely knotted, scarred, or otherwise injured, you may wish to discard the bush. All the pruning in the world won't perform miracles on an unhealthy bush.

But, if the overall health of the plant appears okay, your first step is to remove all dead and spindly growth back to the base of the bush. Keep only the strong, stocky, healthy canes.

Even some of the strong canes may need to be removed if they're growing toward the center of the bush. Your objective is to open up the middle of the bush by directing growth to the outside. If there is too much growth in the center of the bush, sunlight cannot penetrate and pest organisms are provided with a haven by the thick growth.

Retain only four to six strong canes, depending on the vigor and the growth habits of the bush. Keep a lower number of canes on less vigorous plants and more on plants that don't grow so fast. Try to leave no canes smaller in diameter than a pencil.

When you make the cuts to remove canes, cut all the way back to the base. Don't leave stubs. Stubs won't heal and will provide entry points for disease and insect pests.

Once you've removed all unnecessary canes, then you must shorten the remaining canes. When you prune back canes, look for an outwardly facing bud. Make your pruning cut about a quarter inch above that bud. Make the cut at a 45 degree angle with the high side of the cut on the same side of the branch as the bud. If the center of the stem is not a healthy light color, look for another outwardly facing bud six inches or so lower and make another cut. Before making this second cut, though, be sure to sterilize your clippers with alcohol.

Pruning should encourage new canes to come from the base of the rose plant and from the canes that are left. Don't be so overly concerned about making mistakes that you totally avoid pruning. Rose bushes are forgiving plants and, if healthy, will survive your mistakes. But they need your pruning to give best performance.

Be sure to use sharp pruning clippers and loppers. You may need a small pruning saw to remove large canes. If you don't have the proper tools, buy them. You'll need them for other pruning jobs around the landscape.

PRUNING CRAPE MYRTLES

Pruning crape myrtles follows the same principles as pruning most other plants. Just as you wished to open up the center of the rose and remove crossing and rubbing branches, you'll need to do the same for crape myrtles. Then remove all twiggy or weak growth and water sprouts.

You have probably seen crape myrtles that are just cut back to about five feet tall every year. This destroys the natural tree form of the crape myrtle and results in a huge proliferation of weak, spindly branches. You must then go back and thin out a lot of this growth. Better yet, don't cut the crape myrtles back to five feet. Let them grow into their natural tree form and show off their beautiful bark and attractive branching structure in the winter when they are bare. Only prune the rubbing and crossing branches as mentioned above so that you will have a better formed tree. If you want a shorter crape myrtle, just purchase one of the many dwarf varieties.

13

House Plants
Growing Plants Indoors

Though this book is primarily about growing plants outdoors in the landscape, I thought it worthwhile to include a section about growing plants indoors. Plants grown indoors offer various benefits, from air quality to emotional benefits. So many people enjoy house plants, or at least try to enjoy them.

Unfortunately, though, growing plants indoors can be difficult if you don't understand the factors in the indoor environment that make it so.   The primary factors which cause difficulty in growing plants indoors are low light levels, low humidity levels, and water or soil moisture management.

LIGHT LEVELS

Simply put, the light levels in most places inside most homes are not adequate for the growth of most plants.   But then there are locations such as south, east, or west-facing windows that have quite a bit of light... light that may even be too direct for some house plants.

So, one of the keys to growing house plants is selecting ones suitable for the light levels with which you are dealing. Examples of plants for low light areas are ***Aglaonema or Chinese evergreen, Aspidistra,***

Chamaedorea palms, Pothos, Sansevieria, and Zamioculcas zamiifolia (ZZ plant).

Plants for <u>high light</u> areas include **Philodendron selloum, African violet, Areca palm, Ficus benjamina, Norfolk Island pine, Peperomia, Dracaena, Fiddleleaf Fig, English ivy, spider plant, waxplant or Hoya, croton, jade plant, ponytail palm, and schefflera.**

Plants for <u>"average"</u> light areas include most of the **ferns, grape ivy, schefflera, Dieffenbachia, Dracaena, pothos, Ficus pumila, Fiddleleaf fig, English ivy, Arrowhead vine or Nephthytis (Syngonium podophyllum), spider plant, and rubber tree (Ficus elastic).**

Some plants such as **Pothos, Sansevieria, Heartleaf Philodendron, and ZZ plant** will grow well under all light conditions.

The ZZ plant will grow under all light conditions.
Everyone should have a ZZ plant.
They are extremely easy to grow.

HUMIDITY

With air conditioning and heating, the air inside most homes simply does not contain enough moisture to be favorable to the growth of most plants. Possible solutions are buying a humidifier or misting the plants with a mist bottle every day or so.

WATER AND SOIL MOISTURE MANAGEMENT

It's often been said that the most common cause of house plant death is overwatering. Overwatering robs the soil of another critical component, oxygen. So the plant roots die.

When growing house plants, it's best to use a soil mixture that drains quickly. You can always add more water to a well-drained soil mix. But a soil mix that holds too much water will stay wet for long periods of time, depriving the plant roots of needed oxygen.

Pre-bagged soil mixes aren't always well-drained enough. If a mix seems too heavy or poorly drained, you may add ingredients such as perlite to improve the drainage.

Also, all plant containers need to have drainage holes to allow excess water to escape.

How often should you water? It's impossible to answer that question here because there are so many factors involved, from time of year, to type of plant, to type of soil mix. You have to be willing to stick your finger in the soil from time to time to feel how dry it's getting.

With most plants, you want to water as soon as the soil becomes dry to the touch. Water thoroughly, until water runs out the drainage hole at the bottom. You may have to take the plant outside to water or put it over the sink. Or, if the plant has a saucer under it, you may water until water runs into it. However, empty the saucer after watering. Don't allow the plant to stand in the water-filled saucer.

Don't water again until the soil becomes dry again. A few plants (you'll just have to learn as you go) like for the soil to stay a little more moist. And a few plants (cacti being a prime example) can go for much longer periods between waterings.

Signs of underwatering are generally browning of the leaf tips and margins. However, the signs of overwatering can be the same because overwatering damages the root system, which is required to take up water. So, if you get the browning of leaf tips and margins, the corrective action you take depends on whether you think you have been overwatering or whether you have been underwatering. If you think you have let the plant get a little too dry between waterings, water a little more often. If, on the other hand, you never let the soil get completely dry, let it dry a little more between waterings.

FERTILIZING

Most house plants don't grow rapidly. So they don't need a whole lot of fertilizer. Don't overdo it.

There are many commercial house plant fertilizers. Most do a good job when used as directed.

It depends on the type of fertilizer you use, but you'll normally only need to fertilize once a month.

14

Container Gardening
Expand Your Options

Growing plants in containers gives you options. Suppose, for example, that you want the warmth of plants on your front porch. Or on your pool deck. Or you want to grow a tropical that you know you will need to protect during cold winter nights. Containers are the answer.

Containers can be beautiful in themselves. Visit your garden center to see the options available. There are the traditional clay plots, light-weight plastic pots, and beautiful glazed ceramic works of art. Even an old wheelbarrow or a discarded toilet can be turned into a container to grow plants. Use your imagination and have fun. Container gardening truly does give you options... to grow plants where you couldn't otherwise grow them, and to use your creativity.

Here are a few suggestions to help you succeed in container gardening:

- Your container needs to have drainage. Otherwise it's very difficult to water enough without ending up with standing water in the bottom of the container. And the lack of oxygen in the lower part of the pot can result in root rot.
- Use a soil mixture that has good aeration. Check the soil mix you buy. Take a handful of it and make

a fist. Does it clump together in a tight ball? Or does it not hold together at all? You want something in between. It needs to hold some moisture, but it needs to have aeration too. If it doesn't have aeration, add some finely ground pine bark, some peat moss, or some other material that will give aeration. Mix the materials well until you have the right mixture.

- When selecting plants for containers, don't forget to consider the light conditions where you will place the container. For example, if the container will be in shade all day, the plants you select will have to be shade plants. Of course, one of the beauties of growing plants in containers is that you can temporarily put them in light conditions where they may otherwise not grow. That way you can have the color of roses, for example, on a shaded porch for a special occasion. But just don't expect the plant to grow long-term under such unsuitable conditions.
- To determine when to water, don't be hesitant to stick your finger in the soil to see if the soil is dry below the surface. Water whenever you find the soil dry, but don't water if it's already moist.

There are many plants that can be grown in containers. Shrubs, groundcovers, annual and perennial flowers are all possibilities. Even some small trees can be grown in large containers.

Many container plantings just consist of a single plant in the container. But some of the most interesting container plantings are made up of several plants. For example, there may a tall, upright shrub, a groundcover spilling over the edge of the container, the vertical lines of an ornamental grass, and a clump of color provided by flowers. See the color photos in Volume II of this book for some examples.

The following are a few ideas just to get you started. But the possibilities are endless. Just use your imagination. Experiment, and have fun!

LOW-GROWING GROUNDCOVER TYPES
'Purple Pixie' loropetalum
Mondo grass
English or Algerian ivy
Perennial or ornamental peanut
'Marguerite' sweet potato
Portulaca
'Tricolor' oyster plant
Creeping Jenny

SMALL TO MEDIUM SHRUBS
'Mojo' pittosporum
'Soft Caress' mahonia
Dwarf nandina
Texas sage
'Mountain Snow' pieris
'Orange Blossom Special' dwarf pomegranate
'Yewtopia' plum yew
'Delta Jazz' crape myrtle
'Drift' roses

PLANTS WITH STRONG VERTICAL ACCENT
Aspidistra
African iris
Miscanthus grasses
Purple fountain grass
Dianella
Liriope
Helianthus hirsuta 'Peru'
Yucca
Agave
Cordyline australis 'Red Sensation'
Sanseviera (snake plant, mother-in-law's tongue)

LARGE SHRUBS, SMALL TREES
Weeping yaupon holly
'Little Gem' magnolia
'Twist of Pink' variegated oleander
'Early Bird' crape myrtle
Dwarf Japanese maples
Upright Junipers such as 'Spartan'
Needle palm
Lady palm (*Rhapis excelsa*)

BOLD TROPICAL LOOK
'Elena' elephant ear
'Lime Zinger' elephant ear
'Black Magic' elephant ear
Croton
Variegated shell ginger
'Tricolor' Stromanthe

Ti plant
'Tropicana' canna
Split-leaf philodendron
Alocasia 'Calidora'
Red-leafed banana
Sago palm
Philodendron 'Xanadu'

COLOR
Ornamental peppers
Coleus
Alternanthera
Trailing torenia
Supertunias and petunias
Melampodium
Thryallis
'Profusion' zinnia
'Caliente' and 'Calliope' geraniums
Pentas
Pansies and Violas
Dianthus
Erysimum 'Citrona' orange and yellow
Euphorbia 'Silver Fog'
Impatiens
Trailing verbena
African daisy
Kalanchoe

Container plantings may contain just one type of plant

Or they may consist of a variety of plants

15

Greenhouses & Cold Frames
Protection through Winter

In the lower South, there really aren't that many winter nights where the temperature drops much below freezing. If it weren't for those cold spells, many tropical plants could survive the winter. So it makes a lot of sense to have a small greenhouse to protect sensitive plants for those short freezes.

Tropicals in pots can easily be brought into the greenhouse. But a few years back, I discovered that it even is feasible to dig tropicals that are growing in the ground. They can be crammed into a pot and cut back to fit into the greenhouse. Then it's just a matter of the roots and the lower trunk surviving the winter. In the spring the plants can be set back out in the garden. They will take off a lot faster than a small replacement plant you may buy in the nursery, if you can even find the replacement plant in the spring. Most garden centers don't receive many tropicals until mid-summer. So, you can get a jump on the growing season and without having to buy new plants if you can carry over plants from the year before.

The greenhouse doesn't have to be elaborate or expensive either. You can build one of 2x4's, pvc pipe, and an old window and screen door, and cover it with plastic, for under $200. You can use a portable electric space heater to heat it when necessary. And the window is for ventilation when needed. You will actually find it necessary to open the window, and sometimes the door too, on warm winter days. It's a good idea to have a thermometer inside the greenhouse to monitor the temperature. It's even more helpful to have a maximum-minimum thermometer to record maximum and minimum temperatures reached. That way you can better adjust the heating during the night and the ventilation during the day.

I have also found it very helpful to have the heater on a simple timer. Set the heater thermostat low and the timer to come on about 5 p.m. and to go off at 7 a.m.

Here are the instructions for the under $200-greenhouse that I have used, http://leon.ifas.ufl.edu/lawn_and_garden/Green%20Ho use%20Expo%202009.pdf

But if you do an internet search using the words, build inexpensive greenhouse, you will find a variety of options, such as:

http://doorgarden.com/10/50-dollar-hoop-house-green-house

http://www.albertahomegardening.com/how-to-build-an-inexpensive-hoop-style-greenhouse/

You can leave the frame of these inexpensive greenhouses up all year, or you can disassemble it in the spring. Either way, you will need to put on new plastic covering each fall.

This is the inexpensive greenhouse being built.

Of course you could opt for a more expensive and more permanent greenhouse of glass or rigid plastic also. There are many kits on the market, or you can build your own.

Besides overwintering plants, a greenhouse can be handy for starting seeds in late winter so that you will have plants ready to set out in spring. The greenhouse can even be used in the summer if covered with shade cloth to reduce heat buildup.

If you only wish to overwinter a few plants, you can make the greenhouse on a much smaller scale. Or you can just build a cold frame.

http://www.organicgardening.com/learn-and-
grow/make-your-own-coldframe

A cold frame with heat is sometimes referred to as a hotbed. The internet has many plans for these relatively simple structures.

So consider building one of these options for giving winter protection to tender plants. You will enjoy the ability to carry plants through the winter that you couldn't otherwise.

16

Month-by-Month
Maintaining Your Landscape

Knowing when to do things is just about as important in landscape maintenance as knowing what to do. Although it doesn't include every little detail, the following timetable is intended to give you an idea of the timing for various landscape maintenance activities throughout the year. This timetable was written for Zone 8b. So, if you're in Zone 8a, everything may be delayed, on average, a couple of weeks. Similarly, if you're in Zone 9a, most things will happen a couple of weeks earlier.

Keep in mind that you can be flexible with most of the pointers on the timetable. For example, if you don't fertilize your lawn in April, you can still do it in May. Or you may even decide not to fertilize at all. The schedule is only a guide.

JANUARY-FEBRUARY
Weather: January and February are the heart of our winter. Low temperatures can vary from very rare hard freezes in the single digits to mild weather where the low is in the 50's. Similarly, high temperatures can range from a few rare days where the temperature may stay near or below freezing to days with highs in

the 80's. Highs in the 50's or 60's are more common though, as are lows in the 30's or 40's.

Rainfall amounts will vary across the zone. However, January and February are not typically dry months. Rainfall is usually sufficient enough that little supplemental irrigation will be required on established plants.

In flower during this period may be Taiwan cherries, Japanese magnolias, red maples, redbuds, red buckeyes, Carolina jessamine, camellias, spireas, pansies, dianthus, erysimum, and spring flowering bulbs such as daffodils or tulips. If the weather is mild, petunias and snapdragons may be flowering also.

Planting/transplanting: Plant or transplant woody plants such as shrubs or trees. Now, while it's cool and plants are somewhat dormant, is one of the best times of the year for planting and transplanting. Remember, though, that plants sill need water during the winter. Irrigate if rainfall doesn't supply adequate water.

Plant fruit trees and roses.

Pruning: Prune fruit trees and grape vines before late February.

Prune crape myrtles, if needed, so they'll be ready in spring for setting buds for summer bloom.

Most evergreen plants can be pruned in late February. For spring-flowering plants, such as azaleas, wait until after they finish flowering.

Prune roses in mid-February.

Late in the month you can begin removing cold damage on perennials, getting ready for new growth that will emerg in spring. Scrape stems to determine the extent of the cold damage and cut back to that point. Many perennials will have stems that have been killed back entirely. When you cut those stems back, it's still a good idea to leave six inches or so of stem remaining just to mark the location of the plant and to remind you it's there so you won't damage it by stepping on it before new growth sprouts out.

Fertilization: Fertilize most fruit trees in early to mid-February.

Pest Management: In January, dormant oil sprays may be applied to fruit trees that had a problem with scale insects the previous year.

In February, as fruit tree flower buds begin swelling, start preventative pest control sprays with fruit tree sprays (combination insecticide and fungicide) available from your garden center.

MARCH-APRIL
Weather: Depending on your exact location, the last killing frost should be in mid to late March.   The further north you go, though, the more likely you can still have a freeze into April.

By late April, daytime temperatures have usually become quite warm, well into the 80's in much of our zone.

Though rainfall is not usually plentiful at this time of year, it is often adequate for established plants because temperatures haven't become extreme. But new plants will require regular watering.

In flower: in early March may be loropetalums, plums, crabapples, pears, peaches, and Carolina jessamine. Those cool-season annuals that were planted in the fall such as petunias, dianthus, nemesia, diascia, erysimum (Citrona Yellow and Orange), chrysocephalum (Flambe Yellow and Orange), snapdragons, pansies, larkspur, sweetpeas, and poppies will be blooming now. By mid-March, the dogwoods, silverbells, hawthorns, and azaleas have often started flowering. And by mid-April, the fringe trees are usually blooming. Roses will start in March, and depending on the type of rose, may go until cold weather stops them in late fall.

Planting/transplanting: In mid to late March you can begin planting warm-season vegetables and flowers. In April is a better time for planting caladiums, vinca, and many other plants that like warmer soil. March is a good time to divide crowded clumps of perennials.

You can continue planting shrubs and trees in the warm spring weather. The sooner in spring you plant, though, the better, so that the plants will face less heat stress.

Pruning: Before mid-March you should complete any needed pruning of landscape plants with the exception of spring-flowering plants such as azaleas. Wait until they've finished flowering to prune them.

March is the ideal time to do any drastic renovation pruning of overgrown shrubs.

If you didn't trim the cold damage from flowering perennials in late February, you can do so in March.

You can probably tell where the new growth will be emerging and can cut back to that point. Many perennials will have stems that have been killed back entirely. When you cut those stems back, it's still a good idea to leave six inches or so of stem remaining just to mark the location of the plant and to remind you it's there so you won't damage it by stepping on it before new growth sprouts out.

Fertilization: Fertilize trees and shrubs as needed in early March or late February. Roses will need monthly fertilization throughout the spring and summer.

Fertilize flowers, both perennial and annuals. Continue to fertilize most annuals monthly through the spring and summer.

Sidedress most vegetables with fertilizer a month or so after they are up and growing.

Lawn Care: Don't fertilize your lawn until after mid-March. Early April is even better, especially for centipedegrass. The general rule is not to fertilize the lawn until at least three weeks after it completely greens up. There's no rush. The lawn will fare just fine if you wait until April to fertilize it.

Don't worry so much about the weeds in your lawn in March. Most of them are probably winter annuals that will soon go to seed and die. Just keep your lawn mowed. If you wish to apply a pre-emergence herbicide to your lawn to prevent the emergence of summer weeds, do so in March when the dogwoods are in flower. The exception would be for chamberbitter, the weed that looks like little mimosa seedlings with seedpods on the underside of the leaves. Wait until May for that. Follow label directions carefully when using any herbicide.

Lawngrass can be planted from sod or plugs. Plant from plugs now and you can have a filled-in lawn by the end of summer.

Aerate compacted lawns with a mechanical core-type lawn aerator.

As you begin mowing the lawn, sharpen the mower blades every 4-6 weeks.

Live oak leaves are falling now. Use them for mulch in flower beds and around trees and shrubs.

MAY

Weather: Basically, May's activities are about the same as April's. Freeze danger is past. But, the rising temperatures, into the 80's and 90's, begin to make starting plants a little more difficult. New plantings will require careful attention to watering. Though there may be enough rain in May, often there are some dry periods and you may even need to begin watering established plantings and the lawn.

As the cool-season plants that were blooming in March or April finish their flowering now, they can be replaced by warm-season annuals such torenia and narrow-leafed zinnia.

Planting: You can still plant most shrubs, flowers, and trees from containers. But, pay special attention to watering because of the warm weather.

It's really too late to plant most warm-season vegetables, though some heat-loving vegetables such as eggplant, okra, southern peas, peppers, and sweet potatoes can still be planted.

Fertilization: Don't forget to fertilize annual flowers and roses monthly throughout the growing season.

Apply side-dressings of fertilizer to most vegetables.

Lawn Care: Soil temperatures have risen, so now is a good time sodding or plugging. Pay careful attention to watering.

JUNE-JULY

Weather: This is the heart of our summer. Temperatures may be well into the 90's and humidity will be high. July is usually our wettest month. Still, you will have to pay careful attention to new plantings because the rootballs can dry out quickly if it doesn't rain for a couple of days. But, plants with deeper roots such as lawns or established shrub plantings will probably be fine as long as the rains come once or twice a week.

In flower: All of the typical summer-flowering annuals and perennials should be in bloom now. (See the chapter on flowers for more details.)   Crape myrtles, Jerusalem thorns, and goldenrain trees are among trees that may be in flower now. Hydrangeas and gardenias flower during this season.

Planting/transplanting: Because of the heat, it's not our peak planting season. You can still plant container-grown trees and shrubs, but water faithfully. You can still plant flowers successfully, but you should plant only those that can really take the heat. (Again, see the chapter on flowers).

Pruning: Be pinching back chrysanthemums, salvias, and other fall-blooming perennials now so that bushier plants and more flowers will result. Stop the pinching in late August.

Groom perennial flowers that have finished flowering.   Remove old flowers, cutting back to vigorous growth. Prune shrubs now as needed.

Fertilization: Continue fertilizing annual flowers and roses monthly.

Many fruit trees should be fertilized again now. (See fruit tree chapter for details.)

Lawn Care: Watch for chinch bug problems in sunny spots in St. Augustine grass lawns.

AUGUST

Weather: By August, our landscape is usually beginning to show signs of wear from summer's heat and humidity. The weather is very similar to that of July, hot and humid, usually with plenty of rain, but not always.

In flower: Abelias, crape myrtles, oleanders, altheas, chaste trees, and Jerusalem thorns may be in flower now. Also, many annual and perennial flowers will be blooming, too, if you have selected the ones that thrive on the heat. **Planting/transplanting:** You can begin preparing the soil in your fall vegetable garden in late August. Some plants can go in.

As in June or July, August is not the most ideal planting weather. Still, if careful attention is given to watering should rainfall not be adequate, most container-grow trees and shrubs can be planted.

Heat-tolerant flowers such as pentas, torenia, vinca, or *Zinnia angustifolia* can be planted.

Pruning: Because summer can be hard on many flowering plants, we need to spend a little extra time grooming plants now. If you take the time to cut back annuals, such impatiens, that have become leggy over the summer, they'll soon be much more attractive and their flowering life will be extended.

Trim the old faded flower stems off hydrangeas.

Give shrubs with lanky, untidy growth their last major pruning of the season.

Fertilization: Now is a good time to fertilize shrubs and small trees again if you're trying to encourage growth.

Don't forget to fertilize annual flowers and roses.

Lawn Care: If your lawn looks fine, you may not want to fertilize it again now. But, if it looks a little weak, now is a good time to fertilize again. This is more important with St. Augustinegrass than with centipede. The nutrients from the spring fertilization have long since been used or washed away.

Watch for chinch bug problems in St. Augustinegrass lawns.

SEPTEMBER

Weather: Temperatures begin to drop slightly in September, especially during the night. In the air, there's a slight hint of fall and cooler weather to come, especially during late September evenings. Rainfall amounts also decrease quite a bit. You may have to water established plantings should we go for an extended period without rain.

In flower: September finds many of the same warm-season flowers blooming, but a few new perennials such as pineapple sage, firespike, Mexican sage, lion's ear, candlebrush senna, chrysanthemums, and forsythia sage join the list for the next couple of months.

Planting: Plant chrysanthemums and other flowering perennials for fall bloom.

Renew tired annual plantings by adding crotons, marigolds, torenias, pentas, coleus, or others that will last until cold weather in late November.

September is a good time to divide crowded clumps of perennials.

Start cool-season plantings such as collards, broccoli, and lettuce in your vegetable garden.

Most trees and shrubs can be planted now.

Fertilization: Continue monthly fertilization of annual flowers and roses.

Lawn Care: If you didn't fertilize your lawn last month, you may use a 5-0-20 or 5-0-15 winterizer on it this month.

Watch for sod webworm problems in lawns.

Continue watering your plants and lawn as needed. Don't neglect them now, thinking they should be going dormant and needing no water. It's still early.

OCTOBER
Weather: October is our driest month.   Though

days can be still be quite warm, in the upper 80's or into the 90's, there is a trend toward cooling. By the end of the month, nights can be cool, though we usually don't reach freezing temperatures in October.

In flower: October finds many of the same plants flowering as in September. The fragrant tea olive perfumes the garden as do also the large hanging Angel Trumpet flowers. The golden yellow flowers of the candlebrush senna or cassia are spectacular as is firebush. Swamp sunflower, with its bright yellow flowers, also demands attention.

Planting/transplanting: Continue planting your fall vegetable garden. Now is the time to plant strawberries. As temperatures begin moderating again, it is a good time for planting trees and shrubs. Just remember to water.

Now is still a good time for transplanting or dividing perennial flowers.

Plant cool-season annual flowers such as petunias, pansies, diascia, nemesia, erysimum (Citrona Yellow or Orange), Flambe yellow or orange chrysocephalum, snapdragons, and dianthus.

Fertilization: Continue monthly fertilization of annual flowers and roses.

Don't forget sidedressing fertilizer in the vegetable garden.

Lawn Care: If winter and very early spring weeds are always a serious problem in your lawn, and you need to apply a pre-emergent herbicide, now is the time.

Continue watering as needed. October is often very

dry and water will likely be needed on lawns and other plantings. If your lawn is browning now, it's not likely from cold... more likely you need to water it.

Sod webworms can still be active.

NOVEMBER

Weather: The weather finally really stars to feel like fall in November. There will be some very cool nights. There may even be some frost, particularly after mid-month. Days may be cooler, too, but temperatures can still climb into the 80's during mild weather. Rainfall may be in short supply, but you still probably won't find it necessary to irrigate established plantings much, because the temperatures will also be lower. However, pay special attention to the water requirements of new plantings. And you still may find it necessary to water the lawn a time or two. As in October, if it's brown now, it's probably from lack of water.

In flower: Many of the warm-season annuals and perennials will still be in flower until a good freeze stops them. The perennials such as pineapple sage and Mexican sage that started flowering in September will also still be in flower. Also joining the flowering list this month should be cool-season annuals such as pansies, erysimum (Citrona Yellow and Orange), dianthus, and petunias. Some camellias may also come into bloom this month. Firebush will still be blooming, and its leaves will take on a burgundy-bronze tint.

Planting/transplanting: Lots to do in the garden this month! It's a great planting month: shrubs, trees, perennial flowers, cool-season annual flowers, vegetables, etc.

Plant seeds of spring-blooming flowers such as poppies, bachelor buttons, larkspur, and sweet peas. Plant cool-season annuals such as pansies, violas, dianthus, nemesia, diascia, erysimum, sweet alyssum, and snapdragons.

Plant narcissus or daffodils and other spring-flowering bulbs.

Continue planting cool-season vegetables in the vegetable garden.

Keep pine straw and leaves off the lawn. Use them for mulching trees, shrubs, flower beds, bare areas under large trees, and vegetable gardens.

Lawn Care: If desired, sow rye grass seed for a temporary green lawn during the winter. Remember, though, you'll have to mow it.

DECEMBER

Weather: December's temperatures are not usually too harsh. There will be nights when the temperature drops below freezing, but there will also be unseasonably warm, humid nights when the temperature stays in the 50's. Sometimes, though, especially late in the month, around Christmas, the cold Arctic air reaches into our area, sending temperatures plummeting into the 20's or even lower. Be prepared for anything during our winter. Often mild, but variable, with the emphasis on "variable", is the best way to describe the weather of our winters. Rainfall usually starts to increase a little in December over the drier October and November.

Plants don't use as much water during the winter, but they still need some. So if we don't have much rain, remember that new plantings especially will still need watering.

In flower: Camellias should be very colorful by now.   The cool-season annuals such as pansies, ornamental cabbage and kale, and erysimum should be very attractive now. Hollies with colorful berries will add to the season's color. The tea olive will flower on through the winter as long as it's not too cold.

Planting/transplanting: December is also a good planting month.   Almost everything that could be planted in November can be planted now unless we're having a very cold winter. Even if it's very cold, most trees and shrubs can be planted. In fact, now is a much better time for planting trees and shrubs than is June, July or August. Now is even better than March and April. The heat is more stressful on new plants than is the cold.

Continue collecting mulch materials and renewing mulch in beds.

Pruning: Now is a good time to prune hollies and junipers so that you can use the cuttings for holiday decorations.

Lawn Care: Rye grass can still be seeded in your lawn this month.

Holiday plants: Remember when taking your Christmas tree home to re-cut the base of the stump and place the tree in a bucket of water for 24 hours before placing it inside the house. Keep it watered regularly.

Pick out a poinsettia for the holidays, but keep it out of drafts inside your home so it will hold its bracts longer. Other plants of the season are Christmas cactus, rosemary topiaries, and amaryllis.

PLANT FOR COLOR THROUGHOUT THE YEAR

Each new season in the South is heralded by flowers.   With careful planning, you can have something blooming in your garden throughout most of the year. You must plan ahead, though. Perhaps the following ideas will be helpful. And, if you're observant throughout the year, I'm sure you can add many others to this list.

LATE WINTER (typically January-February to early March)

Camellia – These beautiful evergreen shrubs have a variety of pink, red, white or variegated flowers fall through spring. Visit public gardens such as Maclay Gardens in Tallahassee to see them at their peak in February.

Taiwan cherry – One of the earliest flowering cherries, very dark pink. Late January or early February.

Okame cherry – Lighter pink, early flowering cherry. Late January or early February.

Japanese magnolia – There are various species of deciduous magnolias for which this common name is used. Pink, lavender, wine, or white flowers. Usually start in February.

Redbud – Deciduous native tree with brilliant purplish-pink blooms.

Red maple – Deciduous native tree with red flowers and seeds. Some have better color than others.

Carolina yellow jessamine – Native vine with sweetly fragrant flowers.

Annual, bulbs, and perennials – Pansies, erysimum, diascia, nemesia, 'Flambe Yellow' and 'Flambe Orange' chrysocephalum, petunias, dianthus, sweet alyssum, calendulas, narcissus, daffodils, snowdrops, scilla, tulips, creeping phlox, etc.

EARLY SPRING (typically March – April)

Pears – White flowers. The fruiting pears sometimes bloom in February. The ornamental Bradford pears don't flower well here except after cold winters.

Plums – Chickasaw (shrubby tree) and American plum (larger), both have white flowers. Also are the varieties of fruiting plums.

Crabapple – Small native tree with delicate pink flowers.

Silverbell – Underused small native tree with white flowers.

Dogwoods – Sorry, only the white ones do consistently well in the deep South. Further north, about Atlanta, pink ones do fine.

Flowering quince – Deciduous shrub with red flowers.

Viburnum tinus – Showy white flowers on a mid-sized attractive evergreen shrub. Flowers may begin in February.

Forsythia – Deciduous shrub with yellow flowers (if enough winter chilling received).

Spirea – Several species of this popular wispy, deciduous shrub exist. Beautiful white flowers.

Azaleas – Several species are used here. Most popular are the large Indica types with flowers of violet, red, white or pink. These can't handle the cold of the upper South. Other species are mid-sized or smaller. Several natives deciduous species exist, with orange, pink, or white flowers. Some very fragrant.

Loropetalum – The pink flowers and burgundy foliage of these shrubs are making them almost as popular as azaleas, if not more so.

Banana shrub – Yellow flowers that resemble small bananas and that have a very sweet fragrance.

Sweet shrub – Very fragrant small, burgundy flowers.

Wisteria – Chinese, the common type, and Japanese, both bloom now. But both vines can be invasive. Stick to the American wisteria (*Wisteria frutescens*). May be harder to find, but worth it, because you won't be fighting it years later.

Lady Banksia rose – Numerous yellow flowers on this climbing rose.

Knockout roses – These versatile landscape roses start blooming early and will continue until winter cold comes again next year.

Annuals – Poppies, bachelor buttons, larkspur, and sweet peas will be flowering, but only if you planted from seed in October or November. Petunias, diascia, nemesia, erysimum (Citrona Yellow and Orange), 'Flambe Yellow' and 'Flambe Orange' chrysocephalum, snapdragons, dianthus, verbena, and sweet alyssum are among other cool season flowers blooming now. They're doing best if you planted them in the fall instead of waiting until spring.

LATE SPRING (typically April, May, into June)

Fringetree or granddaddy greybeard – Small native tree with clouds of white flowers.

Satsuki azaleas – Small, late-blooming azaleas.

Southern magnolia – Begins flowering in late May to early June.

Oakleaf hydrangea – Native hydrangea with large clusters of white flowers.

Garden hydrangeas – Common hydrangeas with large blue or pink flowers. Also are lacecap types.

Gardenia – Fragrant white flowers on glossy evergreen shrub.

Confederate jasmine – Small, fragrant flowers on an evergreen vine.

Butterfly bush – Large perennial, attractive to butterflies with its blue, purple, lavender, or white spikes.

Roses – Knockout roses and many other low-maintenance landscape roses will bloom now on through the summer.

Annuals – Pentas, begonias, impatiens, marigolds, salvia, petunias, geraniums, cosmos, cleome, snapdragon, nicotiana, zinnias, torenias, etc.

Perennials – Hidden gingers, daylilies, amaryllis, cannas, lantana, verbena, *Salvia guaranitica*, stokesia, Shasta daisy, agastache, Angel's trumpet, crinum, purple coneflowers, *Thunbergia battiscombei,* etc.

SUMMER

Crape myrtle – Brilliant clusters of red, pink, white, purple, or lavender flowers on these small to medium-sized deciduous trees.

Vitex or chastetree – Small, deciduous tree with purplish-blue, fragrant flowers. Should be used more.

Jerusalem thorn – Small tree, sometimes damaged by cold in severe winters. Brilliant yellow flowers, but also thorns.

Chinese flame-tree – Small tree with showy yellow flowers.

Sourwood – Small native tree with white flowers.

Oleander – Tough, durable shrub for hot, sunny sites. Pink, red, yellow, or white flowers. Don't eat any part of the plant. It's very poisonous.

Abelia – Several types of this durable shrub are available. Flowers are either white or pink. Leaves are very glossy and take on almost a burgundy color in full sun. Types with variegated leaves available also.

Clethra – This native shrub and its various cultivars have very fragrant white flowers.

Althea or Rose-of-Sharon – Pink, blue, or white flowers on this large deciduous member of the *Hibiscus* genus.

Honeysuckles – Several, such as coral honeysuckle, flower from spring through summer with dark pink or gold flowers.

Tough annuals for the summer heat – *Zinnia angustifolia*, coleus, croton, crossandra, trailing torenia, pentas, gomphrena, Burgundy Wine euphorbia, melampodium, vinca, portulaca, *Heliconia hirsuta* 'Peru', four o'clocks, thunbergia (vining), mandevilla, allamanda, variegated tapioca, and pentas.

Perennials – Purple coneflower, jacobinia (shade), shrimp plant, lantana, plumbago, rudbeckia, agapanthus, Mexican heather, Brazilian sage, bush allamanda, variegated shell ginger, caladiums, ti plant, acalypha, agastache, Angel's trumpet, canna, *Cordyline australis* 'Red Sensation', crinum, hummingbird flower, coral cockspur, firebush, thryallis, Dwarf turk's cap, butterfly vine, perennial or ornamental peanut, yellowbells, Thunbergia battiscombei, chaste tree, trumpetcreeper, and others.

FALL

Cassia – Several species of this small tree with brilliant yellow flowers are available. Some will not overwinter as perennials here but are worth planting for the one-year show and will probably come back from seed.

Tea olive – This evergreen shrub has very fragrant, small white flowers not only in the fall, but also in the spring and late winter.

Sasanqua camellias – These are typically the smaller-flowered and earlier blooming camellias.

American beautyberry – Flowers aren't showy, but the bright purple berries in the fall are.   Small native deciduous shrub.

Chinese flame-tree – The yellow flowers of late summer and fall are followed by beautiful salmon colored seed capsules in the fall.

Annuals – Zinnia angustifolia, coleus, croton, crossandra, trailing torenia, 'Burgundy Wine' euphorbia, melampodium, vinca, *Heliconia hirsuta* 'Peru', mandevilla, allamanda, *Caesalpinia pulcherrima*, variegated tapioca,   pentas, marigolds, petunias, pansies, violas, dianthus, pentas, snapdragons, erysimum, and chrysocephalum.

Perennials – Pineapple sage, firespike (*Odontonema*), plumbago, Mexican sage, chrysanthemums, swamp sunflower, Sedum 'Autumn Joy', rudbeckia, shrimp plant, cigar flower, butterfly bush, *Thunbergia grandiflora* (sky vine), butterfly vine, *Salvia guaranitica*, purple coneflower, jacobinia (shade), shrimp plant, lantana, bush allamanda, variegated shell ginger, ti plant, acalypha, agastache, Angel's trumpet, canna, Cordyline australis 'Red Sensation', firebush, Dwarf turk's cap, perennial or ornamental peanut, yellowbells, *Thunbergia battiscombei*, tibouchina, lion's ear, cape honeysuckle

(*Tecomaria capensis*), Philippine violet, and garlic vine are among colorful perennials in the fall.

.

ADDITIONAL INFORMATION SOURCES

University of Florida IFAS Extension publications:
http://edis.ifas.ufl.edu/

University of Georgia Extension publications:
http://www.caes.uga.edu/publications/

Auburn University Extension publications:
http://www.aces.edu/pubs/

Mississippi State University Extension publications:
http://msucares.com/pubs/infosheets/

Louisiana State University Extension publications:
http://www.lsuagcenter.com/

Texas A&M University Extension publications:
http://agrilifeextension.tamu.edu/

Clemson University Extension publications:
http://www.clemson.edu/extension/hgic/

North Carolina State University Extension publications:
http://www.ces.ncsu.edu/

University of Tennessee Extension publications:
https://utextension.tennessee.edu/publications/Pages/
default.aspx

University of Arkansas Extension publications: http://www.uaex.edu/other_areas/publications/default.asp

Oklahoma State University Extension publications: http://www.oces.okstate.edu/

Virginia Tech Extension publications: http://www.ext.vt.edu/

New Mexico State University Extension publications: http://extension.nmsu.edu/

Southern Living magazine gardening info: http://www.southernliving.com/

http://www.floridata.com/index.cfm   Floridata is a photographic encyclopedia of landscape plants, an online plant & nature reference, and a gardening marketplace.